THE JOHN GOULD FLETCHER SERIES

Lucas Carpenter, General Editor
Volume IV

John Gould Fletcher

SELECTED ESSAYS OF
JOHN GOULD FLETCHER

Selected and introduced by

Lucas Carpenter

The University of Arkansas Press
Fayetteville   1989   London

DESIGNER: Chiquita Babb
TYPEFACE: Linotron 202 Baskerville
TYPESETTER: G&S Typesetters, Inc.
PRINTER: Braun-Brumfield, Inc.
BINDER: Braun-Brumfield, Inc.

The paper used in this publication meets the minimum
requirements of the American National Standard for Permanence
of Paper for Printed Library Materials
Z39-48-1984. ∞

Library of Congress Cataloging-in-Publication Data

Fletcher, John Gould, 1886–1950.
   Selected essays of John Gould Fletcher.

   (The John Gould Fletcher series ; v. 4)
   Bibliography: p.
   Includes index.
      I. Carpenter, Lucas.   II. Title.   III. Series:
Fletcher, John Gould, 1886–1950. Works. 1988 ; v. 4.
PS3511.L457   1988   vol. 4   814'.52   88-35336
ISBN 1-55728-078-9 (alk. paper)

Contents

General Editor's Preface

Selected Essays of John Gould Fletcher brings together for the first time a representative selection from Fletcher's voluminous critical writings. Like most of his contemporaries, Fletcher was drawn to criticism (especially critical journalism) because of the opportunity it presented to express his own deeply held aesthetic and philosophical beliefs and to make his living as a man of letters. Ranging in subject from modernist poetics to Oriental art, these essays reveal a keen, insightful intellect coming to grips with the central artistic problems of the most revolutionary period in the development of modern literature, painting, music, and philosophy. This collection is significant and long overdue both in terms of the light it sheds on Fletcher's concerns as poet and critic and of what it reveals about the evolution of the modernist movement.

Acknowledgments

"Preface." *Irradiations, Sand and Spray,* by John Gould Fletcher. New York: Houghton Mifflin, 1915.

"Miss Lowell's Discovery: Polyphonic Prose." *Poetry,* 6(April 1915), 32–36.

"Preface." *Goblins and Pagodas,* by John Gould Fletcher. New York: Houghton Mifflin, 1916.

"A Rational Explanation of Vers Libre." *The Dial,* 66(11 January 1919), 11–13. Reprinted by permission.

"The Impulse of Poetry." In *American Caravan IV,* ed. Alfred Kreymborg. New York: Macauley, 1931.

"The Orient and Contemporary Poetry." In *Asian Legacy and American Life,* ed. A. E. Christy. New York: John Day, 1945.

"Three Imagist Poets" appeared in two installments in *The Little Review:* 3(May 1916), 30–35 and 3(June–July 1916), 32–41.

"Conrad Aiken—Metaphysical Poet." Rev. of *The Charnel Rose,* by Conrad Aiken. *The Dial,* 66(31 May 1919), 558–59.

"Some Contemporary American Poets." *Chapbook,* May 1920, pp. 1–31.

"William Blake." *The North American Review,* 218(October 1923), 518–28.

"The Spirit of Thomas Hardy." *The Yale Review,* 13(January 1924), 322–33.

"Walt Whitman." *The North American Review,* 219(March 1924), 355–66.

"Ezra Pound" originally appeared as an untitled review of *Ezra Pound: Selected Poems,* ed. T. S. Eliot; *A Draft of XVI Cantos of Ezra Pound,* by Ezra Pound; and *A Draft of the Cantos XVII to XXVII,* by Ezra Pound. *The Criterion,* 8(April 1929), 514–24. Reprinted by permission.

"The Modern Southern Poets." *Westminster Magazine,* 23(January–March 1935), 229–51.

ACKNOWLEDGMENTS

"Herald of Imagism." Rev. of *Amy Lowell: A Chronicle,* by S. Foster Damon. *Southern Review,* 1(Spring 1936), 813–27. Reprinted by permission.

"The Secret of Far Eastern Painting." *The Dial,* 62(11 January 1917), 3–7.

"The Future of Art." Rev. of *History of Art,* by Elie Faure, trans. Walter Pach. *The Yale Review,* 14(July 1925), 805–09.

"The Key to Modernist Painting." Rev. of *Cézanne: A Study of His Development,* by Roger Fry and *Cézanne,* by Julius Meier-Graefe. *Bookman,* 67(April 1928), 189–91.

"East and West." *The Criterion,* 7(June 1928), 306–24. Reprinted by permission.

Richard Aldington, copyright Catherine Guillaume.

Collected Poems by Hilda Doolittle. Copyright © 1982 by the Estate of Hilda Doolittle. Reprinted by permission of New Directions Publishing Corporation and Carcanet Press Limited.

Collected Poems 1909–1962 by T. S. Eliot reprinted by permission of Faber and Faber Ltd.

"Journey of the Magi" in *Collected Poems 1909–1962* by T. S. Eliot, copyright 1936 by Harcourt Brace Jovanovich, Inc. and copyright © 1963, 1964 by T. S. Eliot, reprinted by permission of the publisher.

Cadences by F. S. Flint reprinted by permission of AMS Press.

The Poetry of Robert Frost, Edward Connery Lathem, editor reprinted by permission of Henry Holt and Co., Inc. Copyright 1969.

The Complete Poems of Thomas Hardy, edited by James Gibson (New York: Macmillan, 1978).

The Dynasts by Thomas Hardy (New York: Macmillan, 1904).

The Complete Poetical Works of Amy Lowell by Amy Lowell. Copyright © 1955 by Houghton Mifflin Company. Copyright © 1983 renewed by Houghton Mifflin Company, Brinton P. Roberts, Esquire and G. D'Andelot Belin, Esquire. Reprinted by permission of Houghton Mifflin Company.

"Conquistador" in *New and Collected Poems 1917–1982* by Archibald MacLeish. Copyright © 1955 by the Estate of Houghton Mifflin Company.

I am grateful to Gretchen Schulz for her painstaking editorial skills, to Martha Hogan Estes for her patience and advice, and, as always, to my wife Judy for her unfailing understanding and support.

Introduction

When John Gould Fletcher sailed for Europe in the summer of 1908, he was in search of an education that he felt three years at Harvard College had failed to supply. An excruciatingly shy young man from Little Rock, Fletcher had gone to Harvard in 1904 only to fulfill his father's wish that he become a lawyer. Once there, he quickly became disenchanted with the college's regimented curriculum and began on his own an intensive, passionate study of those subjects which would interest him for life: literature, art, music, and philosophy. He also started to write poetry. Upon the death of his father in 1906, Fletcher decided to resign from Harvard and use his substantial inheritance to break free of what he perceived to be a provincial, philistine America and see what the Continent had to offer. He was little prepared for what he found there.

Europe in 1908 was about to experience nothing less than a revolution in the arts: modernism. No one can be quite sure as to how and why modernism happened, and, as is the case with the equally problematic term *romanticism*, satisfactory definitions have proved impossible, although many have been proffered. Most scholars agree, however, that French Symbolism and Impressionism, the Decadence of the English *fin de siécle*, and the intellectual influence of Freud, Darwin, Nietzsche, and Marx created an atmosphere for artistic revolution that encouraged radical breaks with tradition and convention.

The first and most crucial phase of modernism lasted from 1910 to 1925, the years which saw shattering breakthroughs in all the arts in the form of works by Pound, Eliot, Joyce, Stravinsky, and Picasso, to name but the most prominent figures of the movement. The period also encompasses World War I, four years of unprecedented slaughter indelibly etched in the minds and spirits of the first modernists. Fletcher was there for all of it, both as an active and influential participant and as an astute observer and commentator.

After traveling extensively in Italy, France, and England, Fletcher rightly perceived that London was becoming the center of literary modernism and would present him with the best opportunities for success as a writer. Never an effective self-promoter, he languished in obscurity, writing many poems influenced by the French Symbolists and the then popular Georgians (a group he later turned against), but failing in his attempts to find a publisher. Finally, in 1913 he brashly decided to bring out at his own expense five volumes of his poetry under the imprint of four different firms. Although these so-called "wild oats" volumes now seem weak and derivative in comparison with his mature work, this rather dramatic publishing venture was a turning point in Fletcher's career. He began to meet such literary luminaries as Ezra Pound, T. E. Hulme, W. B. Yeats, Ford Madox Ford, H. D., Frank Flint, Richard Aldington, and, on her first visit to England to learn firsthand more about the "new poetry" before appropriating it for herself, Amy Lowell.

After overcoming some initial artistic and personal reservations, Fletcher joined the fledgling Imagist group then collecting around Pound. Pound was impressed by the experimental nature of Fletcher's "Irradiations" series and helped in placing his work with *Poetry* and *The Egoist*. When a quarrel between Lowell and Pound split the Imagist group, Fletcher went with the "Amygist" faction (H. D., Aldington, and D. H. Lawrence). Lowell, in turn, was influential in finding a publisher for Fletcher's first important volume, *Irradiations, Sand and Spray* (1915), the appearance of which brought him, as he put it, "scandalous success" and vaulted him into the limelight of literary modernism. Thus began a career that would include twelve more volumes of poetry and, in 1938, a Pulitzer Prize for his *Selected Poems*.

By the late 1920s, Fletcher saw that the locus of literary modernism was shifting from England to America. He also realized that his own poetic interests were increasingly centered on his native South, and by 1929 he had established firm ties with the Nashville-based Fugitive-Agrarians. In 1933 he returned to America from his self-imposed exile and settled down near his birthplace in Arkansas. However, by 1940 his reputation was in decline, and by the time of his suicide in 1950, he had been virtually forgotten. Only recently have his life and work begun to receive the attention they deserve. Indeed, as the years clear, Fletcher emerges as perhaps the most representative figure of the modernist movement, since the corpus of his work reveals virtually all of the primary characteristics, interests, and tendencies of the movement.

A principal reason for this rise in Fletcher's reputation is to be found in his critical essays. Although he published six significant prose volumes (*Paul Gauguin: His Life and Art*, the first English biography of the artist; *John Smith—Also Pocahontas*, a whimsical account of the classic American colonial love affair; *The Two Frontiers: A Study in Historical Psychology*, a prophetic analysis of the relationships between the United States and the Soviet Union; *The Crisis of the Film*, a consideration of early cinematic art; *Life Is My Song*, his autobiography and a crucial document in the charting of modern literary history; and *Arkansas*, a highly regarded history of his native state), his essays best display the breadth and depth of Fletcher's critical faculty. Like most of the central figures in what has been called "the Age of Criticism," he recognized early on that literary reputations were not to be made by imaginative work alone and that in a time of muddled and sometimes hysterical literary manifestoes, the well-crafted essay was the best vehicle by which to communicate his literary and aesthetic positions. On a more pragmatic level, after an unfortunate financial arrangement designed to lure his future wife away from her husband seriously depleted Fletcher's inheritance, he was compelled to rely on literary journalism in order to make ends meet. In 1914, his first essay, "More War Poetry," appeared in *The Egoist*. By the time of his death thirty-six years later, he had published approximately 250 reviews and essays in dozens of periodicals and anthologies, with *Poetry, The Egoist, The Dial, The Little Review, The Freeman, The North American Review, The Criterion*, and *The Yale Review* comprising his principal outlets for publication.

Viewed in their entirety, Fletcher's essays display exceptional range, knowledge, and intelligence and totally belie Mark Royden Winchell's assertion in the recent *The History of Southern Literature* (1986) that Fletcher "had no interest in any modern art other than poetry." Indeed, Fletcher was considered an authority on modern art and Oriental art and wrote frequently on both. So intense was his interest, in fact, that he once seriously considered becoming a painter himself. His essays are also replete with allusions to modern music, especially the work of Stravinsky and Scriabin. However, to better appreciate the overall significance and import of the essays, it would be best to consider them within the categories employed in organizing the three sections of this collection, i.e., poetry and poetics, appreciations of individual writers, and art and philosophy.

First of all, just as Fletcher's poetry exhibits most of the characteristics of modernist verse, so his essays on poetry and poetics reflect the major concerns of the modernist movement. For example, his prefaces to *Irradiations, Sand and Spray* (1915) and *Goblins and Pagodas* (1916) convey a sense of urgency in their advocacy of the experimentalism employed in most of the "new poetry," especially his own. In clear perception of the revolution he saw occurring in all the arts as a radical reaction to Victorianism, Fletcher acknowledged that the subject matter of the arts was no longer limited by tradition and convention but consisted instead of the entire spectrum of "nature and human life." However, like Pound and Eliot, Fletcher emphasized the importance of craft over inspiration in the creation of a work of art that is a unified aesthetic whole, recommending the French Symbolists as examples of how even the sordid can be rendered beautiful through skilled poetic craftsmanship.

In these prefaces Fletcher advances his belief that all art "aims at the evocation of some human emotion in the spectator or listener" and, consequently, "the good poem fixes a free emotion, or a free range of emotions, into an inevitable and artistic whole." Since Fletcher was active in the Imagist group when those words were written, they are significant in their departure from Pound's dictum that the images "present an *intellectual* and emotional complex in an instant of time" (my italics). Throughout his life, Fletcher remained suspect of poems serving merely as vehicles for ideas and was later critical of his friend Eliot and his fellow Fugitive-Agrarians for having gone too far in establishing an "intellectual school" of poetry.

Both prefaces further express the modernist preoccupation with the interrelationship of all the arts. Fletcher was present at the tumultuous premiere of Stravinsky's *Le Sacre du Printemps* performed by Diaghilev's Ballet Russe in Paris in 1912 and, amid the near-riot of the audience, felt as if his aesthetic vision had been totally altered. He was also an avid supporter and patron of modernist painting and sculpture. In the preface to *Goblins and Pagodas*, he explains how he combined the techniques of music and painting to produce his masterful "color symphonies," which taken together express various stages in the life of the creative artist. In support of his synesthetic method, he evokes the work of Scriabin and the color organ invented by Wallace Rimington, but the crux of the method is Fletcher's conception of rhythm as the "basis of English poetry" and of the poetic line as "musical movement," a conception shared by most of the Imagists and expressed by Pound in this way: "As regarding rhythm: to compose in the sequence of the musical phrase, not in sequence of a metronome." Such a view obviously leaves little place for traditional meter, rhyme scheme, and formal stanzas, and it precipitated the so-called "free verse controversy," which flared at intervals in the little magazines from 1913 to 1930.

An early advocate and practitioner of free verse, or *vers libre* as it was commonly called, Fletcher felt that it was the only form offering the freedom of expression demanded by experimental poets like himself and the other Imagists. He was also convinced that it better enabled the poet to appropriate and employ techniques from painting, music, and sculpture. But in "A Rational Explanation of *Vers Libre*," his most detailed discussion of the verse form, he warns that "there can be no such thing as absolutely free verse" because "a piece of verse must have a certain form and rhythm, and this form and rhythm must be more rounded, more heightened, more apparent to both eye and ear, than the form and rhythm of prose." Thus the poet is "not absolutely but relatively free," and far from being Robert Frost's "playing tennis without a net," free verse in Fletcher's view is more complex and demanding than traditional metrical forms. In illustration of his argument, he provides a sophisticated analysis of how the free verse line functions within a poem, leading up to five "laws governing the writing of free verse" which offer much insight into how the form was practiced at the time.

Fletcher's interest in free verse led him to experiment with other free forms. One of these he termed "polyphonic prose," and in his autobiography he describes how he introduced Amy Lowell to the form only to have her appropriate it as her own and take credit for its invention. However, as evidenced in "Miss Lowell's Discovery: Polyphonic Prose," he set selfish considerations aside and supported her as the "true discoverer" of this form, going so far as to praise her mastery of the "orchestral quality" of polyphonic prose and refer to her creations as "the Beethoven symphonies, the Bach fugues, the César

Frank chorales, of poetry." Ironically, it was Fletcher who went on to become the form's most accomplished practitioner, best demonstrated in such works as "Clipper Ships," "The Passing of the South," and "America 1916."

In "The Orient and Contemporary Poetry," written long after the Imagist group had dissolved, Fletcher considers yet another primary characteristic of early modernist poetry: the pervasive influence of Oriental poetry and thought. He begins by identifying China as more significant than Japan as a source of influence. Although the Imagists popularized and imitated the Japanese *haiku* and *tanka* forms (Pound's "In a Station of the Metro" is the most famous example), Fletcher deems Japanese poetry monotonous as a result of its rigid adherence to form and argues that it owes what strength it has to what it has received through the influence of Chinese poetry, which he considers "more richly endowed" and capable of rendering "the full picture." It was from the Chinese, he suggests, that the Imagists derived their conviction that "the real business of poetry was to state, and state concretely, just what had moved the poet, and to leave the reader to draw his conclusions." If French Symbolism was the "father of Imagism," then Chinese poetry was "its foster-father," and even though Imagism "did not set itself the task of transmitting directly the substance of classical Chinese poetry," the Imagists succeeded in constructing "a poetry more akin to the Chinese *spirit* than the critics have hitherto suspected."

Perhaps the most significant essay in this section is "The Impulse of Poetry," for it is here that Fletcher most clearly and completely expresses his poetic aesthetic. He begins by discussing the "art for art's sake" notion that the artist is primarily concerned with producing what is considered "beautiful." Fletcher proposes instead that "the genuine artist is always concerned with the construction of a complex frame of reference to describe the puzzlingly fugitive, disordered, incoherent nature of reality." If the result is beautiful, it is "due solely to the command he has over his own sensuous and formal means of expression; it is not due to any primary desire to create beauty for its own sake."

Agreeing with Hume's dictum that "Beauty is no quality in things themselves; it exists only in the mind that contemplates them," Fletcher goes on to add that our minds generally arrive at beauty "through the faculties of sight and hearing." Using examples from architecture and music, he establishes the visual arts as "spatial" and the musical arts as "temporal." But inasmuch as no art is "pure," there is always crossover between the spatial and temporal categories, and nowhere is this better illustrated than in poetry, which he considers to be "a temporal utterance of a spatial situation":

> It is temporal in so far as its material is composed of words—that is to say auditory sounds, arranged in rhythm. It is spatial in so far as this material images the external situation, the subject matter of the poem. It is thus both plastic and dynamic in its approach to reality.

Accordingly, he assigns to poetry the "central place in the arts" because "it is by studying poetry that we can most readily grasp the field of architecture, sculpture, painting, on the one hand, and drama, music, and dance on the other."

In an analysis of the roles of image and rhythm in poetry, Fletcher compares two seascapes, one by Winslow Homer and the other by the Japanese painter Ogata Korin. "These two pictures," Fletcher declares, "springing as they do from very different civilizations, give us exactly what their respective civilizations give us." The more realistic American artist "is concerned, whether consciously or not, in stressing those very qualities in his seascape which the Christian religion has tended to stress in the individual, the qualities that describe pure being, that define individuality, the qualities of uniqueness, power, self-reliance." The more minimalist Japanese artist, on the other hand, "is unconcerned with the actual appearance of the wave. What he aims at is what the Buddhist doctrine itself aims at: to disengage the actual quality of an experience from the experience itself."

Fletcher then finds counterparts for the two paintings in a lush description of the sea taken from Swinburne's "Hymn to Proserpine" and in H. D.'s spare "Sea Gods," seeing the former's visual and auditory images as merely descriptive, while viewing the latter as more evocative of "the precise quality of the sea itself," a quality which renders the poem "static and plastic." Although H. D.'s poem, according to Fletcher, is to be preferred, his ideal poem would consist of a merger between the "dynamic sensibility" of Swinburne and the "plastic thought" of H. D.

With regard to the role played by rhythm in poetry, Fletcher emphasizes that poetry, above all, "is meant to be spoken or sung rather than read from the printed page." Defending the modernist practice of free verse as most closely approximating the rhythm established by the "intake and expiration of the breath" characteristic of much primitive poetry, he praises the Imagists for creating "a new form, a form dependent upon immediate visual and verbal intuition of every aspect of its subject. . . . to be achieved not by elaboration of detail, but by a stark stripping off of all detail in order to pursue the essential."

Fletcher concludes the essay with a discussion of the complex relationship between poetry and philosophy, expressing his intention "to show in what manner philosophy has been allied historically to poetry." For Fletcher, the kinship between the two stems ultimately from the fact that both philosophy and poetry deal with reality as apprehended by human consciousness. But consciousness consists of both thought and feeling, and the philosopher concentrates on thought while the poet deals primarily with feeling. Still, philosophical thought is more rooted in human experience than is the abstract thought of science, and it is for this reason that philosophy can be seen as "a connecting link between art and exact science."

Furthermore, Fletcher presents the poet as "a highly conscious voluntary agent working directly upon the full range of his experience as human being, and upon his underlying knowledge of that experience." The poet of necessity seeks "the laws underlying experience," which can only be stated in what Fletcher terms "concrete ethical constants":

> The poet thus approaches philosophy from the side of ethics, the philosopher from the angle of epistemology, the theory of knowledge. The one is concerned with the practical and immediate workings of experience; the other with the theoretic and symbolical presentation of fact, resting on the figured relation of the knower with the known.

Fletcher is very close here to Matthew Arnold in considering poetry to be a "criticism of life," a position also approached, if not occupied, by T. S. Eliot.

Fletcher does acknowledge the existence of "philosophical poets," and cites Goethe, Shelley, and Blake as examples, but while the Romantics had a relatively coherent body of philosophy from which to draw, the twentieth century, according to Fletcher, is philosophically chaotic. The prototype of the modern philosophical poet is his friend

T. S. Eliot, whom Fletcher portrays as "a dualist. . . . who dismisses the material world altogether as pure flux and argues in favor of a new ideal world based on the action of instinct and duration" and who also believes that writing "is essentially an impersonal process." Although Fletcher agrees with Eliot that poetry needs "a good dogmatic ground on which to base . . . poetic perceptions," he disagrees with Eliot's dualism and with his impersonal theory of expression:

> Mind and matter to me are distinct, but not separate, items of perception. What unites them is precisely conscious personality. This I would define not as a fixed entity such as is individuality, but as a variable quality, and all we can say about personality is that it is a quality completely non-individual, in the final sense, in its workings. It is a quality that in its most developed form completely transcends the individual unit by the operation of imaginative understanding; and its aim is . . . self-completion through a fusion of the intellect and the intuition on the plane of human values.

Fletcher's final position, ironically, is more romantic than modernist, but it is the kind of romanticism toward which much modernist poetry and criticism ultimately tend, despite their avowed neo-classical intent. In *Axel's Castle,* Edmund Wilson explained this phenomenon as a consequence of Symbolist influence, which produced an extreme recurrence of romanticism, a "second swing of the pendulum," that tended "to make poetry even more a matter of the sensations and emotions of the individual than had been the case with Romanticism."

In his appreciations of individual writers, Fletcher displays an acuity of insight into both the form and substance of a literary work matched only by his solid sense of "how things stand" at any moment in literary history, especially his own. However, although he was certainly well-read in the novel, Fletcher, like Pound and Eliot, mentioned fiction or fiction writers only infrequently in his criticism (Hardy and Dostoyevsky are the most common exceptions), and he rarely reviewed contemporary fiction. His interest lay instead in poetry and poets, and here his focus was primarily contemporary. Convinced from the outset of the importance of the modernist literary revolution, Fletcher seems to have set himself the task of charting its history as he perceived and experienced it, as evidenced in his essays on individual writers.

In "Three Imagist Poets," for example, Fletcher begins by asking "What is Imagism?" After answering the question with remarkable concision by citing the "four cardinal points or principles" of Imagism with regard to subject, style, form, and "the attitude of the artist to life," he demonstrates the practice of Imagism in the work of Richard Aldington, H. D., and F. S. Flint, all of whom, of course, he knew personally as fellow Imagists. Not surprisingly, Fletcher finds much to admire in their work, including Aldington's "mood of mutability," H. D.'s "purely and frankly pagan" poetry, and Flint's "flavor of supreme irony." Still, Fletcher's praise is not unqualified, and he criticizes them collectively for what he saw as unrelieved pessimism and despair.

Conrad Aiken was another close friend whose work Fletcher saw as central in the modernist canon. He met Aiken in Boston in 1915, and the young Aiken appears to have become something of a disciple of Fletcher. In turn, Fletcher reviewed all of Aiken's early volumes of verse and was certainly influential in establishing the younger poet's reputation. "Conrad Aiken—Metaphysical Poet" is particularly interesting inasmuch as Fletcher's use of the term *metaphysical* anticipates Eliot's revival of the term two years later in his now famous essay "The Metaphysical Poets." The metaphysicals, for Fletcher, were "the poets who, turning within themselves, wrote of the world as mirrored in the human brain."

In "Some Contemporary American Poets," Fletcher addresses the state of poetry in America in 1920. He traces the origin of "the present revival of poetry in America" to the appearance of Edwin Arlington Robinson's *The Children of Night* in 1897, praising his "love for cryptic ironic statement." Fletcher then considers briefly but insightfully the work of Robert Frost (a modern spokesman for Puritanism), Amy Lowell (a poet of "opulent exuberance"), Edgar Lee Masters (too confined by his "method of photographic realism"), Carl Sandburg (possessed of the ability to juxtapose "the sense of free nature with the observation of the tortured, thwarted life of industrial civilization"), Vachel Lindsay (a "reformer," not a poet), Ezra Pound (a "restless seeker after beauty"), Conrad Aiken (who displays a tendency "to balance the romantic with the realistic"), Wallace Stevens ("a dramatist without a theme" and "artist without philosophy"), and Alfred Kreymborg ("gifted with a sense of the ironic side of ordinary life"). The essay is also interesting for its early perception of the significance of regionalism in modern American poetry.

Fletcher's most incisive consideration of the work of his friend Ezra Pound occurs in his 1928 review of *Ezra Pound: Selected Poems* (edited with an introduction by T. S. Eliot) and the first twenty-seven of Pound's *Cantos*. Although Fletcher successfully resisted Pound's early attempts to turn him into a disciple and later went with the "Amygists" when Lowell quarreled with Pound, Fletcher was never stinting in his recognition of Pound's profound influence on modernism. But Fletcher was always critical of Pound's poetic technique. In this essay, for example, he criticizes Pound's use of archaisms, judges "Hugh Selwyn Mauberly" to be lacking "cumulative effect," and considers the *Cantos* to be failures. Fletcher's major objection is to what he terms Pound's "purely aesthetic and non-moral sensibility," but he continues to value the ambitious nature of Pound's poetic experimentalism.

On a lecture tour through the South in 1927, Fletcher became acquainted with the Nashville Fugitives and, having recognized for some time Southern qualities in his own poetry, he soon established a strong relationship with these fellow Southerners (especially Allen Tate and Donald Davidson) that would last for the rest of his life. By the time he returned to his native South for good in 1933, he had already published extensively in *The Fugitive,* contributed the essay on education to the controversial Fugitive-Agrarian manifesto *I'll Take My Stand* (1929), and appeared as an able defender of the Agrarian position at a highly publicized University of Virginia conference on Southern regionalism in 1931.

"The Modern Southern Poets" is Fletcher's attempt to direct attention to the Fugitive-Agrarians because "no critic of discernment or capacity has yet arisen to say anything of importance concerning the present-day Southern poets, in regard either to the value of their achievement, or to the prospects for its continuance." Ranking them with such contemporaries as Frost, Robinson, Masters, and Sandburg, and regarding them as the delayed fulfillment of the "promising beginnings [of Southern poetry] under Poe, Chivers, Timrod, and Hayne," Fletcher provides a brief biographical sketch of each writer, followed by a concise critique of his work. The essay, however, is no mere "puff-piece." The same reservations and suspicions he harbored with regard to the intellectuality of Pound and Eliot are provoked by the Fugitives.

For example, while he praises "the oblique shaft" of John Crowe Ransom's irony, Fletcher fears that the poet "has attempted to borrow too many devices of ellipsis and intellectualized cross-reference from the poets of the Eliot following—and has pushed these devices into realms of abstract thinking far removed from the 'simple, sensuous, passionate' thing that is poetry." Likewise, Allen Tate garners Fletcher's approval for his attention to craft, but the "metaphysical" nature of his poetry remains suspect. Donald Davidson is the only one of the major Fugitives to escape relatively unscathed, largely because of his "impenitent Romanticism," with which Fletcher was in profound sympathy. In concluding the essay, he warns that Southern poetry runs the risk of becoming "distorted, fragmentary, obscure, the more the poets I have discussed here find their stock of subjects running low, or the more they speculate on the *intellectual* content as opposed to the emotional, or *sensible,* content of their subject-matter."

The poet with whom Fletcher was most closely associated during his career was Amy Lowell, and although he frequently wrote about Lowell's poetry, "Herald of Imagism," a review of S. Foster Damon's *Amy Lowell: A Chronicle,* is his most detailed attempt to consider both her life and work. Concurring with Damon that the essence of Lowell's personality is to be found in her illustrious New England heritage and that "as she grew to womanhood . . . she was getting more and more maladjusted to the world in which she had been asked to live," Fletcher suggests that poetry became the only outlet for a "vivid but undisciplined imagination." The crystallizing event in her life was her meeting Pound and the Imagists in London in 1913, for it was through them that she discovered the freedom offered by modernist poetry and proceeded to become one of modernism's most outspoken and effective advocates. Her poetic reputation, according to Fletcher, will rest on her brilliant experimentalism in giving voice to her knowledge and perception of her Brahmin existence.

The remaining essays in this section are appreciations of the work of three poets who, along with Shelley and Poe, were the principal individual influences on Fletcher's art: William Blake, Walt Whitman, and Thomas Hardy. In the case of Blake, Fletcher acknowledges the power of his visionary faculty but considers it "entirely subsidiary to the revolutionary nature of his message." Indeed, Fletcher reserves most of his admiration for Blake's "uncompromising rebelliousness" and for his opposition to the tyranny of scientific reason. Walt Whitman draws Fletcher's praise, as one might expect, for his pioneering efforts in free verse, his own naturally rebellious nature, and his desire "to save democracy by exalting personality." And to Thomas Hardy, who was still alive when "The Spirit of Thomas Hardy" appeared in 1924, Fletcher frankly grants the title of "the greatest writer in the English-speaking world of the present day," perceiving a connection between his poetry and prose based on an ability to transmit "character and scene from the particular to the universal." However, Hardy remains "essentially a poet" who, although a fatalist, endeavors "to accept the tragedy of life not so much as a ghastly mockery but almost as a triumph."

The essays on art and philosophy which comprise the third section of this collection are indicative of the kind and quality of the scores of essays he published on both subjects. Like their counterparts in the preceding sections, they display many of the central characteristics and concerns of the modernist movement, including the interrelationship of the arts, an emphasis on craft and technique over and above inspiration in the creative process, a high regard for experimentalism in all the arts and a corresponding distaste for the conventional, a commitment to the objective rendering of complex emotional and intellectual states, an aversion to urban industrial existence, and a belief that the West has much to learn from Oriental art and thought. Also in evidence are Fletcher's keen analytical technique and his ability to extract the universal from the particular of a given moment in intellectual and aesthetic history.

"The Secret of Far Eastern Painting" is a significant early attempt by Fletcher to articulate the basis for his lifelong fascination with Oriental art. "The most extraordinary point about Chinese and Japanese painters," Fletcher says, "is that, although they were trained to observe nature and life, their work looks to us altogether artificial and conventional." This paradox can be resolved only if one realizes that "the act of receiving inspiration from nature and the art of rendering it again, are altogether different processes." Unlike the Western artist, who tries to absorb all the various detail of a natural scene that serves to produce an emotional effect, the Oriental painter "selects from the whole object or series of objects . . . a few features which contain all the emotional import of that object, and strives to render these in such a way as to suggest all the rest." The major difference between Western and Eastern art he expresses in the following passage:

> The Western artist uses nature as an end, and painting as a *means* to that end; the Oriental uses painting as an end and nature as a means. Western art is a worship of external form; Eastern art is a rendering of internal mood.

A further comparison between Eastern and Western art in terms of composition, perspective, and color leads Fletcher to conclude that style is the "secret of art" because it is both "artistic morality" and "the means by which our consciousness of man's mission asserts and expresses itself." He advocates Oriental art as an antidote to "the shallow pseudo-scientific training of Western artists and art schools" and sees hope in the new work of the Cubists, Futurists, and Post-Impressionists.

Both "The Future of Art" and "The Key to Modernist Painting" are assessments of the development of modern art. In the former, Fletcher is gloomy about the prospects for art in a civilization increasingly urban and industrial and lacking a generally accepted system of belief as a source of spiritual sustenance. In the latter, however, he praises Cézanne as the father of "Cubism, Expressionism, Constructivism, Vorticism, even Futurism." Cézanne, "like all modern artists," had to struggle against the prevailing tide of contemporary taste, and Fletcher sees much to admire in his having been "a romanticist with strongly classical leanings."

In "East and West," Fletcher returns to his preoccupation with comparing Western and Oriental civilization. Here he sets as his central question "Whether the Oriental mind does not work differently, perhaps better [than the Western mind]: whether the present state of Europe, decadent and anarchic, will be further marred or improved by study and contact with Oriental forms of culture and life?" Not surprisingly, his answer is on the side of improvement.

Fletcher chooses to emphasize the passive quality of the Oriental mind as exemplified by Confucius, Buddha, and Lao-tzu and contrast it with the active, rebellious mentality of the West. But Fletcher does not believe that the two need to conflict. Instead, in a sustained attack against M. Henri Massis' Catholic-oriented *Defense of the West*, Fletcher sees both Eastern and Western culture in decline, to be replaced by the ascendant civilizations of Russia and the United States, neither of which is, in his view, entirely Eastern or Western in outlook: "The 'new capitalism' of the one, as the 'nationalist communism' of the other make of them synthetic forces, undermining the last remnants of stability in Europe for the sake of a future world-unity they dimly foresee and seek along parallel but divided lines to create." For Fletcher, it will take the best minds of both East and West working together to save humanity from "the worst evils of the machine-age in which we live."

Finally, Fletcher's essays clearly display a voracious intellect guided by a compulsion to explain what it has deemed important, and choosing which essays to include in this collection was, needless to say, no easy task. Aside from obvious considerations of space, my guiding purpose was to present those essays which are not only Fletcher's best, but which also shed the most light on his primary concerns as both poet and critic. Among those essays which I have reluctantly omitted are the excellent introduction to his translation of Rousseau's *Reveries of a Solitary* and several insightful commentaries on the work of William Carlos Williams, Gerard Manley Hopkins, and D. H. Lawrence. His contribution to *I'll Take My Stand*, "Education: Past and Present," I have not included only because it is readily available in print and is most profitably read in the context of the other entries in that militantly Agrarian collection. Ultimately, the essays I have selected reveal the full range of Fletcher's achievement as one of the first of the Modernist men of letters, and although these highly artistic and intellectual writings are representative of his time, their final value lies in their continued ability to enlighten and challenge. After all, most of their concerns remain recognizably our own.

Lucas Carpenter
Oxford College of Emory University
August 28, 1988

SELECTED ESSAYS OF
JOHN GOULD FLETCHER

PART I

*Essays on Poetry
and Poetics*

Preface to Irradiations,
Sand and Spray   *1915*

The art of poetry, as practiced in the English-speaking countries today, is in a greatly backward state. Among the reading public there are exactly three opinions generally held about it. The first, and by far the most popular, view is that all poets are fools and that poetry is absurd. The second is that poetry is an agreeable after-dinner entertainment, and that a poet is great because he has written quotable lines. The last and worst is that which strives to press the poet into the service of some philosophical dogma, ism, or fad.

For these views the poets themselves, and no others, are largely responsible. With their exaggerated vanity, they have attempted to make of their craft a Masonic secret, iterating that a poet composes by ear alone; that rhythm is not to be analyzed, that rhyme is sacrosanct; that poets, by some special dispensation of Providence, write by inspiration, being born with more insight than other men; and so forth. Is it any wonder that the public is indifferent, hostile, or befooled when poets themselves disdain to explain clearly what they are trying to do, and refuse to admit the public into the privacy of their carefully guarded workrooms?

It was Théophile Gautier, I think, who offered to teach anyone how to write poetry in twenty-five lessons. Now this view has in it some exaggeration, but, at the same time, much truth. No amount of lessoning will turn an idiot into a wise man, or enable a man to say something when he is naturally one who has nothing to say. Nevertheless, I believe that there would have been fewer mute inglorious Miltons, greater respect paid to poetry, and many better poets, if the poets themselves had stopped working through sheer instinct and set them-

5

selves the task of considering some elementary principles in their craft. In this belief, and in the hope of enlightening someone as to the aim and purpose of my work, I am writing this preface.

To begin with, the basis of English poetry is rhythm, or, as some would prefer to call it, cadence. This rhythm is obtained my mingling stressed and unstressed syllables. Stress may be produced by accent. It may—and often is—produced by what is known as quantity, the breath required to pronounce certain syllables being more than is required on certain others. However it be produced, it is precisely this insistence upon cadence, upon the rhythm of the line when spoken, which sets poetry apart from prose, and not—be it said at the outset— a certain way of printing, with a capital letter at the beginning of each line, or an insistence upon end-rhymes.

Now this rhythm can be made the same in every line of the poem. This was the aim of Alexander Pope, for instance. My objection to this method is that it is both artificial and unmusical. In the case of the eighteenth-century men, it gave the effect of a perfectly balanced pattern, like a minuet or fugue. In the case of the modern imitator of Kipling or Masefield, it gives the effect of monotonous ragtime. In neither case does it offer full scope for emotional development.

I maintain that poetry is capable of as many gradations in cadence as music is in time. We can have a rapid group of syllables—what is called a line—succeeded by a slow heavy one; like the swift, scurrying-up of the wave and the sullen dragging of itself away. Or we can gradually increase or decrease our *tempo,* creating *accelerando* and *rallentando* effects. Or we can follow a group of rapid lines with a group of slow ones, or a single slow, or *vice versa.* Finally, we can have a perfectly even and unaltered movement throughout if we desire to be monotonous.

The good poem is that in which all these effects are properly used to convey the underlying emotions of its author, and that which welds all these emotions into a work of art by the use of dominant *motif,* subordinate themes, proportionate treatment, repetition, variation,— what in music is called development, reversal of rôles, and return. In short, the good poem fixes a free emotion, or a free range of emotions, into an inevitable and artistic whole. The real secret of the greatest English poets lies not in their views on life,—which were, naturally, only those which every sane man is obliged to hold,—but in their profound knowledge of their craft, whereby they were enabled to put forth their views in perfect form. Each era of man has its unique and self-sufficing range of expression and experience, and therefore every poet must seek anew for himself, out of the language-medium at his disposal, rhythms which are adequate and forms which are expressive of his own unique personality.

As regards the length of the lines themselves, that depends altogether upon the apparatus which Nature has given us, to enable us to breathe and to speak. Each line of a poem, however many or few its stresses, represents a single breath, and therefore a single perception. The relation between breath and perception is a commonplace of Oriental philosophy. As we breathe so do we know the universe, whether by sudden, powerful gusts of inspiration, or through the calmer—but rarer—gradual ascent into the hidden mysteries of knowledge, and slow falling away therefrom into darkness.

So much for the question of meter. The second range of problems with which we are immediately concerned, when we examine the poetic craft, is that which is generally expressed under the name of rhyme.

Now rhyme is undoubtedly an element of poetry, but it is neither an indissoluble element, nor is it, in every case, an inevitable one. In the main, the instinct which makes for rhyme is sound. Poetry is an art which demands—though not invariably—the utmost richness and fullness of musical effect. When rhyme is considered as an additional instrument of what may be called the poetic orchestra, it both loses and gains in importance. It loses because it becomes of no greater import than assonance, consonance, alliteration, and a host of similar devices. It gains because it is used intelligently as a device for adding richness of effect, instead of blindly as a mere tag at the end of a line.

The system which demands that the end of every line of poetry must rhyme with the end of some one preceding or following it, has not even the merit of high antiquity or of civilized adherence. In its essence it is barbarous; it derives from the stamping of feet, clapping of hands, pounding of drums, or like devices of savage peoples to mark the rhythms in their dances and songs. And its introduction into European poetry, as a rule to be invariably followed, dates precisely from the time of the break-up of the Latin civilization, and the approach of what the historians know as the Dark Ages. Since it has

come into common use among European peoples, every poet of eminence has tried to avoid its fatiguing monotony, by constructing new
stanza-forms. Dante, Petrarch, Chaucer, Spenser, all these were inno-
vators or developers of what may be known as formal meter. But let
us not forget that the greatest of all, Shakespeare, used rhyme in his
plays, only as additional decoration to a lyric, or in a perfectly legiti-
mate fashion as marking the necessary pause at the close of a scene.
Let us also remember that, as he advanced in thought and expression,
he gradually abandoned rhyme for the only reason that an artist
abandons anything; because it was no longer adequate.

The process that began with the Pervigilium Veneris, the mediaeval
hymn writers, and the Provençal troubadours, and which culminated
in the orchestral blank verse of Shakespeare, has now passed through
all the stages of reduction to formula, eclecticism, archaistic reaction,
vulgarization, gramaphone popularity, and death. Milton—Gibbon
among poets—reduced it to his too monotonous organ roll. Dryden,
Pope, and his followers endlessly repeated a formula. Blake, Wordsworth, Coleridge, attempted a return to the Elizabethan and to the
even earlier ballad forms. In the later nineteenth century we come back
to still earlier forms. Ballades, rondeaus, even sestinas appear. Gradually we find the public attention dropping away from these juggling
feats performed with stale form, and turning to what may be called
the new balladist—the street singer who is content to doggerelize
and make strident a once noble form. We have our Masefields, our
Kiplings, and worse. Ragtime has at last made its appearance in poetry. Let us be grateful to the man who invented it—Nicholas Vachel
Lindsay—but let us admit that the force of nature can no further go.

It is time to create something new. It is time to strip poetry of
meaningless tatters of form, and to clothe her in new, suitable gar-
ments. Portents and precursors there have been in plenty. We already
have Blake, Matthew Arnold, Whitman, Samuel Butler, and I know
not how many more. Everyone is talking—many poets, poeticules,
and poetasters are writing—what they call "free verse." Let there be
no mistake about one thing. Free verse that is flabby, inorganic, shape-
lessly obvious, is as much a crime against poetry as the cheapest echo
of a Masefield that any doggerel scribbler ever strummed. Let poets
drop their formulas—"free" or otherwise—and determine to disci-
pline themselves through experiment. There is much to be learned

from the precursors I have mentioned. There is a great deal to be learned from the French poets—Parnassians, Symbolists, Whitmanites, Fantaisistes—who have, in the years 1860 to 1900, created a new Renaissance under our noses. But above all, what will teach us the most is our language and life. Never was life lived more richly, more fully, with more terrible blind intensity than it is being lived at this instant. Never was the noble language which is ours surpassed either in richness or in concision. We have the material with which to work, and the tools to do the work with. It is America's opportunity to lay the foundations for a new flowering of English verse, and to lay them as broad as they are strong.

Miss Lowell's Discovery:
Polyphonic Prose   *1915*

During the past year something has happened in the sphere of the arts quite as important, in my opinion, as the European war in the sphere of politics and international relationships, or the discovery of radium in that of science. A new poetic form, equal if not superior in value to *vers libre,* has made its appearance in English. The discoverer is a woman. Had it been a man, we should probably all have heard by now of the richness of the find. Since there seems to be some danger that only a few will appreciate its significance, I venture to draw the public attention to it.

I do this the more willingly, because in her preface to *Sword-blades and Poppy Seed* Miss Amy Lowell, who is the true discoverer of this form, has modestly and mistakenly stated that it is not altogether her own invention, but was first employed by a French poet, Paul Fort. Now, for the uninitiated, I may say that M. Fort is a poet who possesses great facility in writing the alexandrine, the French classic meter. Unsatisfied with the chill regularity of this measure, he has attempted to fit it to his temperament, which is that of an improvisatore or ballad singer, by interspersing his poems with bits of prose, whenever his rhyme-invention flags. He thus gains a lightness, swiftness, and spontaneity of effect which have made him extremely popular among younger French poets. This popularity might have been greater had M. Fort printed his work as poetry interspersed with prose. Instead, he has chosen to print it as if it were prose alone, leaving the reader to determine the movement of the rhythm and the division into lines.

Upon this purely typographical device in M. Fort, Miss Lowell's imagination fastened itself. She is almost unique among present-day poets in possessing the ability of writing equally well in rhymed meter and in *vers libre*. She has practiced her art long enough to understand that the really great poetry which will survive, depends upon its sound quality and its substance quality, upon its appeal to the ear as well as to the eye. It seemed to her that there must be some way of fusing together unrhymed *vers libre* and rhymed metrical patterns, giving the rich decorative quality of the one and the powerful conciseness of statement of the other. In short, she was seeking some means whereby she might free herself, and other poets after her, from a constant and dogmatic adherence to a single meter throughout a single poem. In this respect, she was acting as the successor of Coleridge, Keats, Poe, who spent their lives trying to make English meter more flexible to mood and richer in sound effect. In M. Fort's work she found a gleam of suggestion to this end.

Miss Lowell had scarcely begun her attempt to follow Paul Fort before she realized that what she was doing consisted not so much in adapting a French form as in creating a new English one. For one thing, she was faced at the outset by the fact that the English language, since the break-up of blank verse, has no form which is standard, like the French alexandrine. She found it possible to vary the rhythm and meter of these strange new poems of hers almost at will, following the inner emotion of the thing she had to say. Swift-flowing metrical passages might be succeeded by *vers libre* recitatives; connecting links of prose could be used as a relief to the ear, and to lead up to some new metrical passage, and so on. In short, here was the opportunity, long sought, of displaying, within the limits of a single poem, all the resources of her art.

In my opinion, Miss Lowell has, in her latest examples of this peculiar form, resolved in a great measure the difficulties which confront all English poets who attempt to say something new today. The quandary which faces the earnest creator of poetry in the English-speaking countries is, that while he has at his disposal in the English language, the most superb instrument of sense and sound ever forged, he is utterly prevented from making use of its resources by the beggarly poverty of certain rhymes and meters which have been worn threadbare by generation after generation of poets, who could find no satisfying means of escape from them. What hope, then, is there for the young poet who feels he has a new music to express, when the only recognized means of expressing it has been developed to its utmost capacity over three hundred years ago? He is like a man who would try to play Richard Strauss or Debussy, or any of the modern composers, on a harpsichord.

It is true that a few brave young spirits have tried to face this difficulty and to rid themselves of it by writing exclusively in an old form called *vers libre*, which is dependent on cadence, and not on rhyme or metrical pattern. But a critical examination of the work of the best of these young poets—Aldington, H. D., Flint, Pound—proves that their attempt has not been altogether successful. The art of poetry demands as great a mastery of sound-quality as of substance-quality. Intense and concise grasp of substance is not enough; the ear instinctively demands that this bare skeleton be clothed fittingly with all the beautiful and subtle orchestral qualities of assonance, alliteration, rhyme, and return.

This orchestral quality Miss Lowell has developed to the utmost. Therefore it seems fitting that a new name should be given to these poems of hers, which, printed as prose, or as prose and verse interspersed, display all the colors of the chromatic palette. The title that fits them best is that of Polyphonic Prose. Here are the Beethoven symphonies, the Bach fúgues, the César Franck chorales, of poetry. It is an art most difficult of attainment, and not easy of appreciation. But it has come to English poetry, and its effect will be lasting and unmistakable.

Toscanelli drew a chart, but it needed a Columbus to make the voyage. Just so, Miss Lowell, with happy and characteristic daring, has essayed her voyage, and has found a new poetic continent in place of M. Fort's France, to which she at first thought she was steering. It is the old story of Whistler and the Japanese print over again. While a few connoisseurs scarcely dared to admire Japanese prints in secret, Whistler boldly made them the basis of a new art. Some day people will probably be saying that Miss Lowell was quite as important a figure for American art as Whistler. That is always America's little way of doing things. While Europe is jawing, and the American public remains supremely indifferent, some cheeky Yankee goes out and gets a thing done without anyone taking notice.

Preface to
Goblins and Pagodas   *1916*

I

The second half of the nineteenth and the first fifteen years of the twentieth century have been a period of research, of experiment, of unrest and questioning. In science and philosophy we have witnessed an attempt to destroy the mechanistic theory of the universe as developed by Darwin, Huxley, and Spencer. The unknowable has been questioned: hypotheses have been shaken: vitalism and idealism have been proclaimed. In the arts, the tendency has been to strip each art of its inessentials and to disclose the underlying basis of pure form. In life, the principles of nationality, of racial culture, of individualism, of social development, of Christian ethics, have been discussed, debated, and examined from top to bottom, until at last, in the early years of the twentieth century we find all Europe, from the leaders of thought down to the lowest peasantry, engaged in a mutually destructive war of which few can trace the beginnings and none can foresee the end. The fundamental tenets of thought, art, life itself, have been shaken: and either civilization is destined to some new birth, or mankind will revert to the conditions of life, thought, and social intercourse that prevailed in the Stone Age.

Like all men of my generation, I have not been able to resist this irresistible upheaval of ideas and of forces: and, to the best of my ability, I have tried to arrive at a clear understanding of the fundamentals of aesthetic form as they affect the art to which I have felt myself instinctively akin, the art of poetry. That I have completely attained such an understanding, it would be idle for me to pretend: but I believe, and have induced some others to believe, that I have made a few steps towards it. Some explanation of my own peculiar theories and beliefs is necessary, however, to those who have not specifically concerned themselves with poetry, or who suffer in the presence of any new work of art from the normal human reaction that all art principles are so essentially fixed that any departure from accepted ideas is madness.

II

The fundamental basis of all the arts is the same. In every case art aims at the evocation of some human emotion in the spectator or listener. Where science proceeds from effects to causes, and seeks to analyze the underlying causes of emotion and sensation, art reverses the process, and constructs something that will awaken emotions, according to the amount of receptiveness with which other people approach it. Thus architecture gives us feelings of density, proportion, harmony; sculpture, of masses in movement; painting, of color harmony and the ordered composition of lines and volumes from which arise sensations of space; music, of the development of sounds in melodic line, harmonic progression, tonal oppositon, and symphonic structure.

The object of literature is not dissimilar from these. Literature aims at releasing the emotions that arise from the formed words of a certain language. But literature is probably a less pure—and hence more universal—art than any I have yet examined. For it must be apparent to all minds that not only is a word a definite symbol of some fact, but also it is a thing capable of being spoken or sounded. The art of literature, then, in so far as it deals with definite statements, is akin to painting or photography; in so far as it deals with sounded words, it is akin to music.

III

Literature, therefore, does not depend on the peculiar twists and quirks which represent, to those who can read, the words, but rather on the essential words themselves. In fact, literature existed before writing; and writing in itself is of no value from the purely literary sense, except in so far as it preserves and transmits from generation to generation the literary emotion. Style, whether in prose or poetry, is an attempt to develop this essentially musical quality of literature, to evoke the magic that exists in the sound quality of words, as well as to combine these sound qualities in definite statements or sentences. The difference between prose and poetry is, therefore, not a difference of means, but of psychological effect and reaction. The means employed, the formed language, is the same but the resultant impression is quite different.

In prose, the emotions expressed are those that are capable of development in a straight line. In so far as prose is pure, it confines itself to the direct orderly progression of a thought or conception or situation from point to point of a flat surface. The sentences, as they develop this conception from its beginning to conclusion, move on, and do not return upon themselves. The grouping of these sentences into paragraphs gives the breadth of the thought. The paragraphs, sections, and chapters are each a square, in that they represent a division of the main thought into parallel units, or blocks of subsidiary ideas. The sensation of depth is finally obtained by arranging these blocks in a rising climacteric progression, or in parallel lines, or in a sort of zigzag figure.

The psychological reaction that arises from the intelligent appreciation of poetry is quite different. In poetry, we have a succession of curves. The direction of the thought is not in straight lines, but wavy and spiral. It rises and falls on gusts of strong emotion. Most often it creates strongly marked loops and circles. The structure of the stanza or strophe always tends to the spherical. Depth is obtained by making one sphere contain a number of concentric, or overlapping spheres.

Hence, when we speak of poetry we usually mean regular rhyme and meter, which have for so long been considered essential to all poetry, not as a device for heightening musical effect, as so many people suppose, but merely to make these loops and circles more accentuated, and to make the line of the poem turn upon itself more recognizably. But it must be recognized that just as Giotto's circle was none the less a circle, although not drawn with compasses, so poetic circles can be constructed out of subtler and more musical curves than that which painstakingly follows the selfsame progression of beats, and catches itself up on the same point of rhyme for line after line. The key pattern on the lip of a Greek vase may be beautiful, but it is less beautiful, less satisfying, and less conclusive a test of artistic ability than the composition of satyrs and of maenads struggling about the center. Therefore I maintain, and will continue to do so, that the mere craftsman-ability to write in regular lines and meters no more makes a man a poet than the ability to stencil wallpapers makes him a painter.

Rather is it more important to observe that almost any prose work of imaginative literature, if examined closely, will be found to contain a plentiful sprinkling of excellent verses; while many poems which the world hails as masterpieces, contain whole pages of prose. The fact is, that prose and poetry are to literature as composition and color are to painting, or as light and shadow to the day, or male and female to mankind. There are no absolutely perfect poets and no absolutely perfect prose writers. Each partakes of some of the characteristics of the other. The difference between poetry and prose is, therefore, a difference between a general roundness and a general squareness of outline. A great French critic, recently dead, who devoted perhaps the major part of his life to the study of the aesthetics of the French tongue, declared that Flaubert and Chateaubriand wrote only poetry. If there are those who cannot see that in the only true and lasting sense of the word poetry, this remark was perfectly just, then all I have written above will be in vain.

IV

Along with the prevailing preoccupation with technique which so marks the early twentieth century, there has gone also a great change in the subject matter of art. Having tried to explain the aesthetic form—basis of poetry, I shall now attempt to explain my personal way of viewing its content.

It is a significant fact that every change in technical procedure in the arts is accompanied by, and grows out of, a change in subject matter. To take only one out of innumerable examples, the new subject matter of Wagner's music-dramas, of an immeasurably higher order than the usual libretto, created a new form of music, based on motifs, not melodies. Other examples can easily be discovered. The reason for this is not difficult to find.

No sincere artist cares to handle subject matter that has already been handled and exhausted. It is not a question of a desire to avoid plagiarism, or of self-conscious searching for novelty, but of a perfectly spontaneous and normal appeal which any new subject matter always makes. Hence, when a new subject appears to any artist, he always realized it more vividly than an old one, and if he is a good artist, he realizes it so vividly that he recreates it in what is practically a novel form.

This novel form never is altogether novel, nor is the subject altogether a new subject. For, as I pointed out at the beginning of this preface, that all arts sprang practically out of the same primary sensations, so the subject matter of all art must forever be the same: namely, nature and human life. Hence, any new type of art will always be found, in subject matter as well as in technique, to have its roots in the old. Art is like a kaleidoscope, capable of many changes, while the material which builds up those changes remains the same.

Nevertheless, although the subject matter in this book is not altogether new, yet I have realized it in a way which has not often been tried, and out of that fresh and quite personal realization have sprung my innovations in subject as well as technique. Let me illustrate by a concrete example.

V

A book lies on my desk. It has a red binding and is badly printed on cheap paper. I have had this book with me for several years. Now, suppose I were to write a poem on this book, how would I treat the subject?

If I were a poet following in the main the Victorian tradition, I should write my poem altogether about the contents of this book and its author. My poem would be essentially a criticism of the subject matter of the book. I should state at length how that subject matter had affected me. In short, what the reader would obtain from this sort of poem would be my sentimental reaction towards certain ideas and tendencies in the work of another.

If I were a realist poet, I should write about the book's external appearance. I should expatiate on the red binding, the bad type, the ink stain on page sixteen. I should complain, perhaps, of my poverty at not being able to buy a better edition, and conclude with a gibe at the author for not having realized the sufferings of the poor.

Neither of these ways, however, of writing about this book possesses any novelty, and neither is essentially my own way. My own way of writing about it would be as follows:

I should select out of my life the important events connected with my ownership of this book, and strive to write of them in terms of the volume itself, both as regards subject matter and appearance. In other words, I should link up my personality and the personality of the book, and make each a part of the other. In this way I should strive to evoke a soul out of this piece of inanimate matter, a something characteristic and structural inherent in this inorganic form which is friendly to me and responds to my mood.

This method is not new, although it has not often been used in Occidental countries. Professor Fenollosa, in his book on Chinese and Japanese art, states that it was universally employed by the Chinese artists and poets of the Sung period in the eleventh century A.D. He calls this doctrine of the interdependence of man and inanimate nature, the cardinal doctrine of Zen Buddhism. The Zen Buddhists evolved it from the still earlier Taoist philosophy, which undoubtedly inspired Li Po and the other great Chinese poets of the seventh and eighth centuries A.D.

VI

In the first poems of this volume, the "Ghosts of an Old House," I have followed the method already described. I have tried to evoke, out of the furniture and surroundings of a certain old house, definite emotions which I have had concerning them. I have tried to relate my childish terror concerning this house—a terror not uncommon among children, as I can testify—to the aspects that called it forth.

In the "Symphonies," which form the second part of this volume, I have gone a step further. My aim in writing these was, from the beginning, to narrate certain important phases of the emotional and intellectual development—in short, the life—of an artist, not necessarily myself, but of that sort of artist with which I might find myself most in sympathy. And here, not being restrained by any definite material phenomena, as in the Old House, I have tried to state each phase in the terms of a certain color, or combination of colors, which is emotionally akin to that phase. This color, and the imaginative phantasmagoria of landscape which it evokes, thereby creates, in a definite and tangible form, the dominant mood of each poem.

The emotional relations that exist between form, color, and sound have been little investigated. It is perfectly true that certain colors affect certain temperaments differently. But it is also true that there is a science of color, and that certain of its laws are already universally known, if not explained. Naturally enough, it is to the painters we must first turn if we want to find out what is known about color. We discover that painters continually are speaking of hot and cold color: red, yellow, orange being generally hot and green, blue, and violet cold—mixed colors being classed hot and cold according to the proportions they contain of the hot and cold colors. We also discover that certain colors will not fit certain forms, but rebel at the combination. This is so far true that scarcely any landscape painter finishes his pictures from nature, but in the studio: and almost any art student, painting a landscape, will disregard the color before him and employ the color scheme of his master or of some painter he admires. As Delacroix noted in his journal: "A conception having become a composition must move in the milieu of a color peculiar to it. There seems to be a particular tone belonging to some part of every picture which is a key that governs all the other tones."

Therefore, we must admit that there is an intimate relation between color and form. It is the same with color and sounds. Many musicians have observed the phenomenon, that when certain notes, or combinations of them, are sounded, certain colors are also suggested to the eye. A Russian composer, Scriabine, went so far as to construct color scales, and an English scientist, Professor Wallace Rimington, has built an organ which plays in colors, instead of notes. Unfortunately, the musicians have given this subject less attention than the painters, and therefore our knowledge concerning the relations of color and sound is more fragmentary and incomplete. Nevertheless, these relations exist, and it is for the future to develop them more fully.

Literature, and especially poetry, as I have already pointed out, partakes of the character of both painting and music. The impressionist method is quite as applicable to writing as it is to landscape. Poems can be written in major or minor keys, can be as full of dominant motif as a Wagner music-drama, and even susceptible of fugal treatment. Literature is the common ground of many arts, and in its highest development, such as the drama as practiced in fifth-century Athens, is found allied to music, dancing, and color. Hence, I have called my works "Symphonies," when they are really dramas of the soul, and hence, in them I have used color for verity, for ornament, for drama, for its inherent beauty, and for intensifying the form of the emotion that each of these poems is intended to evoke.

VII

Let us take an artist, a young man at the outset of his career. His years of searching, of fumbling, of other men's influence, are coming to an end. Sure of himself, he yet sees that he will spend all his life pursuing a vision of beauty which will elude him at the very last. This is the first symphony, which I have called the "Blue," because blue suggests to me depth, mystery, and distance.

He finds himself alone in a great city, surrounded by noise and clamor. It is as if millions of lives were tugging at him, drawing him away from his art, tempting him to go out and whelm his personality in this black whirlpool of struggle and failure, on which float golden specks—the illusory bliss of life. But he sees that all this is only another illusion, like his own. Here we have the "Symphony in Black and Gold."

He emerges from the city, and in the country is reintoxicated with desire for life by spring. He vows himself to a self-sufficing pagan worship of nature. This is the "Green Symphony."

Quickened by spring, he dreams of a marvellous golden city of art, full of fellow workers. This city appears to him at times like some Italian town of the Renaissance, at others like some strange Oriental golden-roofed monastery-temple. He sees himself dead in the desert far away from it. Yet its blossoming is ever about him. Something divine has been born of him after death.

So he passes to the "White Symphony," the central poem of this series, in which I have sought to describe the artist's struggle to attain unutterable and superhuman perfection. This struggle goes on from the midsummer of his life to midwinter. The end of it is stated in the poem.

There follows a brief interlude, which I have called a "Symphony in White and Blue." These colors were chosen perhaps more idiosyncratically in this case than in the others. I have tried to depict the sort of temptation that besets most artists at this stage of their career: the temptation to abandon the struggle for the sake of a purely sensual existence. In this case, however, the appeal of sensuality is conveyed under the guise of a dream. It is resisted, and the struggle begins anew.

War breaks out, not alone in the external world, but in the artist's soul. He finds he must follow his personality wherever it leads him, despite all obstacles. This is the "Orange Symphony."

Now follow long years of struggle and neglect. He is shipwrecked, and still afar he sees his city of art, but this time it is red, a phantom mocking his impotent rage.

Old age follows. All is violet, the color of regret and remembrance. He is living only in the past, his life a succession of dreams.

Lastly, all things fade out into absolute grey, and it is now midwinter. Looking forth on the world again he still sees war, like a monstrous red flower, dominating mankind. He hears the souls of the dead declaring that they, too, have died for an adventure, even as he is about to die.

Such, in the briefest possible analysis, is the meaning of the poems contained in this book.

A Rational Explanation
of *Vers Libre*   *1919*

The world is in need of a reasonable explanation of the perplexing phenomenon known as *vers libre*. Since the Imagists came upon the scene about five years ago, with their talk about cadence and their disposition to experiment freely in all sorts of forms, a great deal has been written for and against *vers libre,* and a great many writers—good, bad, and indifferent—in England and America, have shown a disposition to revolt from the old forms of metrical verse. But no one has yet attempted to explain clearly and simply, for the benefit of the man in the street, just what "free verse" is.

The latest theory that holds the field in America merely leaves the confusion worse confounded. This is the theory of Professor William Morrison Patterson, which has now the backing of no less a person than Miss Amy Lowell. Miss Lowell's earlier theory—of the strophe's being in itself a complete circle, part of which could be taken rapidly and part slowly at will—was difficult enough for the uninitiated to grasp; but this new theory of Doctor Patterson's is worse. We are told that verse contains no less than six species: metrical verse, unitary verse, spaced prose, polyphonic prose, mosaics, and blends. In the future the public will apparently have to recite every poem they like into a phonograph in order to find out what it is. Having examined and registered its time-intervals, syncopations, and so forth, they will classify it by one or the other of the above labels. The idea is ingenious, but one wonders if anyone will take the trouble to waste so much time in these hurried days.

Let us then leave this atmosphere of the laboratory, and try to find out for ourselves what the poets mean when they talk about *vers libre*.

The first point to be noted is that, logically, there can be no such a thing as absolutely free verse, any more than there can be such a thing as absolutely free prose. A piece of verse must have a certain form and rhythm, and this form and rhythm must be more rounded, more heightened, more apparent to both eye and ear, than the form and the rhythm of prose. Take a corresponding instance from the art of music. An aria by Mozart may contain two or more distinct melodies, but these are combined together, repeated, ornamented, and finally summed up in such a way that the aria is in itself a distinct and separate whole. On the other hand, any long stretch out of Wagner's Ring reveals the fact that there is nothing but a series of linked musical phrases—motives we may call them—in constant progression. Mozart's method is, then, the method of the poet: Wagner's is the method of the prose writer.

This distinction being made, and it is an important one, we may next ask ourselves the question: Why do poets speak of *vers libre* at all? If there can be no verse logically free—except verse written without form, without rhythm, without balance, which is impossible—then why all this fuss over something that does not exist? This very same argument, by the way, appeared in an English journal about a year ago, and I happened to be the only man to reply to it. My reply was that the importance of *vers libre* was that it permitted verse to be not absolutely but relatively free. It gave scope for the poet's own form-constructing ability, but did not hamper him with a stereotyped mold, like the sonnet. It permitted him to vary the rhythm at discretion, so long as the essential rhythm was preserved.

To illustrate. Here is a short piece of free verse, the structure of which is comparatively simple. I have set the accents above the lines in order to show how they fall:

> I have fléd awáy into déserts,
> I have hídden mysélf from yóu,
> Ló, you álways át my síde!
> Í cannot sháke myself frée.
> Iń the frósty evéning
> Wíth your cóld eyes you sit wátching,
> Láughing, húngering still for mé;
> I will ópen my heárt and gíve you
> Áll of my blóod, at lást.

The first thing to be noticed about this is that there are exactly the same number of beats in every line—that is to say, three. The number of syllables between the beats varies—so that the incidence of the beat is different, sometimes iambic, sometimes trochaic, sometimes anapaestic, and so on—but the first principle of unity, that the number of beats should be the same throughout, is preserved.

Now to take each line separately. The first is comparatively simple, and gives the main beat of the poem. This is repeated with slight variation in the second line, and again repeated in the next to the last line:

> I have fléd awáy into déserts,
> I have hídden mysélf from yóu . . .
> I will ópen my héart and gíve you.

These lines give an effect practically identical; and herein we have the second principle of unity, the principle of basic rhythm, displayed.

But what, one may ask, is to be made of the rest of the poem? Here in lines three to eight, and again in the last line of all, there is a group as definitely trochaic and dactylic in formation as the others are iambic and anapaestic. Does this not destroy the unity of which you make so much?

Not at all. With this second group we come precisely to the most important law of *vers libre*—the law of balanced contrast. Lines of different metrical origin are used in *vers libre* precisely as the first and second subjects of a symphony by Beethoven or Mozart. Let us examine.

The first line which announces the second subject of the poem is as follows:

> Ló! you álways át my síde!

This line is the exact opposite, not only in metrical form, but in *mood,* to the line announcing the first subject:

> I have fléd awáy into déserts.

These two lines between them contain the essence of the poem. The rest is variation, amplification, ornament. For instance:

> Lo! you always at my side . . .
> Láughing, húngering still for me.

Are not these two lines, separated from each other by four lines of text, of exactly the same metrical pattern? And is not the same theme, with a slightly different middle, repeated in the line "I cannot shake myself free," and also with a different close in "In the frosty evening," and also in "All of my blood at last"?

If I had written:

> In the frosty evening
> All of my blood at last
> Sorrowing and grieving
> For the vanished past.

I should have been writing doggerel doubtless, but I should have been doing just what the metrists ask poets to do—I should have preserved the regularity of incidence which they regard as necessary to poetry. How, then, can anyone say, as some have said, that there is no metrical unity to *vers libre*, no basis of regularity upon which the poem stands? The basis is there, but it is concealed. *Ars est celare artem.* We cannot measure poetry with a metronome, or even classify it with a phonograph, as Dr. Patterson would have us do.

There remains one more line to be considered. This is:

> Wíth your cóld eyes you sit wátching.

I have marked this line above as having three beats, but it is obvious that this way of reading it may be unpleasant to some people. "With" is that phenomenon, not uncommon in English verse, of a long syllable which is unaccented in itself but which obtains a light stress from the fact that the voice dwells upon it. "Cold" is probably the same thing. One recalls the celebrated line of Macbeth:

> Tóad that únder cold stóne.

"Eyes" is probably accented also, like "stone" in the line just quoted. We therefore have:

> Wíth your cóld eyés you sit wátching,

a reading which gives us four beats—or three and a half, if we recognize that the stress upon "with" is not so important as that upon "cold" or "eyes" or "watching"—and a reading which probably will be more satisfactory to most readers.

What is important for us to know is that this line is, in a sense, a *suspended* line, that it partakes somewhat of the characteristics of both the first group—comprising the first, second, and next to the last lines—and also of the second group, comprising the rest of the poem. It is especially allied to the next to the last line:

I will open my heart and give you.

It needs no expert in verbal music to see that the movement of this is closely paralleled by the movement of:

With your cold eyes you sit watching.

We have here, then, what might be called in musical phrases, a *resolution*. The line:

With your cold eyes you sit watching

is the keystone of the verbal arch we have constructed. It binds the two contrasting subjects, moods, musical phrases, of the poem together and welds them into one.

We may therefore deduce from this analysis the following laws governing the writing of any piece of *vers libre:*

(1) A *vers libre* poem depends, just as a metrical poem does, upon uniformity and equality of rhythm; but this uniformity is not to be sought in an even metronomic succession of beats, but in the contrasted juxtaposition of lines of equal beat value, but of different metrical origin.

(2) When a meter in a *vers libre* poem is repeated it is usually varied, like the thematic material of a symphony. These variations and nuances are designed largely to take the place of rhyme. Rhyme therefore in most cases is undesirable, as it interferes with, rather than assists, the proper appreciation of these nuances. But occasionally it may be necessary to stress some complex variation, or to hold together the pattern of the poem.

(3) Suspensions and resolutions are common. The poet writing in *vers libre* is guided not by any fixed stanza form but by the poem as a whole (if the poem consists of one strophe, as in the case discussed above) or by each strophe (if the poem consists of a number of strophes). Unity within the bounds of the strophe is his main consideration. It will be found in almost every case that the strophe consists of two parts: a *rise* and a *return*.

(4) Every poet will treat these laws differently. Since in English it is

open to the poet to write, with equal facility, verses of two, three, four, and five beats so *vers libre* in English must necessarily be a more complex and more difficult art than in French, where so much current *vers libre* is merely modified Alexandrines. Every poet will therefore construct his strophes somewhat differently according to his own taste. That is what we mean when we speak of "free verse."

(5) As for "spaced prose," "polyphonic prose," "mosaics," "blends"—and all the other more or less experimental forms which I and others have attempted—they are not and should not be called verse at all. The difference between them and true *vers libre* is this: *vers libre* derives from metrical verse and from the old stanza forms. Throughout all its variations, unity of rhythmical swing and the dynamic balance of the strophe is preserved. These other forms derive from prose, which does not possess unity of swing and which substitutes for the strophe the paragraph. These forms may be confused with true *vers libre*, but the fact remains that the origin of each is different. With *vers libre* the starting point is the repeated rhythmical phrase; with these other forms the starting point is the prose sentence.

The Impulse of Poetry   *1931*

I

The Central Art

In his introduction to Worringer's *Form in Gothic,* Mr. Herbert Read has pointed out that, in aesthetics, "the necessity of a psychological groundwork has been firmly established, and it is realized that no general theory of aesthetics will be possible until the relation of the sensuous and formal elements in aesthetic perception has been generally established." And Mr. Wyndham Lewis, in his *Time and Western Man,* has written a volume to show that from his point of view, the artists, no less than the philosophers, scientists, and historians of the present day, have been unduly influenced by the concept of time, to the neglect of the spatial and plastic. These opinions from two divergent and independent critics of the present day, as well as some measure of practice and study of the arts on my own part, have tempted me to outline roughly what in my view is a valid basis for aesthetic, not yet stated in any of the books on the subject that have come my way, and of peculiar applicability to an art I have frequently practiced; that is, poetry.

Historians of art and authors of aesthetic handbooks generally start their investigation into the troublesome problem of what art is, by making a definition of the beautiful, and by applying, or attempting to apply it to art's complex reality. I shall not attempt to define the beautiful, for I hold that no artist has been primarily concerned with the production of what can be immediately recognised as the "beautiful," in the same way as a modern manufacturer produces a foolproof motor car. Only the artists of the nineties, with their gospel of "art for art's sake," aimed directly at the manufacture of the beautiful, and that is why we cannot look at them now. The genuine artist is always concerned with the construction of a complex frame of reference to describe the puzzlingly fugitive, disordered, incoherent nature of reality. He is an instrument engaged in extracting the essence of that reality for our benefit. That he does so beautifully is due solely to the command he has over his own sensuous and formal means of expression—it is not due to any primary desire to create beauty for its own sake.

As human beings we are all of us equipped with certain senses. Unless we are unfortunately blind or deaf, or are unable to coordinate our senses with our faculties of reasoning, as in the case of idiots and insane people, we constantly verify reality by reference to our senses of sight and of hearing. These two senses, used as instruments for the verification of what surrounds us, are the ultimate crown of our heritage as human beings. It may be doubted whether other animals, for all their reputed keenness, either possess or make use of them to the same degree. A dog, for example, will prick up his ears at a sudden sound; but there is nothing to tell him, as it tells us, whether that sound is a footstep or the fall of an apple from a bough. The same dog will howl equally at the sound of a piano or at thunder. A cat will detect the slightest movement in the grass, and will stalk it; but there is nothing apparently to tell the cat whether it is merely the movement of a falling leaf, or a bird, until investigation has taken place. A horse will equally start at a shadow beside the road, or at the movement of a railway train. All the higher animals verify the evidence of their sight and hearing through the employment of their extraordinarily keen sense of smell. Perhaps because we adopted the upright carriage of the body, some thirty thousand years or so ago, the sense of smell has progressively weakened in us. We have achieved our status as men by depending on our sight and our hearing, in conjunction with our hands, ever ready to execute the bidding of these higher agents.

"Beauty is no quality in things themselves; it exists only in the mind that contemplates them," as Hume long ago pointed out. Our minds, in so far as they are employed at all in the process of aesthetic contemplation, generally arrive at beauty through the operation of the faculties of sight and of hearing. But it is a peculiarity of our status as human beings that we are also impelled to do something with our hands in regard to the objects we contemplate. A life of pure contemplation is, except for some few Oriental mystics, practically impossible to man; the balanced life is one that combines contemplation and action. Human art is the final resultant of the faculty of pure disinterested contemplation when combined with action in a given material: stone, wood, color, words, or the human body itself.

For example, let us take the normal inquisitive child. Such a child will draw on a slate, will make up some sort of a croon or tune and sing it, or will spend hours in banging tunelessly away on a toy xylophone or piano. All this is art of some sort: art in its undifferentiated, natural state; art one degree lower in its grasp of technical principles than the art of savages, to whom the principles of selection and differentiation have already displayed themselves. Most children, probably, have at some period shown an aptitude for art in this respect, and have taken the first steps in the long voyage of discovery of the relationship between the material world of outer reality, and the world of intellectually ordered form. The child's tentative strummings, chantings, and drawings are what culminate in a Michelangelo, a Shakespeare, a Beethoven. That the child's powers seldom advance beyond this primary stage is probably due, not to its upbringing, but to the operation of that mysterious curse laid on Adam in Genesis. It is not by the balancing of form against feeling, but by the mechanical sweat of his brow, that man is forced to eat his bread.

Let us, however, revert to the child, drawing upon a slate, or making up a sort of rude chant and singing it. In the drawing, the child is creating a diagram of the world as it affects his sight; in the chant, or croon, he is creating a diagram of the world as it affects his hearing. The one represents the measure of his visual, the other the measure of his auditory approach to the world. If we examine the drawing closely, we will generally note the child has used lines, dots, scratches, however inaccurately, to define areas of space; if we listen to the chant closely, we will generally discover, for all its toneless monotony, some sense of rhythmic unity. In other words, the drawing is actually an embodiment of a certain feeling for space; the chant is equally an embodiment of a certain feeling for time.

Let us now take two further examples, drawn not from childish experiment, but from art in its most complex manifestations. Let us take first a great building—not some modern commercial structure, for most modern commercial structures are simply devices for making money, absolutely utilitarian in aim, and without any dignity, order, or proportion, except as utilitarian aims dictate—but some building that is the culmination of a long racial and social expression in architectural form, such as the Parthenon at Athens, Santa Sofia at Constantinople, Chartres Cathedral, or to take a modern example, the new Town Hall at Stockholm. What such a building aims at is, above all, a powerful stimulation of our sense of space. In the proportioning of the columns and their relationship to the base and the entablature, in the soar and spread of the dome above the piers, in the complex interplay of ribbed vaults, clustered columns, buttresses and windows, in the relation of side wings, arcades, courtyards, to the central mass, and of all these to the tower, we achieve a conception of human life as moving through space, dominating space, transforming space from emptiness to solid units of effort and repose. This sense of space, of space brought into actual measurable relation with ourselves as human units living within a certain landscape, is, psychologically speaking, the basis for all architecture. In the actual building, it is powerfully reinforced by the sense of touch, which practically limits the visual to forms that are geometrically definable to our fingers: the cylinder, the cone, the cube, the upright tetrahedron, the sphere or hemisphere, the pyramid. All this spatial and geometrical definition makes architecture, above all, plastic in its aim. It makes the building akin to sculpture in so far as sculpture is organized form, and to painting in so far as painting is organized composition. If we grant that man, as a conscious voluntary unit, is "the measure of all things," in the arts as well as in the sciences (and unless we grant this we cannot make any progress at all), then we must grant further that the arts of architecture, sculpture, painting, primarily derive from man's attempt to measure space with his eyes, and that their mode of expression is through sight confirmed by touch. For this reason we call them the plastic arts.

Now let us take another art which stands at the opposite pole to the art of architecture, namely music. Here again we shall not take as an example a modern popular song, or a dance for a jazz band, but a great classical composition, a cantata by Bach, an opera by Mozart, a symphony by Beethoven, or, simply, a folk song.[1] The function of such music is obviously not to give us any sense of space at all; that is better done by the building in which the music is played, and it frequently so jars with the notes played, that many music listeners prefer to keep their eyes closed rather than think of it. The object of music is rather to stimulate our time sense to the utmost degree, so that if it means anything to us, we dance with the scherzo and mourn with the andante. "All music is what awakes in you when you are reminded by the instruments," said Walt Whitman. We have to be carried along by the music in order to be able to enjoy it; it does not stand still, except as the printed notes on the page. Its constructive element is an element of contrasted rhythm. In this respect it resembles dance and drama, in so far as dance is organized movement and drama is clash of contrasting character. These three arts depend upon hearing, upon man's attempt to measure time with his ears, and their chief mode of expression is through hearing combined with articulate expression, the expression of the body muscles or of speech itself. I shall therefore call them the dynamic arts.

Now, in thus allotting certain arts to space and others to time, it is fitting that we should enquire: what is time and what is space, considered in relation to human life? It is quite obvious that we have to define both time and space with some care if we are thus to admit them to a commanding position over the whole hierarchy of the arts. Mr. Wyndham Lewis has already protested against the preoccupation with time of most of our artists and philosophers; and we have all of us heard, during the past twenty years, objections from various sorts of people against the distortions of proportion and the deviations from the path of photographic reality practiced by such modern artists as Mr. Lewis. Einstein has, however, shown us that, scientifically speaking, neither time nor space need be taken as constant and absolute values. The question is, what are they? I suggest that to the psychologist they are really extra senses, developed by the combined use of our normal five; time depending on our hearing taken in conjunction with our powers of articulation, space on our sight combined with our sense of touch. Art exists largely not for the gratification of one of these senses, as Mr. Lewis supposes, but for both. I am, of course, unable to finally prove this statement, except by psychological experiment; but it would be interesting to know whether good judges of time are not primarily "auditory" in type, as good judges of space are undoubtedly "visual."

No art is, strictly speaking, entirely pure. Thus in architecture, for example, one building may strike us as austere and restrained, and another as exuberant and rich and joyous, thanks entirely to the employment of decorative motifs, or to the juxtaposition and repetition of certain structural devices. The wall surface may be kept entirely plain and simple, as in the case of the Egyptian temples, the Parthenon, or the Byzantine; or it may be broken up in a free play of bosses and hollows, as in the case of the Hindu temples, the Cambodian, or much of the Baroque. The dynamic effect of one type of architecture is not the same as another; by the arrangement of spatial proportions an effect of time is obtained; in the case of the Gothic, of time aspiring to eternity at a single leap, and in Russian church architecture with its superimposed bulbous domes, of time ascending into eternity in overlapping waves. All these qualities that suggest time in architecture, strictly speaking, have nothing to do with the plastic sense of form inherent in the art; they are secondary qualities. Secondary also are the qualities that convey the sense of space in music. Western music at its most complex has, indeed, a complete plastic unity of design. The interplay of contrasting themes in a symphony, their repetition, discussion, and return, produces precisely the same effect as the free movement of space in compositonal unity which a great building or a picture possesses. Thus it is better to say with Mme. de Staël that "architecture is frozen music," than with Pater that "all the arts tend towards the condition of music." All the arts tend to embody some condition of the other arts, inasmuch as art in itself is a synthesis of all our sense knowledge concerning the world, in which synthesis first one and then the other of our senses are predominant. Art is not, as Mr. Clive Bell mistakenly supposed, pure form-organization, but is rather form enhanced by its appropriate emotion. In the case of the plastic arts which derive from static form, the superadded emotion is necessarily dynamic; in the case of the dynamic arts, which derive from shifting emotion, the superadded form is plastic.

In an age like the present, when the foundations of social morality, enshrined in family life, as well as the sacramental appeal of religion, enshrined in ecclesiastical dogma, are alike weakened, the arts necessarily become confused with each other. Such a confusion of the fields in which art achievement is possible may be witnessed at the present day in the development of the motion picture. The motion picture began as an attempt to combine the rhythmic urge of music with the visual appeal of form in motion. Unfortunately the fusion

33

was never perfectly achieved, and before the limits of the respective spheres were discovered, the "movies" decided to add still a third art, that of the spoken word, to their imperfectly achieved combination. The result has been a fresh outburst of chaos and confusion, dependent on accident rather than on disciplined selection for whatever aesthetic achievement is possible to this field. In the great ages of art, a sharp distinction was drawn between the immobile walls of the temple, the attitudes of the worshippers at the service and the rhythmic chanting of the choir. The combined motion-picture camera and sound-recording apparatus simply confuse these respective elements of aesthetic perception, up to a point where they become out of control.

The arts tend to synthesize and heighten reality by relying upon the concrete evidence of our senses, confirmed through human experience; the sciences tend to analyze and ultimately destroy reality by relying upon the abstract knowledge we have of natural law, confirmed by the study of the way all matter works. To the artist, everything is in the play of human experience. I am not at all sure that these two fields of activity are closed compartments; an artist and a scientist may subsist under the same skin, and produce valuable results in either field. Goethe and Leonardo are examples that immediately occur to the mind, and I have heard that Einstein takes an equal interest in music as in mathematics. The quarrel between artist and scientist is, therefore, largely due to the misapplications of art and of science; it is actively fomented by those scientists who suppose that science will radically alter the nature of man or the quality of human experience, and by those artists who maintain that art can be entirely explained by the study of some scientific canon of pure form. One cannot protest too strongly at the tendency in the present day of some scientists to usurp the entire field of the poetic and creative imagination, or the contrary tendency of certain art theorists to suppose that every achievement of the human spirit is amenable to immediate scientific analysis.

Mention in the preceding paragraph of the function of the poetic imagination, leads us naturally to the question of the relationship of poetry to the other arts. Is poetry primarily dynamic or plastic in its intention? The answer to this question will be found if we investigate the conditions under which the poem ethnologically developed from the hymn makers of primitive races to the later and more sophisti-

34

cated writer of epic, dramatic, lyric, and narrative poetry. The primitive poem (as displayed in the songs of most American Indian tribes) was an attempt to control the seasonal rhythm of nature, the rain, the sunlight, the wind, the pollenation of flowers, the supply of abundant food and game, by the repetition of certain words arranged in rhythmic sequence. In order to create this sort of poem the poet was obliged to keep in his mind a picture of the exact physical situation his poem was intended to produce. Thus, for example, a modern Navajo rain chant runs as follows, in translation:

> Yellow butterflies
> Over the blossoming virgin corn,
> With pollen-painted faces
> Chase one another in brilliant throng.
>
> Blue butterflies
> Over the blossoming virgin beans,
> With pollen-painted faces
> Chase one another in brilliant streams . . .
>
> Over your fields of growing corn
> All day shall hang the thunder-cloud;
> Over your fields of growing corn,
> All day shall come the rushing rain.

It is obvious that the poet who sang this song aimed at invoking, by the sympathetic magic of his words, the desired rain, by means of picturing the result that the rain would eventually produce; blossoming fields full of butterflies. And this interpretation of the intention of this particular poem is strengthened by the fact that the transcriber of this particular lyric actually asked the young Indian singer who made it what his song meant. The reply shows, once and for all, how much picture or image-making of a desired situation goes into the production of poetry of this type:

"My song," he said, "is about the butterflies flying over the corn-fields and over the beans. One butterfly is running after another like the hunt, and there are many." (Cited by Nathalie Curtis Burlin in *The Book of the Indian.*)

It follows, therefore, that poetry is a temporal utterance of spatial situation. It is temporal in so far as its material is composed of words—

that is to say, auditory sounds, arranged in rhythm. It is spatial in so far as this material images the external situation, the subject matter of the poem. It is thus both plastic and dynamic in its approach to reality. Homer may serve as a good example of this. The specific rhythm of Homer, the dactylic hexameter, was probably derived from an attempt to imitate the sound of the falling of waves on a beach; the specific materials of Homer were all the folk tales of Greece and of Troy, transformed into a connected narrative of events. The words in themselves were neither mere mathematical signs of things, nor empty sounds. In the formation of language itself, as Professor Jesperson and others have pointed out, there is an element of picture-making. Gestures with the tongue and lips replace gestures with the hands, and the word in its elementary form is a metaphor describing an objective physical reality. Let us also remember that the first writing was entirely picture-writing, and we will see the actual reason for the priority in art of poetry over prose. The poet transforms into auditory and dynamic rhythm the primarily plastic imagery presented to him by the visual and plastic world; and the only distinction we can draw between poetry writing and prose writing is that poetry can be more complete in its fusion of both visual and auditory interests than anything except the most "poetical" kind of prose. The difference between poetry and prose is therefore akin to the difference between three-dimensional and two-dimensional form, between a statue and a bas-relief, a great mural painting and a piece of patterned wallpaper.

Poetry, therefore, if my theory of the arts be correct, is in the happy position of occupying the central place in the arts; and it is by studying poetry that we can most readily grasp the field of architecture, sculpture, painting, on the one hand, and of drama, music, and dance on the other. Whether this new theory of the relation of the arts to the one I happen most chiefly to practice is true, is a question that I must now leave to the reader; but if it is true, then it follows that its correct application to the other arts should lead to an immediate revolution in all our educational practice and theory. For poetry ought to become thereby the main field of our educational interest, instead of being, as it is at present, the province of a few fanatics. I have no expectation that this sort of revolution will ever take place; but I cannot take leave of the subject without remarking that it is only by mentally admitting poetry to be the central mode of the arts that we can understand why the ancients thought the poet to be divinely inspired, and why most of the moderns think of him only as something too silly for words.

II

Image and Rhythm in Poetry

On the desk at which I am writing this essay there stand two pictures. Each is a seascape, painted by an artist of considerable repute in his particular time and place, and each represents the same subject: the play of breaking, storm-lashed waves over a rocky coast. Yet the handling of the two subjects is so different that they might have been composed by two people dwelling on different planets. In the first, a mass of slatey-blue, purple, and rust-red rock slopes down across the left foreground. Towards this charges the full weight of a wave, deep sea-green and freaked with creamy foam. It bursts in a dense explosion of snowy-white vapor rising to the left-hand top of the picture; to the right, the full hollow of the wave is exposed, with its toppling crest blown back in a twisted arabesque of white and pale green. A lowering leaden-colored sky completes the upper background. The entire effect is that of a lucky snapshot, except that no camera ever invented could give us all the play of light and color that this picture contains, nor render so accurately in purely local tone the sense of weight and infuriated onward drive here presented, so that the eye, looking on it, seems to call for confirmation on the part of the ear, and we listen for the boom and swish of the water. The picture is by Winslow Homer and is called *Maine Coast.* It is in the possession of the Metropolitan Museum in New York City.

The second picture also is owned by the Metropolitan Museum, and also presents a seascape of the same sort, as I have said. But here neither the local color, nor the light effect, nor the actual physical configuration of the waves themselves, have been particularly respected. On a background of dull yellow-brown, two yellow-brown shapes, cream-yellow at the top, detach themselves. They are separated from each other, and from the background, by a deep band of bottle green which silhouettes their outlines against the background. Their shapes

37

dimly recall clutching claws, thrashing streamers, the fury of tossed branches. Yet they are waves, because nothing short of waves could wash to and fro in this way, though no specific waves were ever capable of such contradictory movements. The long ravelled lines of foam of the preceding picture have become tooth-shaped, scalloped edges; the uprise of water against the rock looks like the trunk of a gnarled twisted tree; some of the crests are travelling from right to left and others from left to right simultaneously; the forward moving yet suspended beards of spray take the form of claws stretching out to grasp something; one wave is piled above another in a position that defies the laws of probability, and of realistic perspective alike. Yet for sheer control of linear arabesque, and for ability to evoke a certain mood, this last picture is perhaps superior to the former. We know that no Western artist has felt nature in such a way; and our suspicions are confirmed by the Japanese signature that appears decoratively placed in the right-hand corner. It is that of Ogata Korin.

These two pictures, springing as they do from two very different civilizations, give us exactly what their respective civilizations give us. The American artist is concerned, whether consciously or not, in stressing those very qualities in his seascape which the Christian religion has tended to stress in the individual; the qualities that describe pure being, that define individuality, the qualities of uniqueness, power, self-reliance. These qualities he has plastically set down by the use of the strongest possible realistic representation. His picture gains a tragic force, apart from its realistic technique, in the contrast between the solid and motionless weight of the blue-brown rock, the greeny-white wall of advancing water, and the dove-grey neutrality of the sky. The result is gained by juxtaposing elements of divergent dynamic speed. It is gained by treating the whole picture as a contrast of three planes behind each other, the rock, the wave itself, and the sky.

The Japanese artist is unconcerned with the actual appearance of the wave. What he aims at is what the Buddhist doctrine itself aims at; to disengage the actual quality of an experience from the experience itself. Therefore he tells us nothing about the sea except that it moves and upheaves and tosses itself about, lashing its own tops to fury. He presents us, in line and mass, the quality of pure becoming, of endless flux and flow, that the sea possesses, and expects us to make the required connection in our minds between the forms he has painted and the forms implicit in water. If we fail, it is not his fault; he has shown us the essential, or just enough of the essential to stimulate our sensibility. Thus his result is gained not by juxtaposing different dynamic elements, but by treating the entire space of the picture plastically, as a study in spaced forms.

The question that we have now to settle in regard to these two pictures is whether it may be possible that they have their counterparts in poetic technique. Let me take two examples. In the famous "Hymn to Proserpine," in Swinburne's *Poems and Ballads,* published in 1866, the following description of the sea occurs:

> Where, mighty with deepening sides, clad about with the seas as with wings,
> And impelled of invisible tides, and fulfilled of unspeakable things;
> White-eyed and poisonous-finned, shark-toothed and serpentine-curled,
> Rolls, under the whitening wind of the future, the wave of the world.

Sixty years after Swinburne's book was published we find H. D. writing as follows, in *Sea Gods:*

> For you will come,
> You will yet haunt men in ships,
> You will trail across the fringe of strait
> And circle the jagged rocks.
>
> You will trail across the rocks,
> And wash them with your salt,
> You will curl between sand-hills,
> You will thunder along the cliff,
> Break, retreat, get fresh strength,
> Gather and pour weight upon the beach.

In the Swinburne passage we feel that what the poet has been primarily concerned with is the rhythm of the statement. He is concerned with describing the effect, the purely dynamic effect of the sea breaking on the beach. He invents a swift galloping rhythm to convey the irresistible movement of the sea, and skilfully varies it in the last two lines so as to suggest the sudden fall of a breaker, and the continued onward movement of the next. What his sea is actually doing beyond moving and falling is a question that Swinburne refuses to ask. So little does he concern himself with the quality of his wave, that it is possible, here as elsewhere, to transpose and alter detail with little loss of effect:

> Where, shining with foam-dappled sides, upborne by the winds as
>   with wings,
> And fulfilled with immeasurable tides, and impelled by invisible
>   things,
> White-finned and poisonous-eyed, snake-toothed, seaweedily curled,
> Falls, under the blackening blast of the tempest, the wave of the world.

On the other hand, H. D.'s picture does not depend upon dynamic rhythm at all. Her rhythms, dependent not on repetition of stress-accent, but on subtle variations in quantitative value, seem to arrest the sea, to make it stop moving, in order to discuss what precisely it is doing. And it is doing various things: it is trailing across the fringe of strait, circling the jagged rocks, curling between sand-hills, thundering along the cliff, gathering and pouring weight on the beach. In other words, the actual movement impelling the sea forward is disregarded, and the sea itself becomes the active agent, achieving its own forms. The effect is plastic, and we cannot shift the words about in H. D.'s passage as we can in Swinburne's, though we might recompose the rhythm into another pattern.

"Literature," said the late T. E. Hulme, in his *Notes on Language and Style*, "is never an absorption of meditation, but a deliberate choosing and working-up of analogies. The continued, close, compressed effort." And, further, "The art of literature consists exactly in this passage from the eye to the voice. The readers are people who see things and want them expressed. The author is the voice, or the conjurer who does tricks with that curious rope of letters." The fact that Swinburne, in passing from the eye to the voice, has concentrated, in his description, on the movement of one single wave, without concerning himself overmuch about the subtle qualities of water in general, makes his work dynamic and rhythmical, while the fact that H. D. is interested in noting the precise quality of the sea itself, makes her work static and plastic.

Let us return now to our two seascapes. The Winslow Homer seascape escapes from the realism of its method by the use of color-contrast: the white foam against the dark rock, the deep-toned hollow of the wave against the white crest, the dark stormy horizon with the paler zenith. The Japanese artist, on the other hand, paints in monochrome, but is not less successful in conveying the savage mood of the sea, in the arbitrary forms he has chosen. In other words, the Winslow Homer seascape recalls Swinburne's description; the Korin screen is akin to H. D. For the color rhythm, the shifting from dark to light in the Homer, is the same in feeling as Swinburne's galloping stresses; whereas Korin's colorless counterpoint of form recalls the delicate contrasts of H. D.'s static statements about the activities of the water.

Thus we have it established that poetry can not only be dynamic or plastic at will, but that the degree in which the poet wishes to convey auditory or visual phenomena conditions the rhythm employed. We know that H. D. is in poetry an Imagist, that is to say she aims at what T. E. Hulme, another Imagist, describes as "the passage from the eye to the voice." But this description of literature covers only half its function. It is also possible to make the passage from the ear to the voice, as Swinburne does, with practically no interference on the part of the eye. Or it is possible to fuse auditory and visual imagery in such a way that they become practically inseparable, as in some of the greatest—but only the greatest—passages of Shakespeare. The two types of poetic utterance that I have described, that which is based upon dynamic sensibility, and that which is derived from plastic thought, become one.

But this does not answer the question that now obtrudes itself, viz: from which side of reality, the plastic or the auditory, does the poet's mind approach his subject? The answer to this question will be found if we investigate the nature of language itself. Among all primitive races, spoken language has preceded written language, as language itself has succeeded miming and gesture. The fact is that all language passes through three stages, mimetic (sign language), auditory (spoken language) and visual (written language), and of these, the second stage is by far the most important. Moreover we must remember that poetry, above all, is meant to be spoken or sung rather than read from the printed page. From the time when that bard was preferred above all others who could remember more clearly and distinctly the entire epic of the clan, down to the present day, when most people frankly prefer spoken jingles of any sort to the kind of poems that they are obliged to study from the pages of their school books, poetry has depended on the appeal to the lips and the ear rather than the eye. It may be that at some primitive stage of mankind's history, when humanity depended on the hunt, certain hunters were better at tracking the game by sight and others by ear. It was certainly among the latter then that poetry developed. However that may have come about, the value of poetry is that it fixes the continuous flow of the world in a rhythmic pattern of verbal sounds primarily; secondarily, that these verbal sounds take shape as analogous and visible facts. The poetic statement is a rhythmic balance of sound and of sense. But the sound comes first in the poet's mind. Afterwards he may, like the young Navajo bard mentioned above, visualize his work as a picture.

That is not to say that the Imagists were wrong in their insistence on the plastic faculty of the poet. It was necessary to break down the elaborate spell which Rossetti, Swinburne, Morris, and the later nineties had woven about poetry. Their poetry tended to elaborate rhythm without due regard to sense. The Imagists were forced to insist upon sense again; the hard, rocky, definite picture, the "exact word." In so doing they were obliged to defend against these melody-makers of the past, the concept of "free verse." Now no verse is, strictly speaking, entirely free; all verse depends upon some balanced rhythm of accent-beat or quantitative value which exists in the author's mind and can be communicated to the reader. But by demanding absolute freedom of expression for the poet, the Imagists threw open the gate to new rhythmic experiment. No longer was it necessary for the poet to speak in the idiom of Keats, Coleridge, Wordsworth, and Shelley, exhausted as that idiom had been by Tennyson and Swinburne. Such precursors of new rhythm as Matthew Arnold in England and Whitman in America were fully vindicated by the Imagist experiment.

Nor was this all. The natural rhythm of human song is based upon the intake and expiration of the breath. This intake and expiration has been responsible for two of the earliest and most universally employed poetic forms: the couplet, common to Sanskrit, Hebrew, Arabic, Egyptian, and other early classical languages, and the quatrain, which may be looked upon as a development of two couplets tied together. In many early languages the nature of the couplet has been determined by what may be called parallelism; that is to say, a statement is made and is repeated, with slight variation. This parallelism is the basis for some of the greatest poetry this world contains: the Hebrew religious poetry. Its effect appears even in the authorized version of the English Bible. Let anyone read the Psalms, or the Book of Job, with attention to the connective links in sense, and the effect is clear.

> The heavens declare the glory of God
> And the firmament showeth his handiwork;
>
> Day unto day uttereth speech
> And night unto night showeth knowledge.
>
> There is no speech nor language
> Where their voice is not heard.

This type of poetry may be elaborated into fugue-like stanzaic forms, as in some of the sublimer passages of Job, or the parallelism may be not a parallelism of likes at all, but one of opposites, as in much Chinese poetry:

> You have coats and robes
> But you do not trail them;
> You have chariots and horses
> But you do not ride them;
> By and bye you will die
> And another will enjoy them.

The same quality of parallelism is to be found in late Latin poetry, notably in the famous Pervigilium Veneris, and it dominates all the mediaeval Latin poetry of the Church. Its origin, like the origin of rhyme, which entered Western poetry from the Middle Ages, is obscure. It may have derived, as has been argued, from the East. Or it may have been a device known and frequently used by the Greek and Latin orators and transferred to poetry, once the art freed itself from the artificial system of eye-scansion and began to be scanned according to the ear. It evolved along with rhyme which was at first used to mark off the ends of the parallel statements, and it only died out in the Renaissance, when artificial and courtly stanza-forms took its place.

Imagism was a return to poetic forms of a more natural and primitive kind than the poetry that preceded it. The evolution of art forms is always the same: a new way of looking at life creates a new form of art, and this form is elaborated up to a point where it becomes artificial, when it has to give way to a fresh outburst of creative genius, or perhaps I had better say, creative sensibility. It was so in the Middle Ages, again in the Renaissance, and again in the so-called Romantic movement. The poetry of the Romantic Epoch had degenerated from the freshness of Blake, Coleridge, and Wordsworth into the mere juggling with aesthetic and verbal counters that went on in the nineties. Like its contemporary, poetic realism of the Masefield-Frost-Masters-Sandburg type, but in a more uncompromising fashion, Imagism marked "the return to nature." It aimed at creating a new form, a form dependent upon immediate visual and verbal intuition of every aspect of its subject. This new form was to be achieved not by elaboration of detail, but by a stark stripping off of all detail in order to pursue the essential:

> Be in me as the eternal moods
> Of the bleak wind, and not
> As transient things are;
> Gaiety of flowers.
> Have me in the strong loneliness
> Of sunless cliffs
> And of grey waters.
> Let the gods speak softly of us
> In days hereafter;
> The shadowy flowers of Orcus
> Remember thee.

Such a poem is not only interesting as presenting a new aspect of reality, reality conceived of as depending upon the duration of perception in the mind of the beholder, but it is also valuable as supplying for us what is a perfect definition of Imagism. The "nature-worship" of the school of poets inaugurated by Wordsworth, had lost itself in meaningless gestures of awe and wonder at the details of nature—"black as ash-buds in March." With the breakdown of the supposed connection between nature and human sensibility, under the demolishing attack of the Darwinian school, led by Huxley, the nature school could not continue, and there arose the cry of "art for art's sake," which practically amounted to saying "sentimentality for sentimentality's sake." Against this viewpoint Thomas Hardy was almost alone in his protest, but Hardy's view of nature was fatalistic, and offered no new possibilities of a harmonious reconciliation. It is to the credit of Imagism that it at least attempted a way out, by showing nature subject to the same law of contingency as man, and by seeking for the essential link of feeling that binds man with nature, in the "eternal moods." The question why such changes in poetic form as that introduced by Imagism have to occur, why revolutions in poetic practice exist at all, can only be settled by referring to the complex relationship that subsists between poetry and philosophy.

III

Poetry and Philosophy

The moment when man conceived of the world of life in which he lived as existing under one law or one system of laws, that moment philosophy was born. Philosophy, like every other form of human expression and communication, has two sides: a creative side and a critical side. The creative side of philosophy is what the Germans call the *Weltanschauung,* or the general picture of the world presented by the philosopher. The critical side of philosophy is the philosopher's detailed analysis of reality and of knowledge, including his analysis of the work and the worth of the work of his predecessors. Whether mankind are entitled, by the nature and failings of humanity in general, to have or to express any view of the universe as a whole, is a question that has been debated over and over again by philosophers. I do not intend to discuss that question now, but to show in what manner philosophy has been allied historically to poetry.

In the first place, the philosopher's attempt is to seize on the reality of the world by means of his consciousness; to show the direct operation of the life principle in so far as it operates on our thoughts and our feelings, which stand in an analogous relation to each other, so far as the philosopher is concerned, as the plastic image stands to the dynamic rhythm in the construction of a poem. Both thought and feeling are, to the philosopher, aspects of consciousness, but unlike

45

the poet who bases his work upon the organization of feeling primarily, the philosopher is concerned with the organization of thought. Thought in its highest reaches is an entirely impersonal principle. It moves from understanding of the individual fact to the linking up of fact with fact in an abstract scheme. It has therefore mathematical affinities. For the philosopher's thought, like the purely abstract number, is a ratio of space and of time. The number three, for example, may be considered as three units, occupying a certain space; it may also be considered as later in the series of numbers than one or two, or earlier than four. Similarly the philosophic concept may be considered in its relation to some side of ordinary human experience, that is to say, as having certain spatial relations to the events of our lives, or it may be thought of as more immediate in its effect on life itself than another concept. This is what Spinoza meant when he divided the attributes of reality into the two fields of extension and thought.

Philosophy, then, stands midway as a connecting link between art and exact science. In the previous essay I tried to point out that it was possible for a man to be both artist and scientist, though the number of those who have shown greatness in both fields may be very few. It is only possible, however, to move from art to science by means of the bridge of philosophy; and this bridge, linking together abstract cause and effect with concrete reality and experience, is, historically speaking, anterior to the development of science. In the present day, which has shown a great advance in technological science, it is generally assumed that all the great scientific discoveries have been made during the course of the past century. This may flatter our belief in human progress, but it is entirely untrue. Many of the great scientific discoveries of our time have been grasped long ago by the philosophers, by sheer intuition, long before they could be scientifically demonstrated. Thus the Greek philosopher Democritus long ago announced that matter was composed of atoms—though the demonstration of the atom scientifically was not made until the nineteenth century. The still earlier Ionian nature philosophers, in their discussion of what was the primary element, fire, water, or the aether, displayed a realization that some primary element must be posited; a realization that the modern physicist, reducing all matter to forms of electrical energy, has only recently fulfilled. Heraclitus' doctrine that "all things flow" finds its echo in the wavelength theory of the most recent physics. Similarly, evolution was held as a possible principle by many, long be-

46

fore it could be fully scientifically demonstrated. As early as the Latin poet Lucretius we get a clear picture of the evolution of society, and Goethe in his investigation of the presence of the intermaxillary bone in man and the higher apes, clearly anticipated Darwin.

The poet is a highly conscious voluntary agent working directly upon the full range of his experience as human being, and upon his underlying knowledge of that experience. This he aims at setting out not as a series of abstract concepts, but in concrete form and rhythm. But in so far as no side of experience is disdained by the poet, the poet necessarily seeks the laws underlying experience. These laws can only be stated, so far as poetry is concerned, in the terms of concrete ethical constants. Thus the poet is primarily didactic and practical, while the philosopher is primarily idealistic or critical in his approach to reality. This last point must be insisted upon, as the idea has got abroad since the nineties that the poet does not aim at teaching anything, that "pure poetry," i.e. poetry that exists solely in virtue of its own aesthetic appeal, is the highest possible form of the art. But this is not the case. To a greater degree than Milton, the great poet must essentially aim at Milton's aim, "to justify the ways of God to men." Some of the greatest poetry the world possesses, such as Aeschylus' Agamemnon trilogy, or the *Bhagvad-Ghita,* has been written for no other purpose. As Confucius stated in regard to the Book of Odes that he had collected from the folk songs of his time, "they are adapted to rouse the mind, to be used for purposes of self-contemplation, to make people sociable, to regulate feelings of resentment. They speak of duties far and near." The poet thus approaches philosophy from the side of ethics, the philosopher from the angle of epistemology, the theory of knowledge. The one is concerned with the practical and immediate workings of experience; the other with the theoretic and symbolical presentation of fact, resting on the figured relations of the knower with the known. A great philosophical principle like Einstein's general theory of relativity, or Spinoza's identification of God with the natural process, rests on a long mathematical development, just as a great ethical principle, like Confucius' "In self-completion the superior man completes other men and things also," or Jesus' "The Kingdom of Heaven is within you," is the fruit of centuries of poetic evolution.

In so far as man is a conscious voluntary agent, he aims at establishing a series of relations with other conscious voluntary agents. This aim can only be expressed in a system of ethics. The achievement of such a system is a social act of primary importance. Thus the poet, in so far as he tends towards the ethical side of life—and one may say that all poets in so far as they are mature have so tended—is a more important social agent than the scientific philosopher, concerned primarily with the problem of knowledge. His consciousness is not detached from life, but imbedded in its workings. But in so far as a poet is bound by his consciousness of words sensed as objects to the immediate and the concrete, he is a poor philosopher. His work is more frequently a running commentary, a criticism on life (often on his own life) than an ordered chain of reasoning. Thus it happens that most philosophy which we find embodied in poetry has been evolved prior to the poetry, and is derived from some source outside the poet himself.

This general law may be historically illustrated from the development of almost any people that have given to the world a considerable body of poetry. Apart from epic, which as Professor Chadwick has shown, is the product of a special "heroic age" during which the wars of contending feudal and invading states make the bard dependent for his material support on his ability to narrate these wars, all great poetry essentially presupposes a background of philosophic development. Thus the Greek tragedy of the fifth century post-dated the great development of the Ionian nature-philosophers in the sixth century, the greater of the two Indian epics, the Mahabharata, rests upon developed Vedantism, the full-tide of Chinese poetry in the 'Tang epoch came after several centuries of Taoism, and Dante represents, on the intellectual side, the culmination of the Scholastic movement as summed up in Thomas Aquinas. Nor is this general law disputed by the development of English poetry. Although it is impossible to point to any considerable body of philosophical thought as a source-background for the Elizabethan poets, yet one cannot understand their peculiar development without some reference to Seneca's stoicism and Montaigne's scepticism; and in regard to the later "metaphysical" poets (Donne, Herbert of Cherbury, Marvell, Vaughan) it is necessary to think of the rising tide of Platonism in the epoch; while with the later "classical restoration" poets (Dryden, Pope, Johnson, Swift) it is equally necessary to understand the prevailing influence of Aristotelian and less idealistic and more political conceptions.

The most interesting example of a philosophical poet whose work contains both an idealistic and a political *Weltanschauung,* is unques-

48

tionably Goethe. But Goethe is at once the most difficult and the most unsatisfactory of philosophic poets, owing to the fact that so many different and conflicting strains of philosophy met and mingled in him. One has only to compare him for a moment with such a philosophical poet as Shelley, who consistently followed Godwin's optimistic idealism, in order to see that Shelley is the clearer and the less limited of the two. As a poet, Goethe was endowed with a richly animal and warmly passionate nature, strongly lyrical in impulse, but crossed by a strange vein of saturnine scepticism. In his early life he deeply studied the philosophy of Spinoza, and this influence persisted up to the time of the French Revolution, which following after his Italian journey in 1787, made a complete breach between the earlier and later development of his mind. In his Later Period he was more influenced by the combined scepticism and encyclopaedic range of Voltaire. Under the influence of Spinoza's noble pantheism, he conceived of his figure of Faust—who is, in the scenes written before 1789, the type itself of the "God-intoxicated man" as Novalis called Spinoza—the man seeking God in the processes of nature, who can declare that "if we love God it is not necessary for God to love us in return," aiming at an universal science which is "of life not of death" and considering evil as mere lack of knowledge. Against this sublime and Titan-like figure, wishing to translate contemplation into action, Goethe sets the image of Mephistopheles, representing primarily the sceptic force in his own nature, reinforced by the influence of Voltaire. Mephistopheles easily tricks Faust by substituting the fleshly love for the naïve and unsophisticated Margaret for the transcendental striving for the unearthly ideal. But in the second part of the poem, written forty years later, Goethe is possessed of a philosophical idea more akin to that of Hobbes or Helvetius than of Spinoza: he has accepted the limitations of knowledge, the imperfection of the human species, and is concerned primarily with immediate problems of human politics and social life. Faust himself shrinks in importance, and becomes more and more of a lay figure, Mephistopheles gains in good sense and dignity, especially in the scenes at the Emperor's court, and the optimistic conclusion, necessitated by the original scheme, appears both artificial and arbitrary. Thus the great philosophical poem that bridges the gap between the eighteenth and nineteenth centuries remains a baffling juxtaposition of two very divergent ways of looking at the world.

It has been generally assumed, particularly by critics of the neo-classical school, that the poets of the Romantic movement in English literature lacked a philosophic background. This is not the case in regard to Shelley, whose philosophy was consistently an attempt to put Godwinianism into practice, nor is it altogether true of the others. It is increasingly certain that in Blake we have to admit an attempt to fuse in poetry the scattered fragments of much Kabbalistic, Gnostic, and seventeenth-century Occultist speculation about the universe: the fact that Blake himself tended to alter the meaning of his symbolic myth, and to bury its main outlines under the increasing weight of subsidiary figures, should not blind us to this truth. Nor can we grasp Wordsworth, or the more instinctive Keats, without some understanding of the current of nature-philosophy that had been running in England throughout the eighteenth century, the philosophy of Berkeley, Locke, and Hume, with its defense of the imagination against reason. Coleridge, with his blend of fantasy and fact, recalls Kant's attempt to reconcile reason and religion. It is far more easy, indeed, to give rank to the great English romantic poets as philosophers than to their successors: the Victorian poets, Browning, Tennyson, and Swinburne. In their days, the human spirit which had still triumphed tragically in Goethe, Shelley, and Blake, was again crushed under the new and apparently scientifically valid doctrine of *laissez-faire* materialism, backed by the investigations of Darwin, Spencer and Huxley. The problem before these poets was how to reconcile the apparently casual and accidental workings of nature with the doctrine of an all-wise and beneficent God. Browning simply avoided the problem altogether, Tennyson took refuge in vague generalizations about the future, Swinburne swung back to a Dionysian paganism without much meaning. It is only in figures that were considered "minor" at the time that we find any honest attempt to face the full implications of the theory of evolution in its most materialistic form: such figures as James Thomson ("B. V.") on the radical side, and Matthew Arnold on the side of the Conservatives. Both laid stress on a fatalistic agnosticism that later culminated in such a figure as Thomas Hardy, who may be taken as the final reaction against what has been called the "Victorian compromise," which I think had better be called the Victorian evasion of uncomfortable facts.

The advent of the twentieth century brought about a bewildering variety of changes in philosophy. One after another there have risen up on the mental horizon the sceptical naturalism of Santayana, the optimistic pragmatism of Professor James and his follower John Dewey, the radical empiricism of Mr. Bertrand Russell and the American Behaviorists, the new realism of Professors Whitehead and Alexander, and somewhat more aloof and general than all these, what might perhaps be called the intuitional idealism of Bergson. It is this last—however the future may assess its value—that has perhaps had the largest influence on the poetry of our time, and indeed the Italian philosopher Croce has attempted to construct an entire aesthetic out of a similar point of view. It is not too much to say that Bergson's concept of the comprehensive intuition, passing from the physical and objective to the psychical and symbolized, and conceiving time-space existence as a concrete duration of interlinked parts generating each other, is almost a perfect definition of what Imagism itself aimed at, as stated above in the short poem I have quoted from Mr. Pound. Whether we will not in the long run have to take Bergsonism as the chief philosophical ferment of our time, influencing directly or indirectly such modern poets as Verhaeren, Claudel, Carl Sandburg, Robinson Jeffers, and most Russian and German symbolism, is a question that only future investigation can settle.

In Mr. T. S. Eliot, however, we have an important philosophic poet, as well as a critic of first magnitude, who is entirely opposed to Bergsonism. And it is perhaps worthwhile to investigate the roots of his philosophy, in order to understand just what his reaction to Bergsonism represents, and how it differs from the attitude held by the author of this essay. Mr. Eliot is a dualist, that is to say, unlike Bergson, who dismisses the material world altogether as pure flux and argues in favor of a new ideal world based on the action of instinct and duration. Mr. Eliot takes for granted that matter and mind are separate and indivisible constants. This fundamental belief he derives from study of Professors Irving Babbitt and Paul Elmer More, but Mr. Eliot has applied this idea much more logically and unsentimentally to reality than either of these philosophic critics, and has reached some extreme conclusions, which are important. The first of these is that experience is never whole but fragmentary. For example, I may be suffering, materially, from a toothache while at the same time certain lines from Dante (which have no reference to the toothache) are running in my mind. The two experiences are distinct, and have no bearing on each other. In upholding this belief, Mr. Eliot has simply drawn the correct psychological corollary from Professor Babbitt's and Professor More's doctrine; a psychological corollary that must be grasped before anyone can understand the form of his own most important poem, *The Waste Land.* Mr. Eliot's second postulate is that the poet destroys his own personality by writing; that writing is essentially an impersonal process. "The poet has, not a 'personality' to express, but a particular medium, which is only a medium and not a personality." "The progress of an artist is a continual self-sacrifice, a continual extinction of personality." These phrases, culled from Mr. Eliot's *Sacred Wood,* will serve, I hope, to show that I am not ascribing to Mr. Eliot views which are not his.

It is necessary to point out that this belief, too, derives from Mr. Eliot's dualism. If mind and matter are distinct, and the human organism (which is both) can only realize both apart, then there can be no connecting link of "personality" in the process, unless, indeed, we define personality paradoxically as an entirely impersonal quality. But let us pass on to the latter stage of Mr. Eliot's philosophic theory. It is, briefly, that a dogmatic religious system is practically necessary as a primary postulate for the cultured mind as well as for the ordinary mind. And it is here that Mr. Eliot takes sharp issue with the Neo-Humanists, led by Professors Babbitt and More, for there is nothing in their thinking of which they are so shy as of religious dogma. That dogma was not only necessary as an intellectualist framework for, say, Dante's poetry, but was even necessary before Dante could feel the poetry, is a matter that they are not prepared at all to admit. Yet I am not sure that Mr. Eliot is not here on safer ground than in his previous pronouncements on mind and matter and personality. The chief difficulty about the creation or the understanding of reasonably good poetry in our time, is the lack of a good dogmatic ground on which to base our poetic perceptions. We have to formulate a scheme of poetic values without relation to prevailing theological beliefs, and such a scheme is very difficult, if not altogether impossible.

The reader must not, however, take it that while I can meet Mr. Eliot in holding that dogma may be an essential part of poetry, I can also agree with him in regard to his views on the distinctness of mind and matter, and on personality. Although I am in sympathy with his claim for an intellectualist content for poetry, I do not hold that his philosophy can ever supply it. Mind and matter in me are distinct, but not separate, items of perception. What unites them is precisely conscious personality. This I would define not as a fixed entity such as is individuality, but as a variable quality: and all we can say about personality is that it is a quality completely non-individual, in the final sense, in its workings. It is a quality that in its most developed form completely transcends the individual unit by the operation of imaginative understanding; and its aim is neither the self-indulgence of aesthetic Romanticism, nor the self-restraint of Professor Babbitt's Classicism, nor the mystic self-annihilation (which seems to be the aim of Mr. Eliot and was also the aim of Blake and of Nietzsche), but self-completion through a fusion of the intellect and the intuition on the plane of human values.

The Orient and
Contemporary Poetry   *1945*

I

The diffusion of literature, or—to describe the process more accurately and closely—the way in which a literature has been able to renew itself and to alter its direction by means of contact with some form of literary expression practiced in another part of the planet, is a fascinating subject. Those who are unfamiliar with world literature are likely to suppose that the masterpieces in this field are the product of great minds, who, through their work, cover great areas of human experience, guided by nothing better than their "inspiration." The more eager and persistent student will, sooner or later, come to the deeper problem of why certain literary forms came into being, as well as the question of why certain languages guided them to this achievement—and, allied to this, he will inevitably discover that the attempt on the part of certain literary creators to transpose a given form of literature from one language into another has frequently been responsible for new literary awakenings in lands remote from the birth of the original form.

It is with such a group of literary creators that this essay will mainly deal; a group which originated in England, had its adherents in both England and America, and was known by the expressive name they gave themselves, as the Imagists. Professor Glenn Hughes, in the only complete history written of this literary group *(Imagism and the Imagists,* Stanford University Press, 1931) has stated, correctly, that the Imagist movement began with a meeting of a few people interested in the writing of poetry, at a restaurant in London, in the early spring of 1909. Present at the first meeting were T. E. Hulme, F. S. Flint, Edward Storer, F. W. Tancred, Joseph Campbell, and Florence Farr—the last two being recent arrivals from Ireland. The group were highly dissatisfied with the way that poetry in English was being written, and were determined to do something to improve the general quality of contemporary poetry. Hulme, their unquestioned leader, was a man whose interests were equally philosophic and literary; he had done much independent study in both French and German philosophy and literature, and had undoubtedly read the French Symbolist poets, with their dislike of Victory Hugo's verbosity, to great advantage. Flint, who had carefully taught himself to read and write French, was his able second; he was much interested in the new French *vers-libre* forms.

Within a month of its formation, the group was joined by Ezra Pound, the first American present, who had just published his first book in London, under the title of *Personae*. As Flint and other chroniclers have accurately stated, up to that time Pound's poetry had been mainly influenced by the Provençal troubadours, by the early Italian poets of Dante's circle, by Rossetti and William Morris, Robert Browning and the early Yeats. With his restless desire, natural to an imaginative American expatriate, to conquer new poetic territory, and his flair for discovering new poetic talent, Pound felt at once at home with this group. His mind was intrigued with their "doctrine of the image": a theory whereby the production of poetry was made dependent on the production of new and concrete images in words. Hulme, whose philosophic position in regard to the writing of poetry was already fully worked out, and who was prepared to insist upon such clarity of statement as made his pupils see "each word with an image sticking on to it, never as a flat word passed over the board as a counter" was prepared to demonstrate the "doctrine of the image" by means of examples worked out on a blackboard. He was in full reaction against Victor Hugo, Swinburne, and the other romantic poets who were "always flying, flying over abysses, flying up into the eternal gases." He wanted poetry to return to the hard, the definite, the precise, the dry; he demanded a poetry that would present a continuous working up of pictorial analogies between the real world and the world of the imagination. Poetry to him was not inherent in any given metrical form, and for that reason he was disposed to favor the recent French experiments in *vers libres;* it was inherent in the power of metaphorical expression, which alone could create appropriate images; and for that reason, he favored the shorter poem over the long.

The group, as Flint later stated, "died a lingering death at the end of its second winter"; but before that event occurred, two important incidents in relation to it had happened. In the first place, the American poetess, Hilda Doolittle, whom Pound had known back in his early American days, and who was trying to restore to English poetry something of the metric freedom, as well as the poetic vividness of early Greek lyric poetry, decided—following a brief visit by Pound himself back to America in the winter of 1909–10—to come over and settle in London. She then met the members of the group, and was acclaimed by them, as a perfect example of Imagism—although she made no attempt, as they did, to write on modern subjects. In the second place, the author of this essay, in the same spring of 1910, had himself met Hulme in an editor's office in London. Hulme had fished out of me that I was interested in the writing of poetry, and he promptly invited me to take part in the meetings and discussions of the group. My painful shyness—of which I was acutely conscious—as well as the effort I was then making on my own account, to write poetry according to models provided by the early French Symbolists, forbade my responding to Hulme's invitation. And so my efforts were to continue, single-handed, along somewhat parallel lines, until the day in late May of 1913, when—with my series of *Irradiations* worked out and complete—I was destined to meet Ezra Pound in Paris.

The reader may well ask, at this point, "Just what has all this to do with Oriental poetry and its influence upon contemporary English and American poetry?" The answer is, that it has a great deal, as anyone will see who reads further in this essay. None of these early theorists of the image had, one presumes, read much Oriental poetry, either in the original or in translation. Goethe's *West-Oestliche Divan,* as well as Edward Fitzgerald, and Wilfred Scawen Blunt's adaptation from the Arabic—which Pound admired—were no doubt, familiar territory; but the attempt made by James Elroy Flecker to follow Persian models, as well as the *Ghitanjali* poems of Tagore, which may themselves owe something to the Chinese, and which were enthusiastically hailed by Yeats in the early months of 1913, lay still in the future. On the other hand, we have Flint's word for it that the group was much attracted, from the first, by Japanese *tanka* and *hokku* forms (presumably someone among them had read Lafcadio Hearn or Basil Hall Chamberlain); and as Flint added, "we all wrote dozens of the latter, an amusement." The obvious conclusion is, that something in the conciseness of Japanese poetry, as well as its pictorial quality, early attracted the Imagist group.

We who are aware of the immense cultural debt long since owed by Japanese literature and art to the Chinese, are also aware of how little effect these Japanese forms—which have acted on Japanese poetry as a deterrent rather than as a factor favoring full development—can have had upon developing the Imagist group in the direction of a better understanding of Oriental poetry. They might as well have tried to write poems modeled upon the Persian *ghazel*—as the Georgian poet James Elroy Flecker, actually did a little later—as to have confined their attention solely to the *tanka* and the *hokku*, except for amusement, as Flint says. Whether they were aware or not that a great body of poetry existed in the Chinese language that was very highly Imagistic in its essential qualities, I do not know; but the fact remains that Flint, in his own early account of the genesis of Imagism, makes no reference to Chinese poetry, which would encourage a negative conclusion. However, I myself, though not then a member of the group, was becoming increasingly aware of the importance of Chinese poetry; I make no apology, therefore, for interposing at this point a purely personal narrative.

Sometime about the year 1910, I first became aware of the fact that the Chinese people had known a great literary flowering, and had enjoyed great writers of their own. I do not know how this intimation was first brought to me; I know only that I had been familiar with some of the great products of Chinese pictorial and sculptural art since the days when I, as an undergraduate at Harvard, had first walked into the Oriental Wing of the Boston Museum of Fine Arts, and had looked at the treasures magnificently displayed there. It was during the same early period of my studentship at Harvard (1902–1907) that I avidly read through the writings of Lafcadio Hearn; first as a translator of certain French authors—Gautier and Flaubert—whom I had come to admire, and secondly, as an interpreter of Japan. I did not realize at that time that Hearn, great prose writer as he was, was quite unaware, from the outset, of the immense spiritual and cultural debt which Japan had owed to China; and since he was handicapped, as a man, by the myopia which enabled him to see only the objects nearest at hand, he had necessarily refined upon and exaggerated the contributions that the older culture of Japan (already passing away while he wrote about it) had to make to mankind. What he said concerning a people whose lives were regulated by Spartan self-discipline, but who had continued to make an art out of the minute and the subtle, excited me by contrast with the raucous, bustling America I knew, but it actually influenced me very little at the time. After all, as an eager young student, I wanted a culture which was somewhat broader, which responded more completely to the flowing and diverse interests which underlay mankind.

This broadly human element I finally discovered in the Chinese; but I did not become acquainted with them as a people with a literature of their own, till around 1910, when I had already settled in London. Just what book first introduced me to them, I do not know; but I suspect it was Herbert A. Giles' *A History of Chinese Literature,* published in 1901—a book which I still possess and still find worth reading. This led me to Giles' predecessor, James Legge, and to Confucius; but Legge's more than Scotch matter-of-factness, as well as his utter inability to appreciate any poetical qualities in the Chinese written character, repelled me. I received, at the same time, far more enlightenment from the pages of Judith Gautier's *Le Livre de Jade,* first published in 1867, and revised early in the twentieth century. This I found totally delightful; though Chinese scholars have told me it is quite inexact. Cramner-Byngs' *A Lute of Jade,* published in 1909, and consisting largely of rather romantically colored adaptations of Giles and some French or Latin translators, also charmed me when it first appeared; but with the real pioneer effort in French, the Marquis d'Hervey-Saint-Denys' *Poésies de l'Époque des Thang,* a magnificent piece of scholarship published in 1862, I was quite unfamiliar at the time, and did not see a copy in fact until shown one by Ezra Pound, about a year after I came to know him, early in the spring of 1914.

It is difficult for me to say just how deeply I was affected by the first Chinese poems I thus read in European translation; I am sure however, that although they gave only hints of the great riches of Chinese literature, they acted on me as a revelation. In common with all the advanced poetry writers of that period, I was in full revolt from the Victorians, with the sole possible exception of Browning; it seemed to me that all the English poets, from Shelley and Wordsworth onward, had tried too hard to make poetry teach something, preach something, bear the abstract connotation of a general moral lesson—when the real business of poetry was to state, and state concretely, just what had moved the poet, and to leave the reader to draw his own conclusions. True, the Pre-Raphaelites of the seventies, eighties, and nineties had tried to get away from too much Victorian moralizing, but only William Morris, to whom poetry meant the return to heroic mythology, had made much out of Pre-Raphaelitism; and Morris had the advantage of long familiarity with old folk beliefs behind him. The attempt that the Georgians were then making, in the England where I lived, to revive the pure nature-lyricism of the early Romantics by reliance chiefly on Blake, rather than on Keats, Shelley, and Wordsworth, seemed to me rather artificial and forced; I recall that it was obvious to me that few of the Georgians knew anything concerning French poetry, just then concluding some fifty years of extraordinary development under the Symbolists; and so they seemed merely sentimental and naïve, where the French poets were mature, passionate, and subtle. W. H. Davies' poems were to me minor efforts in a falsely pastoral convention; James Stephens was Irish, a rougher and more erratic kind of Yeats; the early Masefield of the *Everlasting Mercy* seemed merely a cheap flash in the pan; W. W. Gibson was frankly dull; Brooke was clever, but just another precocious playboy; James Elroy Flecker charming, but rather too consciously exotic, in the manner of Leconte de Lisle and his favorite Parnassians. The only Georgian that seemed to me to matter was Ralph Hodgson, of all the Georgians the least fecund in output, but the richest in intensity and charm. All of them would, I felt, be better poets had they ever read this poem turned into my own English from Judith Gautier's French version:

> One day, through the foliage and the perfume of the flowering trees,
> the wind carried to me the sound of a distant flute.
> I cut then a branch from a willow-tree, and fashioned of it a flute, and
> responded with a song.
> Since then, at night, when all are sleeping, the birds have heard a
> conversation conducted in their own language.

This, with its hint that it is only through art that man can aspire to rival nature, seemed to me to contain a lesson that the Georgians would do well to learn. Also there was this, written by the same poet, Li-Po, and found by me later on in Hervey-Saint-Denys' translation:

> Close to the city, enveloped in waves of yellow dust, the crows
> assemble to pass the night.

59

They fly cawing, above the trees; they perch on the branches; the
    males call after their mates.
The wife of the soldier, seated at her task, is weaving figured silk;
The crying of the crows comes to her, through the lattices purpled
    by the last rays of sun.
She stops her shuttle. She thinks with discouragement on him she
    awaits here for long;
She goes silently to her solitary cot, and her tears fall like summer rain.

Both of these poems—and many more like them—seemed to me to
point out the Chinese poets had used their imaginations to identify
themselves with the objects they wrote about. That Li-Po had probably never actually cut for himself a flute, and held conversation with
the birds in their own language; that at best he had only pictured the
wife of a Chinese soldier in a city besieged by Tartar cavalry, was of
minor importance. He had done what Wordsworth had failed to do:
"to choose situations and incidents from common life, and to relate or
describe them throughout, in a selection of language really used by
men; and at the same time, throw over them a certain coloring of the
imagination, whereby ordinary things should be presented to the
mind in an unusual way; and further, and above all, to make these
incidents and situations interesting by tracing in them, truly though
not ostentatiously, the primary laws of our nature."

It was to this conclusion that I had been driven by my own investigations into such Chinese poets as I could find available in either
English or French translation, shortly after completing the series of
my *Irradiations* at the close of June in 1913. As I have said publicly
in another place than this essay, the *Irradiations* themselves owed a
great deal to French Symbolist poetry, notably to Verhaeren, Francis
Jammes, and to a forgotten book—*Les Fêtes quotidiennes* by Guy Charles
Cros. These poets had taught me that the commonplace incidents of
our lives—the vision of a child asleep in a baby carriage, the aspect
of great carts piled high with pots of flowers rumbling off by night
to a city market—were as valuable subjects for poetry as Tennyson's
"Locksley Hall" or Hugo's interminable efforts to match the godlike
sublimity of history. Small wonder, therefore, that when Ezra Pound
told me, sometime in the winter of 1913–1914, that he had fallen heir
to the notes left behind by the late Ernest Fenollosa, who had died in
September, 1908, and that these notes contained the translations of

several quite excellent and important Chinese poems, I was invincibly curious. And sometime during that winter—after I had already finished my own *Sand and Spray; a Sea-Symphony*, the first of a series constructed according to a pattern which was, strictly speaking, my own—Ezra Pound showed me some of these translations, now grouped together in his work under the title of *Cathay*.

To say that I realized that these poems, so far as I was concerned, represented to me an enormous revolution in English poetic technique, would be an understatement. I had already, during the late summer of 1912, made some attempts at something similar, both as regards subject matter and technique. Let me quote two of these, both taken from my *Visions of the Evening*, published in the spring of 1913:

> We will sleep in the high-pillared pavilions of late summer nights,
> Watching the mists take vague and altering reflection
> From the crimson lanterns, the towering tripods of flame
> Set all around the hall, overflowing with golden lights.
> We will slumber or we will drink, while the crimson-robed, dark-eyed
> dance girls
> Weave a few wayward paces 'mid the cups and flowers on the
> floor. . . .
> Let us sleep in the high-pillared pavilions of late summer nights,
> Watching the moon's blue breath on the mirror of the pond.

There were some other lines to this as first written, lines voicing a somewhat Omar-Khayyamish mood in philosophy, but not germane to the chief substance of the poem, which aimed to present the image of a night spent camping in the American woods, in an unfamiliar way. The other poem is even more explicit in its direction:

> The lanterns dangle at the ends of long wires, the breeze bobs them to
> and fro.
> My soul is in love with that lazy lantern dance.
> Oh how the autumn gusts through the dark gardens
> Rattle them together, rending their crimson sides!

This, recalling a far-off garden party I had witnessed as an extremely young man in Arkansas, was actually entitled in my book, "From the Chinese." In reality, its substance was no more taken from any particular Chinese poem than was the substance of certain other

61

experiments in the same book, labelled "From the Japanese," actually taken from that language. I knew nothing of either. What had happened was that I had somehow, as a poet, guessed at the way the Orientals had constructed their poem. The parallelism of construction, casting back and forth from the observer to thing observed, is surely manifest: and the self-same quality is omnipresent in Ezra Pound's *Cathay.*

Unlike Pound, these experiments had been made without the benefit of reference to Ernest Fenollosa's literal translations. I had, though, read carefully through his *Epochs of Chinese and Japanese Art,* but without any explicit reference to my own poetry. The general construction of the metric cadence in these examples is, at least, remarkably similar to the *Cathay* poems. And the point about the *Cathay* translations is this: that every succeeding Chinese translator, beginning with Arthur Waley, whose first book appeared in 1918, has, with very few exceptions, essentially followed the metric scheme set up by Pound. This form—ignoring the "rhymes" and the "tones" of the Chinese originals—directly follows the Chinese construction of the phrase and is therefore the most nearly correct vehicle for translating Chinese poetry we have.

It was only after I had read the *Cathay* translations—taken as Pound said, "from the notes of the late Ernest Fenollosa, and the decipherings of the Professors Mori and Ariga"—that I threw overboard my own scruples, which had forbidden me up to then to take part in the Imagist movement, and proclaimed myself truly an Imagist. The Chinese influence and example seemed to me to fortify the whole case for Imagism, which in H. D.'s early poetry, as in that of Aldington, had depended too closely and exclusively on Greek or Latin models. Greek art had already offended me with its academic naturalism; the work of the early Chinese artists, whether in painting or in sculpture, seemed to me very much superior; could not something of the same sort be said also against Greek poetry? Flint's position, as a modern experimentalist taking off from the achievements of the French Symbolists, was far more sympathetic. Indeed, there was at least one poem by Flint that seemed to me rather Chinese, in its implications:

> On black, bare trees a stale cream moon
> > hangs dead, and sours the unborn buds.
> Two gaunt old hacks, knees bent, heads low,
> > tug, tired and spent, an old horse tram.

Damp smoke, rank mist fill the dark square;
    and round the bend six bullocks come.
A hobbling, dust-grimed drover guides
    their clattering feet to death and shame.

It was, then, thanks to the Chinese influence altogether that I my-self became an Imagist, with all that the term implied. And when Miss Amy Lowell, in April, 1915, published the successor to Pound's *Des Imagistes* Anthology (which had appeared in the spring of 1914) under the title of *Some Imagist Poets,* I was proud and happy to take my place in its pages; for it seemed to me that my own combination of French Symbolism and of Chinese image-making had made of me as much an Imagist, as the influence of Greek poetry had made H. D., or the in-fluence of Latin poetry plus Flint, had made Aldington.

II

It is now clear that the Imagist group, as such, did not derive its impetus primarily from Chinese sources. The initial push to the movement had been given by T. E. Hulme, a speculative philosopher and a critic rather than a poet; he had been ably abetted in his initial purpose of getting rid of the vague rhetoric of Hugo and Swinburne by F. S. Flint, who—like Hulme himself—had dipped deeply into French Symbolism. Ezra Pound, who was trying, even then, to alter the rich but rather over-mythological early style of Yeats into some-thing more vivid and direct, had come and listened, and become con-vinced by Hulme's demonstrations; H. D., who had, with the help of many early Greek lyrists, written herself back into a world which stood out in complete contrast to the world of twentieth-century London, had attended some of the meetings, and her earliest poems—duly printed in *Poetry* of Chicago in January, 1913, and labelled "Verses, Translations and Reflections from 'The Anthology,'" meaning of course, the Greek Anthology—had been agreed upon by all as perfect examples of Imagism. Richard Aldington, as a self-confident young man then just emerging on the career of writer, had entered the group, to be strongly influenced by both H. D. and Flint; I, too, had entered, rather belatedly, in the early months of 1914, only after the first Imagist anthology had been published. Miss Lowell had come to

London in the summer of 1913, having—like most of us—previously read much French Symbolist poetry; she had threatened to take charge of the movement from the start; but had gone back to Boston, and was not expected to appear in London again till the summer of 1914. The main sources of Imagist Poetry were still to be found in Greek, Latin, French, and in Pound's Provençal; the Chinese influence, if it existed, was only a vague something in the background; and I cannot myself recall discussing Chinese poetry with any members of the group except Pound and, somewhat later, Amy Lowell.

But if French Symbolism be taken for the father of Imagism, Chinese poetry was its foster-father. I have already pointed out that, in my own case, it was Chinese poetry alone—in such translations as I could then find—that finally convinced me of the validity of the new school. And Pound, by obtaining from Mary Fenollosa her husband's papers, sometime in 1913, had inevitably taken the same direction. He now had in his possession, besides the *Cathay* material, a long and extraordinary essay "The Chinese Written Character as a Medium for Poetry"—an essay which he jealously guarded as a most precious possession and allowed no one to see for a long time, before giving it out to the public.

Fenollosa's contention in that essay was that the Chinese language was the most perfect poetic instrument to be found in the world, because of its ideogrammatic constituents. It perfectly combined the element of pictorialization and of temporal continuity. Fenollosa agreed that the primary act in the creation of poetry was the forging of metaphor—Hulme had spoken of the "continuous working up of analogies," meaning precisely the same thing. To a reader of Fenollosa's essay, it almost seems that, at times, the author of this remarkable document was ready to argue that the Chinese characters are in themselves metaphors: "Poetic thought works by suggestion, crowding maximum meaning into the single phrase, pregnant, charged, and luminous from within. In Chinese character each word accumulated this sort of energy in itself."

This recalls somewhat the theory set out by Richard Wilhelm, the great German sinologist, in whose work Doctor Carl Jung, the Swiss psychologist, has become so interested: that the continuity of Chinese culture (despite all disasters) has been due to the fact that the Chinese possessed an unbroken record of ideographic language. But it is easy to see in what direction Fenollosa went much further; and how many pitfalls there were in his doctrine, when pushed to extremes by such an extremist as Ezra Pound. For Pound, as the jealous guardian of Fenollosa's legacy, immediately leaped to the conclusion that the thing to do was to reduce Imagism to further intensity, and to pack into every word of his resultant poems all the pictorial overtones which Fenollosa had previously found in Chinese characters.

Whether this new direction on his part was responsible for the coolness that now sprang up between him and T. E. Hulme, I cannot say; but in the spring of 1914, I was destined to hear a great deal, through Pound, of a new art movement he was starting, to be called Vorticism. The new group consisted of Wyndham Lewis, who was writer as well as artist; Edward Wadsworth, a painter; Jacob Epstein, the well-known sculptor; Henri Gaudier–Brzeska, the young Franco-Polish sculptor whom Pound had recently met and befriended; and Pound himself, along with one or two others. Pound worked hard on me to get me to take an interest in the movement, and even offered me a chance to lecture to the public on my own theories of poetry. I had, however, other concerns for the moment, and in July of that year, at the same time that the new group got under way with their famous little magazine *Blast,* which soon after vanished—thanks to the more reverberant blast of the First World War—Miss Lowell did return to London, prepared to push the Imagists further along by bringing out, at her own expense, a series of annual anthologies. She and Pound immediately quarreled over the editorship; with the result that when the first of this series of anthologies came out in the spring of 1915, it had no editor at all, and was deprived of the services of Ezra Pound.

In saying this much, I am, however, already getting in advance of my main story; which is, as far as I am able, to trace the impact of Chinese poetry upon the consciousness of some modern Western poets; which impact, I believe, took place at first exclusively through the group known as the Imagists. My secondary purpose it to trace the same impact through my own work. I had already, at the close of January, 1914, written my "Blue Symphony," which was at first intended as an exercise in the pictorial manner of such Chinese poets as had already come my way; and then—as I have already narrated in my *Autobiography*—had, during the course of writing this poem, suddenly run across, by accident, some of Hans Bethge's German translations of old Chinese poems, serving as a choral background to Gustav Mahler's orchestral symphony, *Das Lied Von der Erde,* then being given its first public performance in London. As I have elsewhere stated, the effect of the discovery of these translations was electric. "As I listened to them [the Bethge translations] it seemed to me that the poem I was now writing was the same poem that many of these old Chinese poets had already written. My modern loneliness, exile, despair, fled across centuries of time and thousands of miles of space and was joined to theirs." This rediscovery of the Chinese made me feel that my chief business was to see to it that the direction taken in my "Blue Symphony" was fully followed up; and accordingly, the whole series of my "Symphonies" was then and there begun. To continue with them was now my chief concern.

Pound, however, was certainly off on another tack. In the spring of 1913, he had been strongly and emotionally moved by the beauty of many faces seen in a city crowd as he descended from his train at a station of the Paris Metro. He wrote a thirty-line poem, according to his own account, about this; six months later, he shortened it, adjudging it work of "second intensity"; a year later, he made the following *hokku*-like sentence:

> The apparition of these faces in the crowd;
> Petals on a wet, black bough.

Flint was also doing much the same thing when he reduced an earlier and much longer poem that had appeared in his first book, into the sixteen-line lyric of his *Cadences,* well known under the title of "The Swan." I was doing something of the same thing when I was condensing my personal emotions as detailed in the "Blue Symphony" into what could be pictorially and vividly stated in a whole series of Symphonies. But the effect of Pound's "one image poem," as he called it, was, as it was more intense, more potent. It really compared favorably with such well-known Japanese *hokku* as the following:

> Fallen flower returning to the branch;
> Behold! It is a butterfly.

The question of the relation of the Japanese *tanka* and *hokku* poems to the Imagist movement, or to the older Chinese poems, is a difficult question; and since I write, not as a professional sinologue, but as a poet who happens to have derived much from reading translations of both Chinese and Japanese poetry, it is one that cannot be fully resolved here. My feeling at the time was that the direction taken by this poem—which was put forth by Pound himself as a pure example of what he meant by Vorticism, was largely wrong. Pound has said, in relation to it: "the image is not an idea. It is a radiant node or cluster; it is what I can, and must perforce call, a vortex; from which and through which and into which ideas are constantly rushing. It is as true for the painting and the sculpture as it is for the poetry." In other words what was produced here was as close an approximation to an ideographic poem as the English language could bear. Pound had not read Fenollosa's essay for nothing.

Nevertheless, the English language, for all that, remains nonideographic; and the relation of certain beautiful faces seen in a Paris Metro station to petals on a wet tree branch is not absolutely clear. Morever, the relation of the Chinese classical poets to the Japanese *tanka* and *hokku* poets is, psychologically speaking, like the relation of full-grown and mature human figures to a group of rather small and temporarily attractive children. The *tanka* or the *hokku* poem is nothing more than a sketch; the Chinese poem presents a full picture. Though many attempts have been made to justify the limitations of Japanese poetry—the best being in my opinion, the book on *The Spirit of Japanese Poetry* by Yone Noguchi, whose poetry also had had, since 1912, some effect on my own—yet the fact remains, that the more Japanese poetry one reads the more one realizes that every Japanese poet is forced, by the exigencies of the form, to resemble every other Japanese poet. It is exactly as if every major English poet had been compelled to write nothing but sonnets—or rather, it is even worse. The Chinese poets, by contrast, are richly endowed; they have in their possession a medium in which all their important experiences can be fully displayed.

While I was writing the series of "Symphonies," during 1914 and early 1915, I was content to abide by the Chinese influences that had been absorbed in the translations I had found accessible; and was prepared to resist Pound's Vorticism, which seemed to me to point in the direction of Japanese *tanka* and *hokku* poetry, rather than towards the fullness of experience which I had already found in Li-Po, Wang-Wei,

Tu Fu, and Po Ch'u-I. Chinese poetry was used by me as a crystalliz-ing influence, an achievement accomplished along parallel lines to modern Imagism, which achievement helped to show Imagism the paths it could follow. It was also so used by Miss Amy Lowell, who—after my return to America in the last months of 1914—became my chief literary mentor, and my closest friend. There are many of the shorter poems in her *Sword Blades and Poppy Seed,* published in Oc-tober, 1914, which betray that preoccupation with the concrete occa-sion which is common to both Chinese poetry and to Imagism. There are even vividly pictorial sonnets here, like "The Temple," and "A Tulip Garden," which could not have been what they were without some reference to Chinese models in their author's mind.

It occurs to me, at this stage to point out that such has always been the way of poets. They obtain much from poetry written in other lan-guages, somewhat in the way that a hungry man is prepared to taste an unfamiliar dish rather than go without food. The same process goes on also in art and in music. Painters learn from other painters, and musicians from other musicians. But in the case of poetry, when certain technical devices native to one language flow over into another one, all that can be transmitted in the long run is, not a direct imita-tion, but a unifying spirit. All the sinological expertness in the world could not have directed the Imagists more clearly to the thing to be found at the core of old Chinese poetry: the attitude of man to na-ture, which was not that of the romantics, nor of the contemporary Georgians, nor—as it proved—that of the more recent intellectualist poets, but was Chinese, and I might even add, Taoistic.

It was only when the "Symphonies" were finished, during the first three months of 1915, that I turned back along the lines already marked out by Pound's Vorticism, and became again attracted to the possibilities of Japanese, rather than Chinese poetry. The poems then written under what might be called the *tanka* influence, are the ones assembled under the general title "The Ghosts of an Old House," in my *Goblins and Pagodas,* published in 1916, and those brought to-gether in my *Japanese Prints* published two years later. The specific oc-casion that prompted me to pursue this path was the memorial exhibi-tion of the Clarence Buckingham Collection of Japanese Prints, at the Art Institute of Chicago, in January and February of 1915. As ex-amples of an art of the people, rather than an art produced for feudal and aristocratic consumption, these *ukiyo-e* masterpieces especially appealed to me, an American. In repeated visits to the Art Institute exhibit, I strove to give to many of them their poetic equivalents.

Let me examine one of these equivalents, based on a print showing a *daimyo* attempting to embrace a lady, who is resisting his ardor:

> Force and yielding meet together;
> An attack is half-repulsed.
> Shafts of broken sunlight dissolving
> Convolutions of turbid cloud.

The reader will immediately note that no attempt is made to follow the Japanese *tanka* or *hokku* pattern of syllables. All I was interested in was all that Pound had been interested in, in his Metro poem: to produce an objective equivalent in words, to the object I saw. With the attempt, made at much the same time by Adelaide Crapsey, to produce a metrical equivalent of the *tanka* form in the so-called "Cinquain," I was then unfamiliar. My poem attempted to state the precise effect of the *ukiyo-e* artists' vision, in abbreviated form.

The difficulty with a poetry such as this is that it confines its creator to the fragmentary impression. The links between impression and impression, as well as the power to contrast one impression with another, are lost. What Fenollosa—mistakenly, as I feel—girds against in his essay under the name of the "copula-sensation," is lost. This applies particularly to my "Ghosts of an Old House" poems. Fragments of what should have been a linked-together experience are arbitrarily juxtaposed. The best of the older Chinese poets have not shared this fault. One feels in them a continuous power to move from experience to experience: they do not adopt what Amy Lowell, reading these Japanese-inspired experiments of mine, called "the unrelated method."

The Japanese manner, or as much of it as I could temporarily employ, soon lost interest for me, in favor of a more complex attempt to relate my own capacities as a poet to my American background; though Miss Lowell herself later produced a brilliant specimen of its use in continuous development in her "Twenty Four Hokku on a Modern Theme." There are probably also other examples of Japanese adaptation to be found in the poetry of Wallace Stevens—who has as well studied Chinese models. I do not feel today that it has much value, except as an exercise. Though poetry should be, as the Imagists said, primarily objective, the subjective element is a fairly continuous undercurrent, and cannot be banished without undergoing the peril of making the poetic process frivolous in itself.

III

The effect of Imagism was not what the Imagists intended; instead of drawing attention to the value of much vivid, direct, objective, and clear poetry in early Greek, early Chinese, or latter-day French periods, the result of the Imagist anthologies published through Miss Lowell from 1915 to 1917 was to promote what may be called the free-verse controversy—which sooner or later degenerated into the succeeding prose-poetry controversy.

A file of clippings now in my possession reveals the fact that the academic critics were chiefly irritated by the novelty of the Imagist form. The Imagists had also, in addition to practicing new forms, forsworn the vague cosmic and optimistically prophetic subjectivism that was so rampant in the works of Tennyson, Meredith, Swinburne, and Whitman. So those critics who did not attack the Imagists on the ground of lacking form, melody, rhythm, took as their ground of attack the Imagists' preoccupation with objects immediately to hand, which they qualified as myopic; while the Imagists' preoccupation with their own personal experiences was a clear mark of their egoism. Whether these critics were named William Ellery Leonard, O. W. Firkins, or Padraic Colum, such was their burden of complaint. Colum even went to the lengths of saying that many of the poems included in Miss Lowell's first anthology were far more egoistic in tone than those of Byron.

Other critics, such as John Livingston Lowes or Conrad Aiken (both of whom later repented), pointed out that the range of experience native to Imagist poetry was at best fragmentary, their lines prosaically insipid, and that models of the same kind of poetry could often be found in many prose works, especially novels, where they were embedded in the narrative. This led directly to the prose-poetry controversy.

The writer of this essay once took part in a discussion of just what was meant by the term *vers libre,* which the Imagists continually employed; though this term was in many cases abandoned in favor of a better term: poems in unrhymed cadence. The discussion occurred in the columns of an English weekly journal in March of 1917, and T. S. Eliot was this writer's opponent on that occasion. Eliot argued that there was a distinction to be made between prose and verse, and that "the ghost of some simple meter should lurk behind the arras in even the 'freest' verse, to advance menacingly as we doze, and withdraw as we drowse. Freedom is only truly freedom when it appears against the background of an artificial limitation."

To this the writer reluctantly agreed, though he denied that there was any fixed and abiding dividing line to be made between prose and poetry. The controversy, however, then went on into the question whether such a thing as the prose poem could, or should, exist. All this is given here as a sample of the reaction provoked by the Imagists in critical circles.

Eliot, however, has repeatedly shown—whatever his critical theories may be—that, as regards rhythm, he stands firmly with the free-verse promoters: while the degree to which he is indebted to Imagist practice may be illustrated by some lines which I now extract from the opening of his "*Journey of the Magi*":

> 'A cold coming we had of it,
> Just the worst time of the year
> For a journey, and such a long journey.
> The ways deep and the weather sharp,
> The very dead of winter.'
> And the camels galled, sore-footed, refractory,
> Lying down in the melting snow.
> There were times we regretted
> The summer palaces on slopes, the terraces,
> And the silken girls bringing sherbet.
> Then the camel men cursing and grumbling,
> And wanting their liquor and women.

Surely the thought here is divided into just such parallel phrases as one finds in most Chinese poems—with the leading constituents of the whole picture pointed up by alliteration, especially in the first lines, according to the Anglo-Saxon practice. Nor can Eliot's poetry, or even this specimen of it, escape the charge leveled at the Imagists, of being too exclusively personal to its creator. There is far more of Eliot's individual and exclusively personal experience embodied in every line he has written, than his critics have yet suspected.

One may say here also that if the Imagists were personal to the point of cultivating their egos exclusively, so too were some of the very best Chinese poets. A great many Chinese poets were, in fact, disappointed office-seekers or fallen favorites of some Emperor's court or the other; retiring into the wilds, they took up the careful cultivation of their egos in the face of nature, as a compensation for their failure in a more sophisticated sphere. The Imagists, similarly, were in many cases seeking some individual way out of the mechanistic barbarism of our times, by writing about nothing but what had directly moved them personally.

Moreover, to confute the pedants and the pedagogues, there is abundant evidence to show that Chinese poetry was not always the matter of "flat" and "deflected" tones, of limited rhyme-schemes, and of overworked classical allusions that it became about the time of the Sung dynasty. Arthur Waley—who once freely acknowledged to me the metrical debt his fine Chinese translations have owed to Pound's *Cathay*—has, in one of his volumes, pointed out the existence of long descriptive pieces, irregular in form, and called *"fu"* by the Chinese; these are in fact, prose-poems, though the prose types employed resemble more closely Amy Lowell's once notorious "polyphonic prose," than straightforward stuff. In short, the Chinese poets only became pedantic in the employment of rules to govern their prosody, as their own impulse towards poetry decayed.

For the rest, Imagism did not set itself the task of transmitting directly the *substance* of classical Chinese poetry. Every generation of poets, Eastern or Western, is faced with the same conclusion, of coming to terms in some way with the times in which they happen to be born. That they not infrequently find themselves at odds with their times is a visible fact, to be deduced not only from Western, but also from much Chinese poetry. My contention throughout this essay is that the Imagists, being dependent on such hints as they could find in accessible translations, constructed a poetry rather more akin to the Chinese *spirit* than the critics have hitherto suspected. Chinese poetry became for them a crystallizing influence, rather than a model to be slavishly imitated.

Moreover, in the case of a language basically so different in its construction from English as classical Chinese, it is easy to see that any translation must, of necessity, be inexact as regards its ability to transmit all the shades and overtones of original meaning. I. A. Richards has, indeed, made this fact the basis of one of his volumes, in which the impossibility of translating Mencius into reasonable English is graphically displayed. The Chinese ideogram, as Fenollosa points out, presumably derives from primitive picture writing; though the question of why certain radicals have been combined to form given words, is still quite obscure in fact. Any attempt to give the complete "feel" of the ideograms in English, is sure to lead to much over-elaboration; which was just what misled Amy Lowell, when with Florence Ayscough's assistance, she produced the translations embodied in her book known as *Fir-Flower Tablets*. The concision of the ancient Chinese is lost, under a spate of English phrases.

No translator, therefore, can render classical Chinese exactly; to do so would require the construction of another language upon the same basis. About all that can be given is an approximation, a hint that, after all, despite all the barriers of language, the Chinese spirit may have its counterparts in the West; and that "all men are brothers," whatever their language, learned at the knees of their parents. Let me therefore conclude this section of my essay by quoting a short piece of old Chinese poetry, by Liu Ch'e, Sixth Emperor of the Han dynasty. Here is how it appears, in the versions of three different translators:

> The sound of rustling silk is stilled,
> With dust the marble courtyard filled;
> No footfalls echo on the floor,
> Fallen leaves, in heaps, block up the door:
> For she my pride, my lovely one is lost;
> And I am left, in hopeless anguish tossed.
> —*Herbert Giles*

> The rustling of silk is discontinued,
> Dust drifts over the courtyard.
> There is no sound of footfall and the leaves
> Scurry into heaps and lie still.

And she, the rejoicer of the heart, is beneath them;
A wet leaf that clings to the threshold.

—*Ezra Pound*

The sound of her silk skirt has stopped.
On the marble pavement dust grows.
Her empty rooms are cold and still,
Fallen leaves are piled against the doors.
Longing for that lovely lady,
How can I bring my aching heart to rest?

—*Arthur Waley*

Each of these poems might be taken by the judicious reader as an acknowledgment of the debt we all owe to Chinese literature, and as a partial promise to repay.

IV

Poetry is an act of communication. What is communicated in poetry is not the emotion of the poet, but the objective equivalent of that emotion stated in words (just as what is communicated in painting is not what the painter sees, but the objective equivalent of his vision stated in colors and in forms; and what is communicated in sculpture is the objective equivalent of the sculptor's vision stated in the formal planes of wood, bronze, or stone). All art is primarily making; and beauty is "that which seen pleases"; a definition on which both East and West can agree. Poetry is therefore an aesthetic object made up out of words, with the purpose in view of communicating something.

Therefore, the good student of poetry must be one exceptionally sensitive to words, both from the point of view of their external musical qualities as sound, and from the point of view of the way they affect one another in the construction of the phrase or the sentence. Poetry might also be termed the highest possible articulation of human speech; that is to say, it is human speech heightened by the sense of rhythm that we naturally derive from the muscular activity of our own bodies, and guided by the creative imagination. As to what the imagination is, and how it works, I must refer the reader to Coleridge, and to that famous passage in Chapter Fourteen of *Biographia Literaria* for the only satisfactory definition. Whatever its imaginative constituents may be, a good poem is so bound up in the language in which it is written, that translations of poetry from one language to another are notoriously difficult, unless the translator happens also to be a poet.

Poetry, through its words, aims at producing in the reader something of the same state of mind the poet recalled when he set down the words which form the external content of the poem. These words usually combine objective observation and subjective feeling in a novel and unusual way. The most accepted method, for poets of the West at least, to combine these mental constituents is by means of metaphor, as Fenollosa long ago pointed out. A metaphor is an image, that is to say it is an analogy drawn between something in external nature and the feeling that arises within the observer. Therefore Shakespeare was producing a perfect short Imagist poem when he wrote, in *Hamlet:*

> But see, the morn in russet mantle clad,
> Walks o'er the dew of yon high eastern hill.

There is, however, one important qualification to be made. Inasmuch as we may suppose the reader of poetry to be a person possessing a wide range and diversity of interests in life, there is no reason why a poet—however Imagistic his intention—should not use his material with the purpose of being philosophic, didactic, satiric, sentimental, or merely vivid. Imagism, in its manifestoes, simply said "Be as concrete as possible"; not "Do not teach anything." However, it is possible to construct poems consisting solely of a single natural observation without commentary of any sort. This is precisely what was done in Japan, first by the composers of *tanka* and later by the *hokku* poets.

With the limitations of the Japanese method I have already dealt; therefore I shall not attempt here any recapitulation. The same limitation does not apply to the great Chinese classical poets. Indeed, theirs is probably the greatest body of poetry arising from natural and familiar fact that we have in the world. However, the Chinese poetry still possesses certain marked limitations in subject matter from our Western point of view, which may have been the reason why so many Western poets have recently been turning away from it, since the days of the Imagist reform. With these limitations I must now deal.

As Arthur Waley in his *A Hundred and Seventy Chinese Poems* pointed out, the love of a man for a woman is not a theme often touched upon by Chinese poets, after the period of the Han dynasty. To the Oriental, sexual relationships were supposed to have nothing to do with either companionship or sympathy; these feelings the classical Chinese poet reserved entirely for his friends; with the result (according to Waley) that fully one-half the poetry in the Chinese language deals with the theme of parting with one's friends. Another large number of Chinese poems deals with the theme, common enough in a country where sexual relationships were entered into purely for biological reasons, of the deserted wife or concubine; such poems, as Waley has stated, were written indifferently by poets of either sex, and were thought of as being vaguely allegorical, as recalling the thwarting of public ambitions on the part of their authors, who belonged to the official mandarin class. Moreover, an enormous majority of early Chinese poems are infused with feelings more closely akin to the Taoist or the Chinese Buddhist conceptions of the interrelations of man and nature, than to the severely social and ethical conceptions of the official Confucianism. Finally, as the older Chinese literature grew, a process took place within it that is closely paralleled by Chinese art; the copying and imitation of older models became universal, leading to the mannered artificiality of almost all Chinese poetry produced later than the twelfth century.

Even more serious than all this, from the Western point of view, is the fact that Chinese poetry deals very infrequently with the supernatural. Such a poem as Po Ch'u-I's "Everlasting Wrong" does indeed stand in "garish isolation," not only to the main body of that poet's work, but to the general tendency of Chinese poetry. Except for Ch'u Yuan's famous *Li Sao,* with its marvelous description of "the genius that roams the mountains, clad in wisteria and girdled in ivy," and its supernatural machinery, I can scarcely recall another Chinese poem that takes the supernatural very seriously. The Chinese Taoist, or the Chinese Buddhist, in distinction alike to the primitive Buddhist or to the Christian ascetic, kept his eyes fixed upon nature, in order to discover the secret workings of her laws. A Chinese Dante would be impossible; such speculations as to the spirit-life of the dead would have been thought of as being both impious and dangerous. Human life, in all its variety and continuity, not the otherworld, was important to the

Sons of Han. Indeed, it is precisely the otherworldly side of Christianity—that blend of Greek mystical speculation and of Hebraic moral precept—that has, for good or ill, set its mark on all Western poetry, and made of it something so much more complex in its mingled intellectual and emotional striving than anything present in the classical Chinese poets, that the Chinese seem naïve by comparison.

For example: the Chinese poet might refer to a seascape as being blue or gray, calm or stormy, but never "terror-stricken." Such metaphorical adjectives are as good as unknown. Also the long, farfetched simile is quite unknown in Chinese poetry. The reason is that the simile was almost undoubtedly developed among European poets in order to heighten the spiritual impression to be made by their work. By referring some material fact to some other fact more extraordinary (and the more farfetched the comparison, the better according to most "moderns"), the poet proved that he was one visited by the Muses, or under the direct inspiration of a God. It is curious to note that no Chinese poet ever laid direct claim to such divine inspiration (except possibly Li-Po, who claimed to find it in drunkenness); that there is a connection between this fact and the absence of long similes in Chinese poetry, is, to my mind, not to be doubted.

The Chinese poet, then, was one readily content with his human limitations: he was not one who "neglected to consider the ultimate fate of the body," to quote a phrase from a quite celebrated Chinese poem.

The Western European poets were not so easily satisfied: they were driven alike by their background of mystical and other-worldly Christianity, as well as by their own ingrown nationalism—even more rampant after 1918 than before—and by the monstrous pride of Western secular science (always promising a new world to be set at man's disposal, and always devising some new brand of sheer hell) into a renewed affirmation of the supernatural element in poetry. They escaped, after 1918, from *Weltschmerz* of a new kind of disordered romanticism, explored only by the Expressionists in Germany and the surrealists of France, by proclaiming for themselves, "a new order." A more introspective and more complex kind of metaphysical poetry, derivable from Rilke, or from Donne, or from Paul Valéry, full of the most farfetched metaphors and similes possible, became fashionable in Western literary circles. This poetry, more and more common since

T. S. Eliot turned aside from his earlier Imagism to explore his own "waste land," has already shown itself to be strong in dogmatic assertion, but weak in powers of communication. And so Imagism, as a opening path that had, from 1910–12 onward, led largely in the direction taken previously by many great Chinese poets, became a neglected path—at worst a passing phase, at best an experiment that might expect to receive a few passing pats from those professors who at least realized that it led to a reconsideration of poetic form.

In the highest poetry of the West that we have—the poetry of the Greek tragedians, of Dante in Italy, of Shakespeare and his contemporaries in England, of Goethe and some of his contemporaries and immediate followers in Germany—the linguistic expressions used by the poet always appear to be fused directly with the thought: the style becomes the man. This is not true of many of the most recent and "advanced" modern poets now writing in English. In their eagerness to get away from anything that smacks of sentimental romanticism, they have attempted to recreate the style of Donne, and to apply it to the material of the present day; forgetting that an intellectually adopted manner, without corresponding emotional stress, makes only for pedantry, not poetry; and that Donne himself most frequently justified his style when his feelings were completely engaged. In these ultramodern poets—I might cite Mr. W. H. Auden, as a good example—thought has so far outrun verbal expression, that the authors concerned seem to be seeking for means of expressing some range of thought that is altogether so peculiar to themselves as to be inexpressible in any definite terms that we know. Poetry, to them, has become a means of communicating, to an increasingly dwindling audience, ranges of experience so far removed from the normal that only the practical and patient reader can make anything out of them. These poets have therefore been forced to defend themselves continually against the charge of obscurity.

A prolonged and a careful study of the Chinese poets, who have always so gracefully and completely succeeded in stating their thought, would do much towards clarifying the muddled intentions of the modern poet. It might even succeed in bringing poetry back into popular favor, as the most natural and complete way we human beings have of defining our attitudes to existence.

However, it is quite useless to deny that there are whole ranges of human experience familiar enough to us, which were seemingly quite foreign to the best Chinese poets of the Han, 'Tang, and Sung dynasties. These poets were, one and all, trained as civil servants under the old Imperial system, on which the stability as well as the continuity of the Chinese people rested. A great number of them, owing to dynastic intrigues or for some other reason, failed of political advancement and took up poetry as a means of consoling themselves. We in the West would find it somewhat comic if poetry were to be practiced widely by disappointed politicians (I am far from saying that our kind of politicians would not be benefited if they only knew a little more about poetry). Our conception of the poet is that of a man who necessarily stands completely aloof from local politics, with his mind fixed on values greater than the temporal. We have even become suspicious of poets who write as events move them, who are moved primarily by external occasions to compose their poetry; forgetting that one of the greatest, Goethe, in his conversations with Eckermann, qualified his own poetry as being entirely "occasioned."

The character of the classical Chinese poet, as a member of the official mandarin class, limited him to themes familiar to this class. The poets of the West, drawn from every class in the community, have long since claimed all human experience as their province. It is useless, therefore, to attempt to create an influx of influence from the Chinese poets upon the West, by means of any strict line-by-line analysis and comparison of specific Chinese poems with specific Western ones. What we have to achieve is a transmission, not of detail, but of general method: and this transmission, I feel, took place not only in such Imagist poets as freely acknowledged their debt, such as Amy Lowell, Ezra Pound, and myself, but also in others who have similarly displayed an objective approach akin to the Chinese. For instance, I might refer the reader to poems by William Carlos Williams, Marianne Moore, and Wallace Stevens. The thing that all these poets have in common with the Chinese, is neither a precise similarity in subject matter, nor a direct imitation of form; it is rather a spirit of intense observation, of patient surrender to truth, of complete identification with the object. Such poems as, for example, William Carlos Williams' "The Red Lily," or Marianne Moore's "The Monkeys," or Wallace Stevens' "The Bird with the Coppery, Keen Claws" could not have been the same poems as they are, if the older Chinese poets had never existed; which is far from saying that any of them bear any external resemblance to any particular Chinese poem.

Since the affinity that may exist between the Chinese poets of the past and the Western poets of the present day is altogether a matter of approach, rather than of detail—and since the Imagist poets largely discussed in this essay were those who felt this affinity most keenly over a wide range of subject matter—it surely follows that for most of us, unfamiliar as we are with Chinese ideograms, the best way that we can assimilate the Chinese influence is through the study of translations, and by comparison of these with the work of the Imagists, as well as with the work of those Western poets—three of whom I have already mentioned—who have felt the Imagist influence most keenly. Such a study, I am assured, would result in giving to the Imagist poets a position far higher than they now have in most academic circles. It may be true, as has frequently been stated, that none of the Imagists were great poets. (No one seems to know just what a great poet is, until a long time after the person most concerned is safely dead; and at least one poet who has recently been proclaimed as great, W. B. Yeats, was undoubtedly influenced in the development of his final manner by Imagism, though to this was added a habit of mind more Celtic than English.) But the Imagists, at least, opened up a pathway between East and West that seems to me, at least, one better worth pursuing than the "intellectualist" direction taken by the most recently discussed group of English poets. That is their historical importance in literary history.

In Chinese thought, from antiquity down to the present day, there has been no separation made between human nature and external nature; and it is for this reason that the Chinese poets have so easily been able to shift their attention from one to the other. The same unity between what is without and what is within has controlled all traditional Chinese philosophy. Confucius and Lao-tzü did not really differ as regards the object to be sought for by wisdom, but only as to the means to be employed to attain it.

We in the West today stand at the end of a long watershed of human history. Since the days of Descartes and of Newton, that is to say for the last three centuries of Occidental development, science—whether pure or applied—has ruled over the Western mind. Western science has been governed by the assumption that all the phenomena of matter, of organic life and growth, of the development of personality, of instinct and of reason, have been controlled by causes external to us; that any gaps in our knowledge concerning these causes can only be remedied by the acquisition of more scientific knowledge; that it is only through such knowledge, not through an instinctive faith or an imaginative vision, that man can become in any way master of his own destiny. Nevertheless, no amount of science can tell us why, in the present conflict, we Americans should take our stand upon the basis of those human rights that we affirmed in the Constitution of the United States. That we should affirm the four freedoms of man in the teeth of Axis opposition, throughout the world, is not a scientific, but an ethical fact; and science is, ethically speaking, neutral. Our ethical direction towards democracy is not given us by scientific knowledge but by instinctive faith and imaginative vision; and this is also true of the direction that has now been taken by the Chinese people.

The Chinese people have been forced, by the external circumstances of the last half-century at least, to take up one Western innovation after another; and they were well in process of making a successful readjustment to the ideals of our Western democratic ways of life when—thanks to Japanese aggression—they were forced to the defense of their soil and their final right to govern themselves; a defense which surely, when the history of this war is written, will outrank any other in the field. With the downfall of the older Imperial system, much of the traditional knowledge and the culture of the Chinese people has inevitably disappeared; so much has already lost its contact with the Chinese earth, like the Chinese objects now scattered and reassembled in our Western art museums, that one often wonders how much can be transmitted to the future, even by the Chinese themselves, concerning one of the greatest and longest lasting civilizations which this planet has ever known. But the Chinese people have, since 1937, shown so strong a principle of instinctive solidarity within themselves, as well as such a stubborn and persistent determination to remain masters of their own destiny, and to endure everything rather than to fall under the control of a military clique directed from Japan, that we now have good cause to hope, not only that full Chinese independence may be restored, but that the older Chinese culture, philosophy, fine art, and craftsmanship may also be revived and revitalized, in forms more appropriate to the needs of today.

We of the Occident can best help the Chinese to this consummation by studying for ourselves and understanding more completely the great fundamental landmarks of Chinese culture, in architecture, sculpture, painting, literature, and philosophy. "Who helps another, helps himself" applies here, no less than in the political and economic sphere, where China's continuance as an active combatant on the side of the Western democracies becomes every day a matter of more critical importance. Thus, in the return for the great cultural wealth that the Chinese have already given to us, we of the West can see to it that this culture is not only preserved but restored to its proper functions and proportions. Such, rather than the restoration of bygone European culture, now—so far as Europe itself is concerned, utterly destroyed and made waste, thanks to the Nazi conceptions of race and nationalism—should be our American destiny, for the next thousand years. "When both our central being and outward harmony are carried to the point of full perfection, heaven and earth are in a state of tranquility, and all things will be nourished and flourish."

PART II

Appreciations of
Individual Writers

Three Imagist Poets   *1916*

I

The question is being asked, re-asked and debated, What is Imagism? The fact that this question is constantly raised anew proves that it is not an academic one. For if we are to see clearly the underlying principles of the new poetry, and to understand the relationship of the group which call themselves the Imagists to those principles, we must first disassociate Imagism, strictly speaking, from all that body of verse now being produced in the free-verse forms. As a critic not long ago pointed out, *vers libre* and Imagism are not to be confused. *Vers libre* can be produced and has been produced which is not Imagistic, but realistic, symbolistic, or merely dull. Imagism is an attitude of mind which can appear just as well under the guise of meter and rhyme, or prose, as in verse itself. What, then, is Imagism?

Briefly, the doctrine we call Imagism has four cardinal points or principles. The first of these concerns presentation of the subject. The Imagist aims to present his subject as an image; that is to say, he presents the sum-total of the emotions in any given subject in such a way that the reader experiences the self-same emotions from them. To do this it is necessary for the Imagist to regard his subject matter from its most imaginative aspect, and to present it visually. For the reader, not having experienced the emotion which moved the author to create his poem, is incapable of grasping that emotion save through a direct and complete appeal to his imagination through his higher senses of sight and hearing. By stimulating these senses, through appropriate choice of words, the Imagist aims to arouse the reader to such a pitch that the reader recreates imaginatively for himself the emotional complex which gave birth to the poem. Imagism is, therefore, first of all a means of arousing the emotions through the imagination. The Imagists must therefore be sharply distinguished from the realistic school, and also from the symbolists of the nineteenth century, from which latter they have, in some sense, derived. Through the constant insistence on emotion as the underlying essence of poetry, the Imagists approach closely to the Elizabethans of the sixteenth and the early romantics of the nineteenth century.

The second principle of Imagism concerns style. The Imagists desire to accomplish that renovation of the English language which is always periodically necessary if good poetry is to continue to be created in it. The Imagists have certain prejudices against inversions, clichés, journalese, high-falutin bombast, literary jargon, messy padding with adjectives. Each word must be an exact word, that is to say the sole word necessary for its particular place and purpose in the poem. This careful consideration for style relates the Imagists to the classicists of the eighteenth century, who undoubtedly rescued the English language from the absurdities of the "metaphysical" school. The Imagists also insist on it as a useful check to too great an exuberance of imagination.

The third principle of Imagism concerns form. The rhythmical form of the poem should not be a mere empty pattern, but should follow, as far as possible, the ebb and flow of the emotion throughout the poem. It should be an integral part of the poem itself, as indissoluble from it as the substance of the words themselves. Therefore the Imagists hold that the theory and practice of *vers libre* is necessary, although they do not go so far as to demand it in every case, or to say that rhyme and meter have not their uses. In their desire to create a full emotional range of rhythmical nuances, inclusive of both rhyme and meter as well as freer rhythmical figures, the Imagists derive direct from the first great romantic poets of England—Blake and Coleridge.

The last principle of Imagism concerns the attitude of the artist to life. The artist should realize that if he is not to be the slave of life he must not attempt to be its judge. He must not obtrude his petty personal judgments and vanities between the reader and the subject he writes about. He must not, in short, moralize about life, or gush over it, or make others feel anything else except what he has felt about it. In this respect the Imagist poets are in very firm reaction

86

against the sentimental and pious optimism of the mid-nineteenth century, against the equally sentimental and fallacious aestheticism of the eighties and nineties, and—it may be added—against a good deal of the wishy-washy suggestiveness and sex-obsession that seems to be getting the upper hand of so many writers of today. The Imagist does not weight the balance, either for "morality" or "immorality": he states, and lets the reader draw his own conclusion.

With these four principles in mind, we may now ask ourselves how the Imagists have carried them into practice. For practice is, after all, the supreme test of any theory of art. There are signs that Imagism is getting itself taken more seriously, not as a mere passing fad, but as something that has at least established certain guideposts and land-marks for future poets, who wish to renew the traditions of good writing. I maintain that it has done more. It has permitted three poets, at least, to start from the same principles and to produce among them a very respectable body of poetry, which in each case is filled with the individual flavor of the personality who wrote it. That the Imagist principles should display such applicability and elasticity is, I maintain, very remarkable. We shall now see who these three poets are.

II

Mr. Richard Aldington, the first of the three to be considered, has recently brought together some thirty of his poems in a small volume, entitled *Images*. That this selection does not represent all of Mr. Aldington's work, must be apparent to all who are familiar with it. His long poem, *Childhood*, is not here; nor is his other long poem on the war, which surely deserves mention as being one of the few really humorous war poems ever written. To come to the shorter pieces, surely all admirers of Mr. Aldington's talent must deplore the absence of "Daisy," "Round Pond," and "The Poplar"—the latter one of the most beautiful poems he has ever written. But whether Mr. Aldington has omitted these pieces from a too severe critical judgment, or whether because they seem to interfere with the unity of his book, the fact remains that they were omitted, but that enough is left to give nearly all sides of his achievement.

Mr. Aldington is a sophisticated, a cultivated, even a bookish poet. He has translated Anyte of Tegea, the Latin Poets of the Renaissance, and even that astounding farrago of poetry and buffoonery called Les Chansons de Maldoror. Recently he has given us, in the columns of *The Egoist*, a glimpse at his library which ranges from Euripides, via Apuleius, Hooker and Crowley, to Ford Madox Hueffer! "And is it for this I have labored?" he cries. "To be the object of derision of some bibliophile looking at his books as cynically and disgustedly as I look at mine?"

No, it is not for this. It is for a handful of strange and satisfying poems that Mr. Aldington has labored. Every artist knows that it takes a great deal of life, an immense amount of experience and appreciation, to make even a little art. Life is like a many-faceted prism. We must walk around it, observe it on every side, see it not as we ourselves would care to see it, but as others have seen it, before we can induce it to show a new side to our efforts, to cast a few rays which it has not already cast before. Matthew Arnold, who was one of the few English critics able to look at literature from the standpoint of its historical development, declared that poetry was a criticism of life. And so it is. The task of a modern poet is not to shut his eyes to the past, but to see the work of the generations that preceded him as an uncompleted structure, the living intention of whose builders is again born in him, and seeks fruition in the additions he can make to it. In this sense Mr. Aldington is a modern poet. He is a poet for the well-read, intelligent, cultivated man or woman.

The first poem of his I can remember seeing in print was the one entitled "Choricos":

> The ancient songs
> Pass deathward mournfully.
>
> Cold lips that sing no more, and withered wreaths
> Regretful eyes, and drooping breasts and wings,
> Symbols of ancient songs,
> Mournfully passing
> Down to the great white surges
> Watched by none—
>
> And we turn from the Kyprian's breasts,
> And we turn from thee,

Phoibos Apollon—
And we turn from the fiery day,
And the lips that were over-sweet;
For silently,
Brushing the fields with red-shod feet,
With purple robe,
Searing the grass as with a sudden flame,
Death,
Thou hast come upon us.

O Death,
Thou art the silence of beauty,
And we look no more for the morning,
We yearn no more for the sun—
We kneel before thee;
And thou, leaning towards us,
Caressingly layest upon us
Flowers from thy thin cold hands,
And smiling as a chaste woman,
Knowing love in her heart,
Thou seelest our eyes
And the illimitable quietude
Comes gently upon us.

There is nothing in all the literature I know which can be safely set beside this poem (of which I have only quoted a few fragments) except a few lines of Leopardi:

In te, Morte, si pose
Nostra ignuda natura;
Lieto, no, ma sicura
Del antico dolor.

Other than that, it is unique. And since it is the fashion to despise a poet because he does not write of aeroplanes and locomotives and socialism, but of the eternal verities of life, death, beauty, irony, let us first of all brush away the shallow assumption that Mr. Aldington is an imitator of the classics and that all his work seems a derivation from the Greek.

The mood of the poem from which I have just quoted is not a

89

mood which can be found in any Greek poet, or which any Greek would ever have understood. I have quoted enough to show what that mood is. It is a mood of mutability, of the sadness that arises in us when we see the instability of all earthly things. The first Occidental poet who ever expressed this mood, to my knowledge, was François Villon. In the East, of course, it was felt and expressed much earlier. For one must have seen kingdoms pass away and empires crumble to the dust and "the owl sing his watchsong from the towers of Afrasiab" before one can feel this mood, which Mr. Aldington has here so beautifully and poignantly expressed.

Throughout his poetry Mr. Aldington has frequently given us this emotion of a civilized man, a modern, brought face to face with some beautiful fragment of the past. Thus he cries to a Greek marble:

> I am thy brother,
> Thy lover of aforetime crying to thee,
> And thou hearest me not.

Surely no one would contend that a Greek could ever have said this! And in some quite recent poems we have the same feeling applied to the Renaissance, and even to modernity:

> I turn the page and read:
> "I dream of silent verses where the rhyme
> Glides noiseless as an oar."

> The heavy, musty air, the black desks,
> The bent heads and the rustling noises
> Vanish—
> The sun hangs in the cobalt sky
> The boat drifts over the bare shallows—
> The oleanders drop their rosy petals on the lawns
> And the swallows dive and swirl and whistle
> About the cleft battlements of Can Grande's castle.

Or take this:

> London, (May, 1915)
> Glittering leaves
> Dance in a squall:
> Above them, bleak immovable clouds.

A church spire
Holds up a little brass cock
To peck at the blue wheat fields—

A pear tree, a broken white pyramid,
In a dingy garden, troubles one
With ecstasy—
And I am tormented,
Obsessed,
Along all this beauty,
With a vision of ruins,
Of walls tumbling into clay.

Such a poet is not what we vulgarly choose to call an optimist. No! Let us admit once for all, Mr. Aldington is a pessimist. (So, by the way, were Sophocles and Leopardi and Shakespeare when he wrote *King Lear,* and Mr. Thomas Hardy, to mention only a few; but I have never heard they were worse poets for it.) At times he gives us a very bitter dose indeed to swallow, as in his *Childhood,* "Cinema Exit," or "In the Tube." Yet he is not devoid of humour, playful and fantastic. Witness "The Faun Sees Snow for the First Time," the "Interlude," the "Evening" (a beautiful grotesque which I am tempted to quote), or for a grimmer note the conclusion of "Lesbia." He will not admit that life is altogether without compensations. Herein he is honest. He even admits sentiment as a compensation, and he treats it delicately, fastidiously, with an unexpected touch of purely fourteenth-century feeling in the following piece:

AFTER TWO YEARS

She is all so slight,
And tender and white,
As a May morning.

She walks without hood
At dusk. It is good
To hear her sing.

It is God's will
That I shall love her still
As he loves Mary.

And night and day,
I will go forth to pray
That she love me.

She is as gold;
Lovely, and far more cold.
Do thou pray with me,
For if I win grace
To kiss twice her face
God has done well to me.

Altogether an unusual poet. One who never takes up the pen except when he has something individual to say, and whose utterance is at times so varied as to make him almost bafflingly individual. But not a Greek, although he has written finely on Greek themes. A modern? Yes; and not only a modern but, *au fond*, a Romantic. Remember the conclusion of the beautiful "*Night Piece*":

"Very faint and shrill and far away the whistle sounds—more like a wild bird than ever. And all my unsatisfied desires and empty wishes and vague yearnings are set aching by that thin tremulous whistle—the post-horn of the Coach of Romance."

III

To pass from the poetry of Mr. Aldington to the poetry of H. D. is to pass into another world. For H. D. not only is a modern poet, she is in the best sense of the word a primitive poet. She deals with Greek themes in the same way as the Greeks of the seventh century B. C. might have dealt with them. She is not like Mr. Aldington, a sceptic enamored of their lost beauty. In a sense she is indifferent to beauty. Something speaks to her in every rock, wave, or pine tree of those sunlit landscapes in which she seems to live. For her the decadence of antiquity, the Middle Ages, the modern world seem never to have existed. She is purely and frankly pagan.

How is it that so many people interested in Imagism seem never to have grasped this essential distinction between her work and Mr. Aldington's? I must suppose it is because very few people have ever tried to analyze and rank the Imagist poets on any other basis than that of form. But as I have already pointed out, the form of the Imagists is, after all, a matter of lesser importance than the spirit with which they approach that form. Aldington writes about life; H. D. is almost completely a nature poet. Nature to her is not mere inanimate scenery or beautiful decoration; it is packed with a life and significance which is beyond our individual lives, and all her poems are in a sense acts of worship towards it. Civilization for her does not exist, in our modern sense; she seeks a civilization based only on the complete realization of natural and physical law, without any ethical problems except the need of merging and compounding all one's desires and emotions in that law. Her poetry is like a series of hymns of some forgotten and primitive religion.

I like to think that this primitive quality in H. D.'s poetry comes from the fact that she is an American. There can be no doubt that we are an uncultivated, a barbarous people. Our ancestors, by migrating to an immense and utterly undeveloped continent, without traditions, were thrown face to face with nature and lost, in consequence, nearly all feeling for their previous culture. If you take a child of civilized parents and bring him up among savages, he will revert to savagery, and in the same way our forefathers, as soon as they ceased to cling to the Atlantic seaboard, changed, through contact with the immense wilderness of the interior, not only mentally but physically. For example, Washington was physically and mentally an English squire of his period; Lincoln, about a hundred years later, was, in appearance and habits of thought, like a man of another race. The Indian, although conquered, gave to his conquerors the Indian way of thinking; or rather the Indian's surroundings—the endless forest—produced in the newcomers' minds something of the same way of thinking as the Indian had before their coming. What a pity it has been for art that we, as a nation, did not admit without shame this return to nature! But instead, we were ashamed of our barbarism, and we have striven and are still striving to outdo Europe on its own grounds, with the result that so much of our art seems merely transplanted, exotic, and false. We might have been the Russians of the western hemisphere; instead of that we were almost the provincial English. Instead of Fenimore Cooper and *The Song of Hiawatha*, we might have given to the world a new national epic. But the opportunity is now lost and whatever fragments of that epic may be written will have to be very sophisticated and in a sense artificial products.

93

To make an end of this long digression, I can truly say that I find nothing transplanted in H. D.'s poetry. She has borrowed a few names of gods from the early Greek, but that was because she found herself in complete sympathy with this people, who, if we are to believe the modern school of archaeology, were quite as barbarian themselves in the Homeric period as the Red Indians, and who lived in the closest contact with nature. Let us take an early example:

HERMES OF THE WAYS

The hard sand breaks,
And the grains of it
Are clear as wine.

Far off over the leagues of it,
The wind,
Playing on the wide shore,
Piles little ridges,
And the great waves
Break over it.

But more than the many-foamed ways
Of the sea,
I know him
Of the triple path-ways,
Hermes,
Who awaiteth.

Dubious,
Facing three ways,
Welcoming wayfarers,
He whom the sea-orchard
Shelters from the west,
From the east,
Weathers sea-wind:
Fronts the great dunes.

Wind rushes
Over the dunes,
And the coarse salt-crusted grass
Answers.

Heu,
It whips round my ankles!

This is only one-half of the poem, but it will serve to show this poet's method. Here Hermes is identified with the yellow barrier of sand dunes which breaks the wind, and splits it into three directions, as it comes in from the sea. The scenery and the feeling are not Greek. In fact, as someone has pointed out, the whole poem might have been called "The Coast of New Jersey." But just as Coleridge found a way to give a feeling of the emptiness of the sea by narrating the tale of a legendary voyage on it, so H. D. has given us the eternal quality of the New Jersey coast by identifying its savagery with Greek myth.

The difference between H. D.'s poetry and Aldington's is therefore a difference between an apparent complexity which cannot be analyzed, since it is really the simplest synthesis of primitive feeling, and a studied simplicity which on analysis, reveals itself as something very complex and modern. Aldington's work when studied carefully, raises questions about our life: H. D. goes deeper and offers us an eternal answer. With the single exception of the *Choricos*, I know of no work of H. D.'s which is not superior to Aldington's in rhythm, as I know of no work of Aldington's which does not seem to have more unsolved problems underlying its thought. Aldington is monodic, H. D. is strophaic: Aldington writes on many themes: H. D. on two or three: H. D.'s art is more perfect within its limits; Aldington's is more interesting because of its very human imperfection.

There is another short thing of H. D.'s which fulfils perfectly the Greek dictum that a picture is a silent poem, a poem a speaking picture:

> Whirl up, sea—
> whirl your pointed pines,
> splash your great pines,
> over our rocks.
> Hurl your green over us,
> cover us with your pools of fir.

A chorus of Oreads might very well have sung that to the wind. Over and over again, H. D. never tires of giving us the sea, the rocks, the pines, the sunlight. There is such a hard brightness of sunlight in some of the poems that it makes us fairly dizzy with its intensity:

O wind,
rend open the heat,
cut apart the heat,
rend it sideways.

Fruit cannot drop
through this thick air:
fruit cannot fall into heat
that presses up and blunts
the points of pears
and rounds the grapes.

Cut the heat,
plough through it,
turning it on either side
of your path.

These poems are like cries to unknown gods. Some are simply stark
in their dramatic magnificence:

THE WIND SLEEPERS

Whiter
than the crust
left by the tide,
we are stung by the hurled sand
and the broken shells.
We no longer sleep,
sleep in the wind,
we awoke and fled
through the Peiraeic gate.

Tear,
tear us an altar,
tug at the cliff-boulders,
pile them with the rough stones.
We no longer
sleep in the wind.
Propitiate us.

Chant in a wail
that never halts;

96

pace a circle and pay tribute
with a song.

When the roar of a dropped wave
breaks into it,
pour meted words
of sea-hawks and gulls
and sea-birds that cry
discords.

Recently H. D. has been giving us longer and more complex poems—condensed dramas of nature and life. Her style has become broader and deeper, and her thought more weighty. I wish I could quote all of a poem of this nature called *Sea Gods*. I can only give a brief analysis of it.

The entire poem is a sort of invocation and service of propitiation to the powers of the sea. In its opening lines the poet cries out:

They say there is no hope—
sand—drift—rocks—rubble of the sea,
the broken hulk of a ship,
hung with shreds of rope,
pallid under the cracked pitch.

They say there is no hope
to conjure you.

In short, the gods are merely broken wrecks of the past. The forces of nature cannot help us, it is useless to cry out to them, for they are

—cut, torn, mangled,
torn by the stress and beat,
no stronger than the strips of sand
along your ragged beach.

But, says the poet, in a beautiful passage:

But we bring violets,
great masses, single, sweet:
wood-violets, stream-violets,
violets from a wet marsh,
violets in clumps from the hills.

Every kind of violet is brought and strewn on the sea. For what reason? Here is the answer:

> You will yet come,
> you will yet haunt men in ships—
> you will thunder along the cliff,
> break—retreat—get fresh strength—
> gather and pour weight upon the beach.
>
> You will bring myrrh-bark,
> and drift laurel wood from hot coasts;
> when you hurl, high—high—
> We will answer with a shout.
>
> For you will come,
> you will answer our taut hearts,
> you will break the lie of men's thoughts,
> and shelter us for our trust.

Has the sea, then, in this poem been used in some way as a symbol of the eternal drift, change, and reflux of our life which we have tried to conceal under theories of ethics, of progress, of immortality, of civilization? Perhaps it has. And the violets—what, then, are they but simply the recollections of our earlier sea-state, of our endless, unconscious drift with the tides of life?

I do not propose here to examine H. D.'s mystic philosophy. That philosophy cannot be disengaged from its context. But from a quite recent poem of hers—a poem very beautiful and baffling, I may perhaps be permitted to quote these few lines, wrenched from their context, without comment:

> Sleepless nights,
> I remember the initiates,
> their gesture, their calm glance,
> I have heard how, in rapt thought,
> in vision they speak
> with another race
> More beautiful, more intense than this—
>
> I reason:
> another life holds what this lacks:
> a sea, unmoving, quiet,

not forcing our strength
to rise to it, beat on beat,
a hill not set with black violets,
but stones, stones, bare rocks,
dwarf-trees, twisted, no beauty,
to distract—to crowd
madness upon madness.

Only a still place,
and perhaps some outer horror,
some hideousness to stamp beauty—
on our hearts.

IV

The third poet whose work I have to examine, Mr. F. S. Flint, was already an accomplished writer of rhymed *vers libre* before he joined the Imagist movement. Mr. Flint's early work is contained in a volume entitled, *In the Net of the Stars,* a volume which is still worth reading. *In The Net of the Stars* told a love story in rather uncommon fashion. The poet and his beloved were presented throughout the book, against the background of the starry sky:

Little knots in the net of light
That is held by the infinite Dragon, Night.

This bringing into relation of a quite human love story, with the impassive and changeless order of the Universe, threw a flavor of supreme irony over the whole book. The work is otherwise remarkable technically. At the date when it was published, 1909, Mr. Flint already revealed that he was an assiduous student of Verhaeren, De Regnier, and other French *vers-librists*. Hence its importance as a document in the Imagist movement.

But to come to Mr. Flint's later work which has been assembled under the title of *Cadences*. We find here a poet, first of all, of sentiment. What, you say, an Imagist who deals with sentiment? My reply to that is, that it is time people understood that an Imagist is free to deal with whatever he chooses, so long as he is sincere and honest

about it. Mr. Flint's sincerity is his finest point. He is in some sense the
Paul Verlaine of the Imagist movement. His work gives one the same
delicacy of nuance, the same fresh fragrance, the same direct simplicity, the same brooding melancholy. He lacks the strain of coarseness which ruined Verlaine; he has, in place of it, a refined nobility.
He has not humor. At times he has attempted irony, but I cannot
think he has altogether succeeded in it. He feels life too poignantly to
ever mock at life. There remains tenderness, wistful pathos, imaginative beauty.

On reading Mr. Flint one obtains a very distinct impression of Mr.
Flint's personality. One pictures him as a shy, sensitive, lonely dreamer
filled with a desire to attain to the noblest and finest life, but somehow
kept back from it. Mr. Flint is one of the few poets I know who have
preserved intact today a spark of the old lyrical idealism. He is, perhaps, though he may not realize it, even closer to Keats and Shelley
than to Verlaine—he might almost be called a modern Shelley. His
affiliation with these earlier and greater romantics is more marked be-
caus it is an affiliation of spirit, not of form. Mr. Flint's form has always been his own, and by holding conscientiously to his own form, he
has come closer, to my way of thinking, to poets like Keats and Shelley
than the innumerable tribe of imitators who have rashly taken the
form for the substance.

Here is an early example of Mr. Flint's work:

London, my beautiful,
it is not the sunset,
not the pale green sky
shimmering through the curtain
of the silver birch,
nor the quietness;
it is not the hopping
of the little birds
upon the lawn,
nor the darkness
stealing over all things
that moves me.

But as the moon creeps slowly
over the treetops
among the stars;

I think of her,
and the glow her passing
sheds on men.

London, my beautiful,
I will climb
into the branches
to the moonlit treetops
that my blood may be cooled
by the wind.

And here is another, equally beautiful:

Under the lily shadow,
and the gold,
and the blue, and the mauve,
that the whin and the lilac
pour down upon the water,
the fishes quiver.

Over the green cold leaves,
and the rippled silver,
and the tarnished copper
of its neck and beak,
toward the deep black water,
beneath the arches,
the swan floats slowly.

Into the dark of the arch the swan floats,
and the black depths of my sorrow
beats a white rose of flame

If Mr. Flint had written nothing else but these two poems he would be immortal for their sake, in spite of his disregard—shared by H. D.— of the convenient device which begins each line of a poem with a capital letter, and of the laws of punctuation. They weave a perfect hypnotic spell in my mind, and they fulfill completely a recent definition of Mr. E. A. Robinson, that poetry is a language which expresses through an emotional reaction something which cannot be said in ordinary speech.

Mr. Flint has given us other poems not less beautiful, but with a strain of greater pathos:

Tired faces,
eyes that have never seen the world,
bodies that have never lived in air,
lips that have never minted speech;
they are the clipped and garbled
blocking the highway.
They swarm and eddy
between the banks of glowing shops
towards the red meat,
the potherbs,
the cheapjacks,
or surge in
before the swift rush of the charging teams;
pitiful, ugly, mean,
encumbering.

Immortal?
In a wood
watching the shadow of a bird,
leap from frond to frond of bracken,
I am immortal,
perhaps.
But these?
Their souls are naphtha lamps,
guttering in an odour of carious teeth,
and I die with them.

Perhaps the last poem in Mr. Flint's book will give the most complete exposition of his art and vision:

THE STAR

Bright Star of Life,
Who shattered creeds at Bethlehem,
And saw
In the irradiance of your vision shining,
Children and maidens, youths and men and women,
Dancing barefoot among the grasses, singing,
Dancing,
Over the waving flowery meadows;

So calmly watched the universe and men,
And yet
So fiery was the heart behind the light;

The creeds have been re-made by men
Who followed as you walked abroad,
And gathered up their shattered shards;
Then with a wax of sticky zeal,
Each little piece unto its fellow joined;
But over the meadows comes the wind
Remembering your voice:

O my love,
O my golden-haired, my golden-hearted,
I will sing this song to you of Him,
This golden afternoon.
This song of you;
For where love is, is He,
Whose name has echoed in the halls of Time,
Who caught the wise eternal music, ay,
And passed it on—
For men to sing it since
In false and shifting keys—
Who hears it now?

But the hearts of those who have heard it rightly,
Grew great;
And behind the walls and barriers of the world,
Their voices have gone up in sweetness
Unheeded,
Yet imminent in the wings and flight of change;
Comes there a time when men shall shout it,
And say to Life:
You have the strength of the seas,
And the glory of the vine;
You shall have the wisdom of the hills,
The daring of the eagle's wings,
The yearning of the swallow's quest.
And, in the mightly organ of the world,
Great men shall be as pipes and nations stops
To harmonize your Song.

O my love,
Like a cornfield in summer
Is your body to me;
Golden and bending with the wind,
And on the tallest ear a bird is piping
The lonely song.
And scarlet poppies thread the golden ways.
Out of the purple haze of the sea behind it
Appears a white ship sailing,
And its passengers are harvesters.
But who dares sing of love?

The jackals howl; the vultures gorge dead flesh.

In despite of the last line, which is undoubtedly true, and, under the present circumstances, certainly necessary to the context of all that precedes it, yet I feel I cannot share Mr. Flint's despair of this world. For as long as there is any poet who can have such visions as this is, in such a world as ours, the earth cannot be altogether given over to crime and slaughter. Which one of the Imagists could have given us with so direct and poignant sincerity—scorning all artifice— such a vision of beauty? Or, for that matter, which one of the poets of today?

Conrad Aiken—
Metaphysical Poet   *1919*

The world is seriously in need of a new classification of poets. Hitherto we have been largely content with the old labels of romantic and realist. But these old labels can no longer satisfy, for the boundaries of poetry have been enlarged since the early nineteenth century to embrace the whole field of scientific speculation which is our legacy from the evolutionists, the anthropologists, the psychologists, the sociologists, and the men of science generally. As we are today, it is evident that there may be quite as much romantic magic in a poet writing from a mind stocked with purely scientific theory, as there is in Shelley; and as much realism in the narrower sense, in a poet of pure romantic tendency, as there is, say, in Masefield. We must seek finer distinctions. What is needed is not a new definition of the incomprehensible mystery called "poetry," but a new classification of the poets themselves.

When we come to examine English poetry, we can, if we observe closely, easily distinguish two main streams of inspiration in it—now parting, now fusing, sometimes clouded, and again distinct. There have been the poets who wrote largely of the aspects of things outside themselves; and the poets who, turning within themselves, wrote of the world as mirrored in the human brain. We may call the first objective, and the second subjective; or we may adopt a more recent nomenclature and label the first imagistic and the second symbolistic. But if the spirit of inquiry is strong within us neither of these labels can completely satisfy our intelligence. They do not completely cover the ground. We are perhaps safer if we say that the first group of poets are externalistic, and the second metaphysical, in tendency.

There have been far more poets of the externalist type in English than of the metaphysical. And these poets have been more widely read and appreciated by their contemporaries—indeed, by posterity—than their neglected antitypes. This is partly due to the mental inertia of most of us—an inertia that seeks to be soothed with pretty, easily explainable pictures and familiar tunes—partly also to the extreme difficulty of writing good metaphysical verse. The good metaphysical poet must be always turning the world inside out, so to speak. And since the faculty of verse writing is based primarily on an immediate emotional response to sensuous impression, it is apparent that the good metaphysical poet must be always battling against his own immediate apprehensions. This will explain the rarity of great metaphysical poets. In England there have been, so far as I remember, Donne— facile princeps in this field—also Vaughan, and possibly Marvell. Shakespeare in Hamlet and Iago, Webster in Bosola and Ferdinand, gave us complete figures illuminated by the same searching metaphysic. Shelley, had he developed in the direction of *The Cenci* and of *The Triumph of Time* might have become one of the great metaphysical poets.

To turn from these figures to a writer of the present day and generation may seem to some an impertinence. But we are not able to estimate the weight and significance of a writer such as Conrad Aiken, either as poet or as critic of poetry, except by making some such transition. On the jacket of Mr. Aiken's latest book, his fifth (*The Charnel Rose;* Four Seas Co.; Boston), I find the following: "There is a strangeness about the art of Conrad Aiken that makes it unique. No one is writing just like him in America today." This remark is not only true, it is probably the one true thing that has ever been said about Aiken. And because of this strangeness, which I think springs from the fact that both in his poetry and in his prose criticism Aiken is a metaphysician, he has been more variously estimated by writers and critics on both sides of the Atlantic than any man I know. He is profoundly disliked by many, mistrusted by some, and admired, if at all, by a few.

I turn to page thirty-one of the poem he calls "Senlin: A Biography" (really I like to think that the subject of this poem is Aiken himself) and cull the following stanzas:

> It is morning, Senlin says, and in the morning
> When the light drips through the shutters like the dew,

I arise, I face the sunrise,
And do the things my fathers learned to do.
Stars in the purple dusk above the roof-tops
Pale in a saffron mist and seem to die,
And I myself on a swiftly tilting planet
Stand before a glass and tie my tie.

I stand before a mirror and comb my hair;
How small and white my face!
The green earth tilts through a sea of air,
And bathes in a flame of space.

It is morning, Senlin says, and in the morning
Should I not pause in the light to remember God?
Upright and firm I stand on a star unstable,
He is immense and lonely as a cloud.
I will dedicate this moment before my mirror
To Him alone, for Him I will comb my hair.
Accept these humble offerings, cloud of silence!
I will think of you as I descend the stair.

Here we have a kind of poetry profoundly unsettling of our cherished conventions and prejudices. Either we are by nature timid anthropomorphists in matters of religion (despite all the evidence that can be urged to the contrary) or we are simply indifferent. But Aiken is neither. He looks beneath the surface of age-old compromises and sees the body of Everyman poised on an unstable helpless planet, carefully arranging his tie, while his soul, darkened and without knowledge, humbly seeks to penetrate to the cause of all things. The cruel clarity of such perception as this startles and horrifies. But none the less it is both beautiful and true. In this mind we find all our minds mirrored. Poetry cannot do more.

Even more profoundly disturbing, more intoxicatingly daemonic, is the insight displayed in the poem which gives this volume its title—"The Charnel Rose." The subject of this poem is sexual desire; and out of desire, the "desire of the moth for the star," the desire that has tormented every great mind from Saint Augustine to Nietzsche, Aiken has woven a vast symphony. Quotation here is useless. We are simply upborne in these mad, delirious waves of drunken music that flow in and out endlessly. We are hurried from one chaos into another, so that we should be in danger of losing our bearings utterly were not the mind and voice directing this orchestra that of a poet. "To shape this world of leaderless ghostly passions,—or else be mobbed by it, that is the question": in these lines is summed up the whole purpose of the poem. Conrad Aiken has shaped this world for us, has striven to make tangible to us the intangible substance of our lives, and we cannot withhold from him a meed of praise as great as that of any poet living and writing in America today.

Some Contemporary
American Poets   *1920*

PART I

I

The present revival of poetry in America had its origin twenty-five years ago, when Edwin Arlington Robinson published his first slender book containing *The Torrent and the Night Before,* a collection which a year later was merged in the better known title of *The Children of the Night.* Before this date, which, be it noted, was but two years previous to the Spanish-American War, the domestically accepted standard of American poetry had been the more polite, optimistic, facile verse of New England, the work of Longfellow, Whittier, Bryant, Holmes, and Lowell. Poe and Whitman had found their audiences abroad rather than at home. It fell to the lot of a son of New England to break with the popular view of poetry as a polite entertainment, and to provide his country with poems which, though conceived and executed with the strictest regard for tradition, contained nevertheless a darker and more poignant gospel.

It is not my purpose here to examine all of Robinson's books in detail, and therefore I must necessarily omit consideration of his prose plays, as well as of his long quasi-narrative in blank verse, *Merlin.* My purpose is rather to concentrate attention on the most salient aspects of the work of certain prominent poets in the United States, with the aim of showing what each has accomplished. For the purposes of this study I therefore adopt the point of view of an average intelligent foreigner who happens to have heard little of American poetry, and who wishes to learn something about it. I am therefore obliged to omit from consideration the small but important group of American poets at present residing in England, for the reason that they are immediately accessible, whereas those with whom I deal are not. A foreigner might require to be told that Robinson is not only first in point of date among modern American poets, but in many respects first in regard to sheer intellectual ability. This intellectual ability is displayed, not in any special versatility in handling the subject matter of poetry (in this respect he is indeed singularly limited), but in a new way of looking at life.

Pick up any book of Robinson's which you will and you will find a great number of poems devoted to the subject of lives, imagined or real, which were actually or apparently failures. John Evereldown, Richard Cory, Miniver Cheevy, Luke Havergal, Cliff Klingenhagen, Charles Carville, George Crabbe, Annandale, Flammonde, Lincoln— the list is endless. Against the American who preaches success, efficiency, "hustle," Robinson has always raised a voice in protest. And his voice is the voice of the New England conscience, or rather of what was left of that conscience after the wave of industrialism, cheap immigrant labour, and dollar-hunting swept over New England in the 'seventies, at the beginning of which period he was born. Robinson's mission to America has therefore been that of a lonely upholder of lost ideals. He has shown us wherein we have failed. The spectacle is not pleasant, and grows particularly painful in the case of such a poem as his upon Lincoln, the concealed deadly irony of which is probably lost upon most Americans.

By this steadfast respect for ideals which proved inadequate to hold back the disruptive tides of scientific commercialism, as by his insistence upon the darker side of life itself, Robinson has shown himself spiritually akin to Thomas Hardy. Certain differences are instructive. Robinson has nothing of Hardy's unfailing delight in nature, nothing of his ability to paint unforgettable landscapes. Indeed, I know only of one poem of his which contains a recognizable American landscape—the aptly named "Fragment" in *The Man Against the Sky,* which is really a fragment of decayed New England. Elsewhere he writes verse which, in almost every case, is that of a dweller in cities. His preoccupation is with men and women, rather than with the unconscious forces which shape them. For this reason, it is as a sharp biting etcher of individual portraits that we read him. In this, as in his love for cryptic ironical statement, he resembles closely the later Browning (the Browning of "Parleyings"). But, on the whole, he is far keener in his outlook upon human defects than Browning. Browning could never have written "The Field of Glory," for instance, or "Cassandra." So it is as a definitely New England product that we must take his poetry—a product owning certain affinities to Browning, Hardy, or Crabbe, but with a sharp, sub-acid, quality of its own.

His last book, if we except the inferior *Merlin,* contains his best work, and reveals more clearly than any other his qualities and defects. The poem which gives the book its title, "The Man Against the Sky," is an epitome of his philosophy. Here are its opening stanzas:

> Between me and the sunset, like a dome
> Against the glory of a world on fire,
> Now loomed a sudden hill
> Bleak, round, and high, by flame-lit height made higher,
> With nothing on it for the flame to kill
> Save one who moved and was alone up there
> To loom before the chaos and the glare
> As if he were the last god going home
> Unto his last desire.
> Dark, marvellous, and inscrutable he moved on
> Till down the fiery distance he was gone,
> Like one of those eternal, remote things
> That range across a man's imaginings
> When a sure music fills him and he knows
> What he may say thereafter to few men,
> The touch of ages having wrought
> An echo or a glimpse of what he thought
> A phantom or a legend until then.

This opening, more rich and full in color than almost anything in Robinson's work, merges into the usual grey doubts and questionings. Faced with this symbol of humanity, the poet frankly confesses that he cannot tell us where he is going, or why he exists at all. All knowledge concerning mankind resolves itself into a series of negatives:

> No soft evangel of equality
> Self-cradled in a communal repose
> That huddles into death, and may at last
> Be covered well with equatorial snows—
> And all for what, the devil only knows—

Will aggregate an inkling to confirm
The credit of a sage or of a worm. . . .
No planetary trap where souls are wrought
For nothing but the sake of being caught
And sent again to nothing will attune
Itself to any key of any reason
Why man should hunger through another season
To find out why 'twere better late than soon
To go away, and let the sun and moon
And all the silly stars illuminate
A place for creeping things;
And those that root and trumpet and have wings
And herd and ruminate,
Or dive and flash and poise in rivers or seas,
Or by their loyal tails in lofty trees
Hang screeching lewd victorious derision
Of man's immortal vision.

So absolute is this skepticism that it seeks to create the very faith it denies. The poet offers no comfort to the world beyond that of "an Orient Word that will not be erased," "the living Word no man has ever spelt." But the concluding passages, with their insistence either upon complete faith or on sheer immediate annihilation, somehow fail to carry conviction. Robinson may have felt the need for faith, but has he found it? The answer is doubtful. But in stating this problem for America, he has done more than any other man living to make a new American poetry possible.

II

If Robinson's poetry clearly presents the mind of New England, the poetry of Robert Frost no less clearly presents its heart. Yet Frost is neither temperamentally nor by birth a New Englander. His father found himself so much at variance with his New England neighbors that he not only sympathized with the cause of the South in the Civil War, but gave to his son the name of the great Southern leader, Lee. And the future poet was not only born in San Francisco, but spent the first ten years of his life there. It was only the accident of a return to New England that fixed upon the sensitive plate of Robert Frost's temperament the scenes and characters with which he has made us familiar.

People in Europe generally suffer from a mistaken impression that the West is the wildest part of America. This is not the case. The West, except for one or two "National" Parks, and a few stretches of desert, is decidedly the most cultivated part of the United States. The true region of wildness lies at the threshold of the European visitor arriving in New York. It is in Northern Massachusetts, Maine, Vermont, New Hampshire, the backwoods of New England; the "North of Boston" of Frost's most famous book.

This part of America has the melancholy charm of a country which was once prosperous and cultivated, but which has since fallen into decay. At the time of the Revolution it was a rich agricultural country. Since the opening-out of the West and the development of New England industry it has been gradually emptied of its population, until what remains of the old New England agricultural stock—the true descendants of the *Mayflower* pilgrims—have dwindled in numbers and in prosperity, and have practically given up agriculture, living on stock-raising, apple-growing, and the like. In the last few years many of the deserted and half-overgrown farms have again become populated by Finns, Norwegians, and the like, thanks to the overcrowding of immigrants into the great industrial centers. But it is not with these people that Frost deals, but with the remnant of the original stock—a remnant tough, obstinate, reserved, weakened in fiber through intermarriage, half-crazed in many cases through the combined spiritual and physical loneliness of long winters, few neighbors, the chill isolations of Puritanism. It is with these people, and with the scenes of their daily lives, that Frost has dealt faithfully. In a sense, he has been but an instrument in their hands.

Throughout his work one is faced with the feeling that Robert Frost is only a recording instrument, and one which functions only under compulsion. He is a fastidiously slow worker, and many of the poems in *North of Boston* have developed from a germ which lay latent in his mind for years. In some cases the first idea of a poem was duly committed to paper, to be printed in the *Youths' Companion,* and was taken up later on to be expanded, subtilized, recast. I believe that "The Death of the Hired Man" was so treated. Thus the composition of many of his poems, and the gradual evolution of them into their final form, has taken a great number of years. Insatiably he seeks the quintessential features of a vanishing state of society. His is the most carefully weighed, the most mature poetry now being written in America.

In order to render with finality what may be called, without irony, the most completely finished and exhausted aspect of America—the aspect of Northern New England—Frost has evolved a form peculiar to himself, and which even he does not always handle with equal success; the rambling quasi-narrative, conversational, blank-verse poem, of which "The Death of the Hired Man," "The Mountain," "A Servant to Servants," "The Fear," "The Woodpile," "In the Home Stretch," "Birches," are the most conspicuous examples.

These poems may owe, conceivably, something to Robinson, who essayed the same type less successfully in his "Isaac and Archibald," which, I believe, dates back to 1902. But to whatever poet Frost may owe the germ of the form that is his, it is certain that he alone has handled it most richly.

This form is based upon commonplace incidents, told as far as possible in the language of common speech. Frost has attempted to revive blank verse by means of restoring the connection, lost since Elizabethan days, between the common tongue and the language of literature. But since the figures with which he is familiar live greyer, more colorless, more confined lives than the Elizabethans, and employ a less rich vocabulary, he employs in the place of dramatic climax a subtler reverberation. His poetry is intended to echo in our hearts, to attract us by a sense of sympathy, rather than to uplift us by a feeling of heroic conflict. It is poetry deliberately written without "purple patches," as the late Edward Thomas, possibly the most sincere follower Frost ever had, long ago recognized. It is poetry filled with a brooding sense of mystical kinship with nature which is almost Celtic (one suspects a Celtic strain in Frost, such as existed in Thomas). And in its deliberate avoidance of definite conclusions about the world, as in its employment of carefully differentiated repetitions of the same thought, it recalls the poetry of the great Chinese poets, familiar to us through Mr. Waley's translations.

For this reason Frost is something more than a New England poet. By his deliberate refusal to employ dialect speech (a wise omission), by

his quiet observation that always shines through his scenes and figures, he has raised himself to universal stature. It is only by accident
that he has been selected by destiny to render New England, or any
part of America. He knows this well enough, and in several more
poignant and personal poems he has looked upon New England as
having been in a sense a frustration of a higher destiny he might have
obtained. These poems, which are, contrary to his usual practice, in
rhyme, are by no means the least of his achievements. To read "After
Apple-Picking," "The Road Not Taken," "The Sound of Trees," and
many pieces in *A Boy's Will* is to understand the brooding, sensitive
soul of a great poet.

III

The third American poet whom I have to consider is one whose
work and personality enjoy a greater vogue in America than that of
either Robinson or Frost. Yet this work, typical as it is of certain strains
in the American temperament which essentially differentiate the in-
habitant of the United States from the Englishman, has never—perhaps for that very reason—been received with favor in England. It is
poetry which neither searches the heart so deeply as Frost's nor stimu-
lates the brain as Robinson's; and yet it possesses the relentless driving
power of an energy which its possessor claims as an inheritance from
her Yankee ancestors. I am referring to the poetry of Miss Amy Lowell.

Perhaps it is necessary to have breathed the light, champagne-like
air of a New England winter to be able to appreciate Miss Lowell's poetry; perhaps it is necessary to have known the sensation of the tourist
who first steps ashore on a blazing day in the midst of New York's opulent exuberance; perhaps it is necessary to be able to sacrifice many
deeper and subtler overtones of poetry for the sake of sheer brilliance
of surface. I do not know, but of one thing I am certain: that Miss
Lowell's poetry *is* a poetry of purely surface appearance. Has anyone
ever read her best and most deeply-felt volume, *Men, Women and
Ghosts*, through from cover to cover? From such an experience the
mind emerges dizzied, the senses aching, the nerves unstrung, by the
endless succession of sheer dazzling surface emotions that are swept

past one incessantly, without hint of a third dimension. And the case is still worse with that book's successor, *Can Grande's Castle.* It is true that in her latest volume, *Pictures of the Floating World,* there is an attempt towards a return to a quieter, more persuasive type of poetry; but even that volume contains such sheer racketing earthquakes of surface sensibility as "Gargoyles," "Motor Lights on a Hill Road," or "The Broken Fountain."

Miss Lowell's poetry springs from the rampant prosperity, the blatant successfulness, of America. Like that prosperity and successfulness, it dazzles the beholder at the outset; later on, he perceives vaguely that something is lacking, some finer shade of meaning, some deeper spiritual ideal, some nobler conception of humanity. But since that prosperity and successfulness are very serious facts in this world of ours, so Miss Lowell's poetry is a very serious fact. One must take it for what it is, and see what one can make of it. Critical England, which has seen the elements of a distinguished novelist in Mr. Joseph Hergesheimer, cannot deny to Miss Lowell (who is in one sense Mr. Hergesheimer's counterpart) the title of an eminent poet.

The first fact, then, about Miss Lowell's poetry is that it is two-dimensional: it has length and breadth, but, with certain exceptions, no depth. On the point of higher spiritual ideals, as regards the possible destiny of suffering, struggling man, it is completely dumb. Miss Lowell dismisses the thought of other worlds than ours with a gesture of contempt. Herein she stands at the opposite pole to another New England poetess, Emily Dickinson, who used the visible world as a medium to see through to that Eternity which she spent her life in seeking. Miss Lowell's poetry, on the other hand, is always poetry of sharp, objective fact. It is even fact made slightly artificial by being deliberately handled by its possessor in such a way as to bring out its most strikingly picturesque side. For this reason she has drawn upon books of history and memoirs for a great many of her themes. There is no doubt that, had she been born, say, in the Elizabethan age, she might have been a great rival in drama of Ben Jonson or Beaumont and Fletcher. But she would never have attained to Webster's moral passion, Dekker's sympathy, Marlowe's or Chapman's grandeur, or Shakespeare's all-penetrative searching of the heart. Despite her energy, she has little to say about this world of ours. She sees it, and that for her is sufficient.

Nevertheless, this ability to see the world—the mere surface of things—is an ability not to be despised, and the mere act of seeing, freshly ventured and continuously repeated, produces certain virtues, even if it does not add to our actual insight into life. It enables us, for instance, to understand something of America's superficial aspect. It shows us that the world is curiously varied, and that there is little apparent connection, on the surface, between these variations. In short, such vision is, as Miss Lowell has said, "unrelated." And the result is this, in the case of a camouflaged troopship:

> Lines:
> Rising from the water,
> Curled round and over,
> Whirled, scattered,
> Drawn upon one another, . . .
> Hair lines incessantly moving
> Broad bands of black turning evenly over emptiness, . . .
> Teasing the eye with indefinite motion,
> Coming from nothing
> Ending without cessation:
> Drowned hair drifting against mother of pearl,
> Kelp-aprons
> Shredded on a yellow beach,
> Black spray
> Sprinkled over cream white wave-tops.

No one could ever have written this, or a hundred other precisely similar poems, who had not been born the descendant of a line of Yankee merchant-princes, each with his eye upon the immediately practical. Cinematographic such art undoubtedly is, but yet we may question whether America's best art is not cinematographic. It must be remembered that neither Frost nor Robinson write as Americans to Americans. Theirs is always the standpoint of the detached mature observer. Miss Lowell, on the other hand, writes always as an American. Even at its most sophisticated, there is always something childlike about her art.

Yet there are hints of a deeper intimacy here and there in her poems, especially in the volume, *Men, Women, and Ghosts*. Not only do we have here four poems definitely dealing with New England life, written in the dialect-speech which Frost has perhaps wisely avoided, but the feeling of New England is present elsewhere also. True, there is no feeling of New England in "Malmaison," which presents Miss Lowell's most successfully-drawn woman, the Empress Josephine (all of Miss Lowell's women are a little like Dresden china shepherdesses, and Josephine is no exception, but she lives in this prose poem). But the feeling of New England floods "A Roxbury Garden": it crosses the Atlantic in the shipbuilding scene in "The Hammers": it half-spoils the background of such a poem as "The Cross-Roads" and wholly spoils "The Cremona Violin." And, strangest thing of all, both sections of the poem called "*1777*" are full of it. The second part of this poem is supposed to deal with Venice. But has anyone ever pictured Venice as a "*City of Falling Leaves*"? Such a city, one may be sure, is much nearer in actual geography to Beacon Hill, Boston, Massachusetts. Pare off the trappings of this poem—perhaps the best thing Miss Lowell has written—and one gets cultivated Boston society as it has existed for the last quarter-century. The same superficiality, the same weariness, the same exhausted concealed hankering of the flesh. And the leaves are falling on it all, forever falling.

PART II

I

The poetry which I have examined, that produced by what we may call the older New England group, did not by any means exhaust the new forces which in America were tending to self-expression. About the period 1912–13, when the New England group first began to attain to some prominence, there appeared also on the horizon another group, the elements of whose nurture had been drawn from the very different scenes and circumstances of the Middle West. As the main directions of the former were towards the cities of New York and of Boston, so this latter gravitated towards Chicago and, to a lesser degree, the city of Saint Louis. But they were unvocal and unknown until the happy founding of two periodicals, *Poetry,* of Chicago, and *Reedy's Mirror,* of Saint Louis, gave them their opportunity.

The Middle West is the backbone of America. It is the force that swung Presidential elections, from the date of Lincoln's coming into power, up to President Wilson's second term in office. Except for the employment of this force, it is otherwise dumb. Stretching from the great lakes southwards to the line of the Ohio and the Ozarks, westward over Kansas, Iowa, Nebraska, until it mingles with the foothills of the Rockies, this great prairie country presents a thousand miles of landscape of which the sole salient feature is its immense flatness and monotony. Except in certain widely scattered centers of population, to which foreign immigration has contributed much, and which are both hideously utilitarian and blatantly industrial, the population of this great plain is definitely Anglo-Saxon and agricultural. Up to the twentieth century, this population had all the characteristic traits of agricultural Protestantism—an insatiable respect only for the externals of worldly prosperity, a narrow inability to see beyond its own horizon, a coarseness of fiber which expressed itself by taking over from Puritanism its ugliest traits—the hatred of beauty, refinement, art. Dickens drew indelible types of its society in Martin Chuzzlewit, and since Dickens' day many an unprejudiced European observer, escaping from the carefully cultivated salons of New York and Boston, has looked upon it and lost hope in a country which could draw its strength from anything so soul-destroying and dull.

Yet the Middle West has produced, accidentally, at least two geniuses—Lincoln, the failure at every job, who learned through failure alone the ability to see into every man's heart: and also Grant, the inarticulate, driving power, who broke, with his raw Illinois farmer boys, the skill and might of the South at Vicksburg and before Richmond.

There is something of Lincoln and Grant in the work of Edgar Lee Masters, but there is also another quality—which was probably responsible for his abandoning law and becoming a writer—the quality of Puritan New England, to which he is akin by inheritance. When Spoon River Anthology was first printed in America, its sheer brilliance as a document unfolding the social life of any small Middle Western community during the generation after the Civil War (from 1870 to 1900) led the public to overlook its defects as poetry, as well as the more important fact that it was in no way characteristic of its author. As a plain record of life lived in the midst of a decayed and vanishing society it is invaluable; its minute exactness of detail, extending even to the proper names, sets America before us more clearly than any other work. But it was written simply as a dispassionate record of what the author knew already by heart, having spent twenty-one years in the midst of the society he describes, quitting it at last because "the pathos of the country depressed my imagination indescribably." In his inmost soul Masters has always striven to write from other motives. We, with three other volumes besides *Spoon River* to guide us, may be permitted to ask what those motives were.

In the first place, Masters is a poet without any traditional background. His education has been haphazard, desultory; during his early years, when the formative influences of literature should have exerted their strongest pressure upon him, he was only able to read by fits and starts; he has always been forced to work independently—to do without the guidance of people of maturer intelligence. For over twenty years, before writing *Spoon River,* he wasted his energy in attempting to imitate other poets—Burns, Shelley, Swinburne, the Elizabethans, Ibsen. This struggle was less an attempt to express something than to escape from his surroundings. Then, finally, at forty-five, he set himself to the task of merely recording his surroundings as they had impressed themselves upon him, and the result was *Spoon River.* But merely to record was not enough. He must build something better. He must express the thwarted, tortured longing for beauty which had burned in his soul.

In this light the most characteristic work Masters has ever done is, I think, to be found in his volume, *The Great Valley.* Here is all the dullness and prolixity of the later Wordsworth. Masters is, unfortunately, one of those writers who are born without a sense of humor. But in the midst of this tedious sermonizing there is also something else, which we can at least respect. There is the flame of Christian charity in the "Gospel of Mark"; there is the fierce Puritanic hatred of conventional morality in "Steam Shovel Cut"; there is ecstasy of a stolen moment of beauty in "The Subway"; and certainly the heart tug of an old memory in "I shall never see you again." Above all, there is a cold, just appraisal of America's material success and spiritual failure. This is brought out most clearly in "Cato Braden," the study of a failure, and in the first eight poems, which form a connected series, carrying the history of the Middle West from the founding of Fort Dearborn, in 1803, down to the present.

These poems are too long to quote, but in the most striking of them—the badly-named "Autochthon"—Masters grapples with a great idea. His aim is nothing less than to contrast European civilization, nourished in tradition, or proceeding by harmonious evolution out of tradition, with the American genius which is so crushed by the poverty of its outward circumstances that it burns inward, feeding on life itself. To accomplish this task, Masters has chosen the careers of three men born in the same year—Alfred Tennyson, Charles Darwin, Abraham Lincoln—and contrasts them, step by step. And the result is the most solidly impressive poem Masters has written. It is a poem which everyone must read who wishes to understand what America is.

Master's method of photographic realism has prevented him from being a great poet; as regards technique he is scarcely a poet at all. "Spoon River" is written in a free verse barely removed from prose, and the later works are mostly in a blank verse of most jogtrot description. But at least, in "The Great Valley," he sees clearly what is needed for poetry to flourish in America—a clearing of the ground. Let those who think that America is uncritical of her own shortcomings read this condemnation:

> You are a hollow thing of steel, a cauldron;
> No monument of freedom.
> You're lettered, it is true,
> With many luminous truths. . . .
> But inside you there is a seething compost
> Of public schools, the ballot, journalism,
> Laws, jurisprudence, dogma, gold the chief
> Ingredient of all, stirred into a brew
> Wherewith to feed yourself and keep yourself
> The thing you are!
> Not wholly slave, not really free,
> Desiring vaguely to be master-moral,
> And yet too sicklied over by old truths,
> The ballot, fear, plebeian spirit, lack of mind. . . .
> Hermaphroditic giant, misty-eyed,
> Half-blinded by ideals, half by greed!

II

The work of Edgar Lee Masters stated the problem of poetry in the Middle West in its most acute form. To the solution of that problem have come two other poets, widely differing in the surroundings of their lives, their circumstances, their traditions.

If variety of experience can make a poet, Carl Sandburg should be a great poet. He has been everything by turns—the driver of a milk wagon, a scene shifter in a theatre, a pusher of a truck at a brickworks, a railway construction hand, a dishwasher, a farmer's hand, a soldier in the Spanish-American war, the tenant of a gaol, a student at college, a social worker, a newspaper man. The outstanding fact about him, however, is not that he has been all these things, but rather that he is the son of an unlettered Swedish immigrant. This at once gives his poetry a different quality from the work of any of those with whom I have already dealt.

The great immigrant masses which were lured to America during the years 1870–1914 came with the notion in their heads that they were about to find the Land of Promise, the land where liberty ruled, where unlimited equal prosperity offered itself, where fraternity was not a vain word. The disillusionment that followed was equal in each case. But, according as the immigrants came from the South and East of Europe or from the North and West, they reacted differently. Those from the South and East reacted the more violently. Some of these, accepting the state of affairs, threw themselves into the task of making enough money to get back to their homes with a fortune, or to become "bosses" of their kind. Others, beaten in the race, became agitators, strikers, rebels. In short, to use an American phrase, they did not make such "good citizens" as did the Teutons and Scandinavians from the North and West. These, after their disillusionment, settled down to make the most of things in their new home. And it is from this latter class that Carl Sandburg has come.

There is a message of endurance written large across his poetry. It is not for nothing that Sandburg stands closer to Whitman's method of handling than any poet in America today. For Whitman endured thirty-five years of obscure poverty before settling down to the task of writing, and about twenty-five more years of obloquy and neglect before the world began to listen to his message. This sturdy quality of individual heroic endurance, which Whitman obtained from his Dutch ancestors, finds an equal in Sandburg's granite-like quality, which he obtains from his Scandinavian forebears.

But Sandburg, unfortunately for us, did not launch himself into

the world with a *Song of Myself*. His apprenticeship at newspaper work
and the fact that America during the years when he grew to maturity
had become a land where public opinion had given place to opinion
created and fostered by newspapers made all the difference. His first
bid for fame was with his poem on Chicago—"Hog-Butcher for the
World, Tool Maker, Stacker of Wheat, Player with the Railroads, and
the Nation's Freight Handler." This poem is in reality nothing but
an expanded newspaper paragraph. It is tainted with the two great
plagues of America—spread-eagle bombast and the inability to distinguish between material prosperity and the finer spiritual values.
Whatever the poet's motives may have been in writing it, it is in no way
characteristic of the finer shades of his work.

Much better, and much more characteristic of America's haphazard juxtaposition of sheer ugliness and beauty, is the following:

> Passing through ugly and huddled walls
> By doorways where women
> Looked from their hunger-deep eyes,
> Haunted with shadows of hunger-hands,
> Out from the huddled and ugly walls,
> I came suddenly at the city's edge,
> On a blue burst of lake,
> Long lake waves breaking under the sun
> On a spray-flung curve of shore;
> And a fluttering storm of gulls,
> Masses of great grey wings
> And flying white bellies
> Veering and wheeling free in the open.

This ability to place in juxtaposition the sense of free nature with the
observation of the tortured, thwarted life of industrial civilization is
Sandburg's most salient feature. It saves him from being a materialist
and a realist. Closely allied to this quality is another, more mystical
quality, which enables him to look on all human life as a spiritual war-
fare, endlessly renewed; a search for the unattainable.

The poems written on this theme are, I think, his best. The two
sections of his first book, which are entitled "The Road and the End"
and "Fogs and Fires," are his most solid contributions to poetry.
There are the poems called "The Road and the End" (perhaps the

most beautiful poem he has ever written), "Graves" (which is almost equally as fine), "The Answer," "Our Prayer of Thanks," "Joy," "Nocturne in a Deserted Brickyard," and the vivid "Young Sea." In these poems Sandburg seizes alternately the facts of nature and of human destiny to see through them to some unknown conclusion. This is the mystic method employed by Blake and others—to see *through* realities, not *with* realities—and Sandburg was the first poet in America to employ it.

These sections of his first volume, as well as the early war poems, led many people to build large hopes on his future. So far he had shown promise of producing the rarest kind of poetry—the poetry which flowers out of experience, out of personality, into the immutable and absolute. But with his second volume these hopes of his admirers became a little dashed. *Cornhuskers,* as this volume is called, brings us face to face with this poet's limitations.

The limitations are many, and first among them may be mentioned the limitations of technique and of style. Sandburg has never been able to get beyond the most elementary rhythmic forms. These rhythms, whether printed as poetry or as prose, shackle his effort and tend to make him short-winded. The attempts in *Cornhuskers* to do long poems—such as *Prairie*—break down for the reason that so many of Whitman's poems break down—they are mere strings of disconnected lines rather than rounded wholes.

There is also a second and more serious limitation. Somewhere in this second volume Sandburg pictures himself as sitting in a chair and reading, forever reading, the newspapers. This appetite for journalism, this preoccupation in the affairs of his own day, has gone far to ruin him for serious and sustained effort. No artist can concern himself exclusively with the ephemeral events of his time without damage to his soul. He must see through them to the eternal, enduring realities. This is what Sandburg seems largely incapable of doing. He has experienced, but he has also imperfectly freed himself from experience.

Yet there are signs still, even in this second volume, that he is capable of breaking free from narrow propaganda into a wider vision of reality. A few, short poems—"Valley Song," "Prayers of Steel," and also "Cool Tombs" and "Grass"—show this attitude. In "Prayers of Steel" he has successfully wrested American effort into a new kind of symbolism:

Lay me on an anvil, O God.
Beat and hammer me into a crowbar.
Let me pry loose old walls,
Let me lift and loosen old foundations.

Lay me on an anvil, O God.
Beat me and hammer me into a steel spike.
Drive me into the girders that hold a skyscraper together,
Take red-hot rivets and fasten me into the central girders.
Let me be the great nail holding a skyscraper
    Through blue nights into white stars.

The same handling of symbolism is to be found in the long poem, *Smoke and Steel*, which appeared in *Poetry* for February, 1920, and which is, so far, the best-sustained effort Sandburg has given us.

III

The difficulties that beset the critic in attempting to appraise the value of the work of Masters or Sandburg cease to exist when one comes to Vachel Lindsay. Here is a poet who, in effect, lays all his wares upon the counter and invites the public, rather than the intelligent, to be judge of them. The result is, that you either like them extremely, in which case you pick Lindsay as the only American poet, or you dislike them so much as to declare that Lindsay is not a poet at all. Neither attitude is, however, altogether the true one.

Lindsay is a reformer first and a poet afterwards. Born of strong Kentucky mountain stock—a Scotch Calvinist by birth and by inheritance (the American *Who's Who* states him to be a member of the Christian Disciples Church)—he is, above all, an itinerant preacher. He recalls, in a different way, another itinerant preacher—Robert Louis Stevenson. The difference between them is simply that Lindsay is less of an artist, more robustious, more democratic. In short, he is an American.

Lindsay's gospel is extremely simple. He believes that America should become not only the most prosperous country on earth but the greatest art-producing country. He wants all Americans to become artists. Linked with this idea is the corollary that art can only be produced by the community at large. With true Puritan intolerance Lindsay has attempted to make all his work an illustration of this prevailing creed. It does not always do so, however. That fact, conjoined to a saving sense of humor, has been his salvation.

It is beyond the purposes of this essay to ask the question whether these theories of art are true or not. What matters is the result of those theories; and in producing his work Lindsay hit upon one unexpected piece of good fortune. It is impossible to produce this community art which he dreams of without first paying attention to the thing which expresses the life of the community—that is, folk lore. Now America has practically no folk lore except the Indian, which requires a very different type of brain from the average Anglo-Saxon to appreciate it. The only other folk lore which America has produced, and which it is in any way capable of instant understanding, was that invented by the American Negro in slavery. And Lindsay lived far enough South to come into contact with the Negro spirit, without living so far South as to instinctively despise it.

The result of his immersion into the stream of Negro folk lore is written visibly across the pages not only of *The Congo*, which is his best book, but also across all the others. The Negro not only gave to Lindsay the peculiar syncopation of meter which is his sign-manual as a technician, but also that mingling of religious fervor with naive grotesque which makes the substance of his poems. Anyone who has heard the old Negro "spirituals" sung must recognize this. For instance:

> When Israel dwelt in Egypt's land,—
> Go down, Moses—
> Oppressed so hard they could not stand:
> Let my people go!
> Thus saith the Lord, bold Moses said,
> Let my people go!
> If not I'll strike your firstborn dead;
> Let my people go!

Does not this contain the germ of "Booth led loudly with the big bass drum / Are you washed in the blood of the Lamb?" or "Mumbo-Jumbo, the God of the Congo / Mumbo-Jumbo will hoodoo you," or any one of a dozen of Lindsay's best known poems?

If the matter had stopped here, no more need be said. But unfortunately Lindsay has not stopped here. It was not enough for him to write "The Congo," "The Santa Fé Trail," "The Kallyope Yell," and dozens of other good Negro or quasi-Negro poems. He must also teach audiences to sing them. His art must be, above all things, democratic. So he invented the poem-game, in which the audience is called upon to join in shouting the refrain, and devised the "higher Vaudeville imagination" to account for not only his own art, but also that of the Greeks. Starved as he is of art of any kind, and admitting only the kind of art that immediately gets into the brains of the multitude, he has gone so far as to bless the cinema, which is the only form of art that most Americans care for, and to write poems to Mary Pickford. And doubtless, in all good faith, he takes such things as *The Daniel Jazz*" seriously.

But it is impossible to take them seriously. We may wish with all our hearts that this age did not show such a serious breach between the artist and the public; we may even hope for America the new birth of democratic art; but art is eternally one thing, and journalism is another. Much of Lindsay's work is journalism, just as, in a different sense, much of Miss Lowell's work is journalism. It does not measure up to the immutable standards of style or subject. It does not quicken the imagination. There is in it immense noise and energy, but America does not need more noise and energy, but rather an escape from them. This escape Lindsay does not provide.

As I have already said, the one thing that saves this poet is his sense of humor. The poem called "The Congo" is better than either "The Santa Fé Trail" or "The Fireman's Ball" (the latter is a particularly vicious piece of moralizing) because it is less ethical, more funny. And better than either are the two Chinese poems, "The Chinese Nightingale" and "The Empire of China is Tumbling Down." Lindsay is thoroughly at his best whenever he is simply playing with rockets, lanterns, and outlandish costumes. He is indeed a superb nonsense poet—a broader Lewis Carroll or Edward Lear—as the recently appearing *Golden Whales of California* will testify.

Rarely does he successfully strike the deeper notes of poetry. The war poems at the end of *The Congo* are samples of his utter failure to see the larger issues of human destiny. He seriously supposes that the war was entirely caused by the mad ambition of certain kings, and that the peasants did not acquiesce in their own slaughter. And it is a well known fact that, when America entered the war, he became an ardent supporter of Conscription and of the Sedition Act, which muzzled the American press. He even dreamed for a time of applying the "family album" test to citizenship—only those being admitted who could show ancestry stretching back to the Revolution.

He has completely failed to learn the lesson of his own early poem, "The Eagle that is Forgotten." With the exception of "The Broncho who would Not be Broken," which is a glorification of the outlaw, it is the most impressive poem he has written. It turns to ashes that creed which he himself preaches, the creed which would make the voice of the majority the voice of God.

PART III

I

From the consideration of the foregoing poets I might go on to other sections of the United States—the South, the Far West—and put the question: Why is it that so little comparatively has been produced by these sections? To answer such a question would involve an otiose discussion, and would add nothing to anyone's knowledge of American poetry. Far better to pass on to another group of American poets who are distinguished from the two preceding not only by being born in the decade succeeding those I have just mentioned, but also because they became, at an early age, either voluntary exiles from the United States or poets expressing themselves by violent reaction to the monotonous uniformity of American life.

The first of the exiles in point of time, and perhaps also in eminence, is Ezra Pound. Pound came to Europe about 1908, and spent a year wandering in Italy, France and Spain before settling in London. There he published in the following year *Personæ*, which was so successful that it was almost immediately followed by *Exultations* in the same year. After a return visit to America in 1911, which only served to disgust him completely with his native country (unfortunately for him, this visit antedated the American revival of interest in poetry by two years), he published *Ripostes* in 1912.[2] In 1913, having been five years in Europe, he collected together most of the pieces later published in *Lustra* (hence the title), and in 1915 he published the results of his work on Fenellosa's manuscript notes (which came into his hands a year before) under the title of *Cathay*. What poetry he has since written will be found in the recent *Quia Pauper Amavi* (1919).

I have made this brief historical note in order to clear away certain misconceptions. In all his work since 1912 (with the sole exception of *Cathay*) Pound has, I think, quite unjustifiably, put greater stress upon his own personal attitude to life, to literature, to members of his own profession, and to society generally, than upon his poetry. He has said in effect that the thing that matters is Ezra Pound and his opinions— not poetry in itself and for its own sake, but poetry for the sake of expressing a man's personal attitude and reaction to what lies about him. This is certainly a mistake on his part. The mere strong expression of one's likes and dislikes does not make any man a poet, and to go about continually thumping the public on its head for its stupidity leads merely to putting oneself on the level of the public, not above it. Nor is Pound in any way well equipped for the job of being a satirist. The earlier volumes show a temperament utterly opposed to the satiric. In these volumes, as in *Cathay*, there is only the restless seeker after beauty—a beauty hard, bright, tangible, vividly American in its abrupt quality of definition, if not in its *mise-en-scène*.

Is it too much to suppose that the search for this beauty, which led Pound back to twelfth-century Provence, to mediæval Italy, to Greece finally and ancient China, came to him primarily from the keen, vivid atmosphere of America, and from his hatred of the prevailing commercial ugliness, so utterly unsuited to that atmosphere? At all events, in *Personæ* Pound had not yet found himself. He was still struggling with vestiges of what he calls the "crepuscular." It was in *Exultations* that he became master of his own material, and in this book he produced poetry such as no Englishman could ever write. The nearest things to these poems by an Englishman are some of Richard Aldington's early pre-war poems. Compare these with Pound, and the difference leaps to the eye. Aldington is cool, detached, impersonal. Pound, though deriving perhaps nine-tenths of his inspiration from Italian or Provençal literature, lives himself a vivid life in each of these poems:

Lo, I have seen thee bound about with dreams.
Lo, I have known thy heart and its desire;
Life, all of it, my sea, and all men's streams
Are fused in it as flames of an altar fire!

This, from the very first poem in *Exultations,* sets the note.

Exultations certainly contains more gold than anything this poet has done. "Sestina Altaforte," "Pierre Vidal Old," "Ballad of the Goodly Fere," "Sestina for Ysolt," "Portrait," "Francesca," "On His Own Face in a Glass," "Defiance," "Nils Lykke," "Alba Innominata"—it seems strange that the hand which wrote these poems could ever have descended to the trumpery smartness of *Homage to Propertius* or to the subfusc pedantry of *Three Cantos.* For these poems have all the vivid energy of a young race. Even at their most bookish, they are bookish in a different sense from European bookishness. The European of the present day when he desires to live in the past surrounds himself with echoes. Pound, you feel sure, might quite easily have lived with Bertran de Born, or even Villon, held rhyming bouts and drinking bouts with them, and broken their pates if necessary.

Strange that the demon of climate, requickening the old shreds of Anglo-Saxon stock, should have produced out of western North America this vivid spirit of flame! Strange, but also tragic. Pound has never been at home in twentieth-century Europe. He can only get life out of books—from the life about him, he can obtain nothing. Something prompts him, therefore, to mock the world he sees, because he hates it; and when he mocks, the vividness utterly abandons him. The smile becomes a leer, the attitude a pose, the dependence on other men's work assumes the dimensions of intolerable pedantry. Technically Pound's later work is even more interesting than his earlier. The *vers libre* experiments of *Ripostes* and *Cathay,* the free, broken blank verse of *Near Perigord* and *Three Cantos,* are fascinating things to study. But except where he follows faithfully some other work, as in *Cathay,* the poems in these last two volumes are almost valueless. They are "a broken bundle of mirrors," the patchwork and debris of a mind which has never quite been able to find the living, vivid beauty it set out to seek. As a pioneer, as a treader in unbroken paths, America can afford to salute the earlier, as it is forced to reject the later Pound; and a whole host of modern American poets could never have done the work they are doing without the inspiration of his influence.

II

There are other American exile poets, no less interesting than Pound, but I have been obliged to omit them, for the reason that, unlike him, they do not lend themselves to a misunderstanding of their position, but reveal more clearly than he has done the completely cosmopolitan European outlook. Without intending a bad pun, I might almost say that Pound's best work is actually provincial. Whatever sort of poetry he may attempt to write, the abiding result will always be found in the picturesque, flamboyant romanticism of his early phase. One cannot therefore omit him from a consideration of American poetry, for the reason that this tendency towards romanticism is just as clearly marked in the work of certain of the younger American poets as in his.

Along with this tendency, suppressed in Pound's case, there has arisen in America recently a clear reaction against the lyrical, and a growth of the impulse towards the dramatic. As this impulse is still in the formative stage, it is almost too early to predict anything concerning it. But in three other poets, two of whom, at least, have been influenced by Pound, it is possible to trace the early stages of this new development of American poetry.

Conrad Aiken might almost be termed a juvenile prodigy of poetry. Though barely past his thirtieth year, he is the author of five books of poetry, not to mention a volume of criticism. Not all in these books is worth reading. His first volume, *Earth Triumphant,* is interesting chiefly because of the strong influence of Masefield's realistic style. In his second (*Turns and Movies*) Aiken turned from Masefield to the sharper realism of Masters, without much success. It was not until his third that he found himself, and began to write the type of poetry which he has since so successfully developed.

Aiken is possibly a romantic, born out of time. The influence of the South upon his childhood probably gave him a bent towards the rich coloring and the sensuous verbal melody of Poe. The influences of his young manhood, spent at Harvard and in wandering about Europe, made him tend towards the realistic type of poetry. Since then he has attempted a fusion of both strains, not always with success. He has been reproached with his submission to so many influences from other poets. But this submission to influences is the mark of many a

131

genuine artist, and Aiken doubtless felt the study of many other poets necessary before he could set himself to the task of exploring the complex richness of his own temperament.

A more just reproach to be made against him is that he has not yet found a subject capable of employing his fullest range of power. Or, to speak better, he has found it merely in glimpses. *The Jig of Forslin,* the first book in which he began to be himself, is characteristic for this defect. Aiken takes the theme of an ordinary man, and seeks to draw the contrast between his actual life and his imaginary fantastic life of dreams. But long before we have finished the poem we forget who Forslin actually is. The range of fantastic experience through which he is made to pass is obviously beyond the scope of any ordinary individual, as Aiken himself admits in a prefatory note. But, he says, Forslin is not any particular man, but man in general. This vagueness and refusal to particularize detracts from the artistic value of the poem as a whole, though it enables us to appreciate certain portions of it, as, for instance, the scenes on Golgotha or the final concluding sections, beginning on page 119.

Already in this poem two tendencies are visible in Aiken. One is the tendency to balance the romantic and the realistic, which is somewhat overborne by his natural unconscious bent for the romantic; the second is the tendency to explore these romantic and realistic strains up to the point of their fusion in life, which makes his work essentially a poetry of dramatic contrast, or of counterpoint welded together only by his own rich sense of verbal melody. It is already apparent that Aiken requires a large canvas for his effects. In fact, he has developed Poe's celebrated theory about a long poem being only a succession of short ones to its logical conclusion. He splits the central theme up into innumerable facets, and sets these facets one against the other to shine by contrast. The result is that the central design is frequently lost (his poem called "The Charnel Rose," which appeared in his last volume, but was written, I think, before *Forslin,* is an example of this).

As I have already said, it is certain that Aiken has the equipment of a poet, but not so certain that he has found the theme which will enable him to make fullest use of that endowment. Living in a country which has produced fewer individual great men than any other, and where the great body of the population are notoriously similar to each other, he is practically confined to the exploration of the fantastic side of such ordinary lives as he sees about him. *Nocturne of Remembered Spring,* which followed *Forslin,* is an example of his inability to find a satisfying subject. A great deal of ability and genius has been wasted in this volume on working out the ordinary marital reactions of two quite ordinary people. The whole volume leaves one only with a vague sense of fatigue and weariness.

Senlin: a Biography, the most recently written poem of Aiken's which has appeared in book form, gives us more clearly than anything he has done the measure of his ability. Senlin is essentially a younger, more definite Forslin. The whole poem arranges itself, like a series of scenes out of drama, under the headings "His Dark Origins," "His Futile Preoccupations," and "His Cloudy Destiny." In many of these scenes a new desire to particularize, to make more definite, is clearly at work. Particularly striking is the scene where Aiken has set himself the task of recording the emotions of Senlin tying his necktie before a mirror in the morning, and relating these emotions to all the facts and surmises about this strange planet the world. In this scene he has succeeded more closely, perhaps, than anywhere else to rendering at once the pettiness and the grandeur of life.

III

The tendency towards the dramatization of psychological experience, already manifest in Aiken, grows more and more apparent as we approach the younger school. I have space but for two further examples.

Wallace Stevens stands in sharp contrast to the poets concerning whom I have already spoken, in so far as he has yet to publish his first volume. Whether this fact is due to a good-humored contempt for the public taste or a feeling that he has not yet completely expressed himself, I cannot say. His poems, scattered largely through the files of *Poetry* and *Others,* are nevertheless highly significant of the tendency of the new movement.

Stevens is an ironist, but the same irony which is coldly stated in Robinson, is half-hinted at in Frost, is insisted upon by Masters or Sandburg, or is implied by Aiken's counterpoint, changes in him to a note of agreeable banter. He is a dramatist without a theme—or perhaps lacking the ambition to find one. His one-act play, *Three Travellers Watch a Sunrise,* although it won an important prize, is a total failure. It barely develops a situation. Far more important is the strange psychological monologue, "Carlos Among the Candles," which can also be found in the files of *Poetry.* It is obvious that in the figure of this "eccentric pedant of about forty" who lights candles in a darkened room in order to fill his life with magnificence, and then blows them all out again because he prefers the darkness outside, Stevens has symbolized much of his own attitude to life.

Stevens has certainly read very carefully a number of modern French poets. Whether he ever lived for a time in Paris I do not know. At all events, he carefully dresses his verses in the latest French mode. Only the vague sense of disquiet, pulsing underneath, proves him to be essentially American.

"Phases," which appeared in *Poetry's* War Number, in November, 1914, gives his measure:

> There's a little square in Paris,
> Waiting until we pass.
> They sit idly there,
> They sip the glass.
>
> There's a cab-horse at the corner,
> There's rain. The season grieves.
> It was silver once,
> And green with leaves.
>
> There's a parrot at the window,
> Will see us on parade,
> Hear the loud drums roll—
> And serenade.

Concealed irony! The same note recurs in the celebrated "Peter Quince at the Clavier," which is probably the finest poem, technically, which Stevens has written, and it dominates the deliberately cryptic "Sunday Morning," which is another "Portrait of a Lady" better and more memorable than T. S. Eliot's. Stevens is so quotable that one can scarcely resist a magnificent passage in the third section of this poem. But I must refer the reader to the appendix.

It is always the strange aspects of life which capture Stevens, and particularly the æsthetic aspect. He is merely a commentator upon them, detached and impersonal. He avoids going below the surface of these aspects, possibly because he feels that it is all only illusion, possibly because he is too sensitive to them. He is an artist without philosophy, and even as an artist his output must always be small, for the reason that so few themes are really fitted for that peculiar blending of the abstract and the objective that is his. His work recalls Mallarmé or Villiers de l'Isle Adam, and in some timeless, ageless drama like *Axél* or *Hérodiade* he might be most at home. But there is no doubt whatever that, whether he ever finds a clear road for his genius to travel on or not, he is a poet.

IV

Aiken and Stevens both tend towards a dramatization of life-experience, but neither has written actual drama. A third poet, richer in some ways in experience than either, but far more severely limited in technique, has sought to cast his vision of life into rudimentary dramatic form. This poet is Alfred Kreymborg.

Kreymborg has had a varied career. Himself the child of obscure immigrant stock—the name is Danish, and Kreymborg is closely akin, temperamentally, to Hans Christian Andersen—he has lived all his life in the most complete poverty. Yet America has neither soured nor suppressed him. He has been editor, lecturer, poet, and filled various other rôles in life. And he has two books to his credit—one of which, *Mushrooms,* is almost entirely a joke; while the other, *Plays for Poem-Mimes,* looks like a joke, but takes on the appearance of something more serious when we understand what Kreymborg is trying to do.

He is trying to revive the theatre. Gifted with a sense of the ironic side of ordinary life, Kreymborg turns the lens of his observation upon men and women, and sees them as diminished, odd little puppets knocking each other about. So he writes his whimsical little plays of which the characteristic features are puckish humor and a limited but very sure control of cadence. It is a small achievement, but it is an achievement—for the reason that it foreshadows what may possibly prove to be a new field for American poetic talent.

Long ago Edwin Arlington Robinson began to pack life dramas

into lyric forms, despairing perhaps of being able to render them in any other way. Kreymborg, a representative of the very latest phase of the movement, is now tending in the same direction of drama, through the medium of puppet-plays. The dramatic impulse in America is not by any means dead—it has scarcely begun to unfold itself. Hitherto the genius of America's poets has been spent either upon the discovery of themselves and their surroundings or on the research into new forms of expression. The two opposing tendencies of poetic realism and of free-verse are now gradually approaching the point of fusion. This point is the starting point of a new poetic drama. But before such a drama is possible in America the stage must be purged from all purely literary imitations of old models, and from the demands of spectacle. Kreymborg is performing one side of this task; perhaps the cinematograph companies, by getting all the regular theatres into their hands, and thereby forcing drama to seek refuge in the hearts of enthusiastic amateurs, are unconsciously performing the other.

William Blake   *1923*

The French Revolution, an event of which the reverberations were destined to dominate the history of two-thirds the inhabited world throughout the nineteenth century, and up to the interval of the Great War in the twentieth, was permitted by one of those ironic dispensations of Providence of which history affords so many examples, to have more intellectual and spiritual effect on France's next-door neighbor than upon France herself. In that country the result of the Revolution was that the bourgeois class took the place of the old aristocracy, and Napoleon, with his purely military genius, replaced the faded glories of the bygone days of Louis the Fourteenth. It was in conservative, reactionary, phlegmatic England, ruled still by the old land holding aristocracy, that the Revolution went immediately to people's heads and produced in literature and the arts generally the effect of a spiritual explosion. Byron, Wordsworth, Keats, Shelley, as well as Turner and Constable, could not have been what they were had the Revolution not unconsciously inflamed their ardor; and the same is true in a still greater degree of the one man who, though largely unknown to his contemporaries, was the most important precursor of the whole Romantic movement in England, and whom we now see to have been, either as poet or artist, at once more radical and more logical in his revolt than any other.

William Blake was born in the year 1757, the same year in which Swedenborg, the strange Northern mystic and visionary, declared that he had been admitted into Paradise, and had received confirmation that the prophecies of the Last Judgment contained in the Apocalypse had all been fulfilled and that the Dispensation of the

Holy Spirit had begun. His father, a respectable hosier, was himself one of the first members of the Church of the New Jerusalem which had come into being as a result of Swedenborg's doctrine, and which had recruited its members largely from dissentient sects. There is a sort of ingrained Calvinism perceptible in Blake's writings and character that leads one to suppose that before he became a Swedenborgian his father may have been a Presbyterian. As a young man, he may himself have seen Swedenborg, who had lived in London during his last years, and who died there in 1772. Blake grew up, the second of a family of three sons and one daughter, in any case, in an atmosphere profoundly impregnated with the spirit of Swedenborg's teachings, and, like his great predecessor, he possessed the gift of "vision," with this exception, that according to his own account it was natural to him from his earliest days. He was wont to say that he had "seen God Almighty putting his face to the window" at the age of four, and "a treeful of angels at Peckham Rye" at the age of seven.

Most of Blake's admirers and critics have spent pages in the effort to describe exactly what he meant by this faculty of "vision," without realizing that in its essence this faculty is something common not only to him and Swedenborg, but also to every imaginative man upon earth who tries to pierce behind the veil of appearances and to state in some artistic or philosophic form the essence of reality. We may therefore accept Blake's visionary faculty, without supposing that it was anything else than a normal faculty, shared by him with thousands of others known and unknown, who do not exercise it so constantly. He spoke, as Crabb Robinson noted, of his visions in the tone of ordinary speech; mentioned seeing Socrates or Jesus Christ in the same tone that you and I speak of seeing Smith or Jones; and probably with better reason, for Blake may really have seen further into the character of Socrates or Jesus than you or I see into the inmost nature of any of our neighbors.

In any case, we must be prepared to accept the visionary form of Blake's writings if we are to understand him at all. When we have once done so, it becomes apparent that in his case the visionary element was entirely subsidiary to the revolutionary nature of his message. Even as regards the dates of his writings, it is clear that, if the French Revolution had not happened, Blake would have been in all probability merely a minor poet and water colorist, with a turn to eccentricity. Apart from the *Poetical Sketches, Tiriel* (the most Ossianic and least interesting of the mythical books) and the fragment of *An Island in the Moon,* he wrote nothing up to 1789, when he was thirty-two years old. But this year, the year of the outbreak in France, produced the *Songs of Innocence* and *Thel.* In 1790 appeared *The Marriage of Heaven and Hell,* a document of primary and decisive importance in the history of his intellectual development. It is apparent that here Blake was risking everything, and ready to appear before the world as the thoroughgoing preacher of the sacredness of rebellion. The year following he projected a great poem in seven books on the French Revolution; the first book being, as appears from the unique copy preserved, actually set up with a view to publication, but not published. Despite the announcement following the title page, that "the remaining books are finished and will be printed in order," I cannot believe that Blake actually wrote more of this poem than we possess.

Yet, as in the case of all honest artists, Blake was unable to keep silence, though the public wanted none of his work. In 1793, the year of the Terror, he wrote *America,* to which he prefixed the significant words "A Prophecy," and the same year he wrote in his manuscript notebook this sentence, so poignant in its revealment of deep suffering and despair: "I say I won't live five years, and if I live one, it will be a wonder." And this note takes on added significance when we reflect that it was about four years after this that he sat down to the great task of producing in carefully written MS. the masterpiece by which he hoped to be remembered if he was to pass out of the world, the poem *Vala.*

As it happened, life had other things in store for Blake, like many great men before or since his day; the crisis passed over, and a change of scene and occupation produced in him other fruits. In 1801, he was rescued from poverty and neglect by Hayley, who, thanks to Flaxman's recommendation, constituted himself his patron. It was probably about this time that Blake presented to Mrs. Flaxman, in testimony of her husband's kindness, the illustrations to Gray's poems which have recently been discovered. Hayley, as is known, took Blake and his wife off to the country, where Blake had an interesting if somewhat hectic time for three years, ending up with quarrelling with his patron, and being committed for trial on a trumped-up charge of sedition brought against him by one Schofield. In later years, he was wont to refer to this period as "his three years' slumber on the banks of the ocean." Yet it was not so much a slumber as an awakening of the poetic fires within which had died down. During this period *Vala* was rehandled, in the light of fresh developments that occurred to Blake, and then became *The Four Zoas, or the Torments of Love and Jealousy in the Death and Judgment of Albion, the Ancient Man,* a title we shall have to refer to later in the course of the necessary discussion and clarifying of Blake's thought. It suffices to say here that the new development of his thought was destined to make his work less personal and autobiographic on one side, and even more complexly allusive and figurative on the other. *Vala* or *The Four Zoas* was never printed, but long fragments and ideas from it were used as the ground-work to the later *Milton* and *Jerusalem*—works both of which bear the title-page date 1804, though *Milton*—which exists in three copies only—was not off the press until 1809, while *Jerusalem,* the single hand-tinted copy actually printed by him, did not appear until 1820.

The later years of Blake are of interest mainly to students of his development as a designer, in which field he has been somewhat better served by his critics than as a poet. Yet he was not altogether silent, though his works have come down to us only in manuscript. The Pickering MS. dates from the period of his residence with Hayley at Felpham, and is fairly accurate and complete. But the poem which well might have been Blake's final masterpiece was never, so far as we know, actually finished. It exists only in rough drafts in the notebook which Rossetti bought for ten shillings, and the second of its sections, partially incomplete, is headed with the title which might well stand as the title of all Blake's literary work: "The Everlasting Gospel."

In all these works, the fundamental quality of Blake's mind is his uncompromising rebelliousness. He is in revolt against the hypocrisy that parades itself as morality, the injustice that masks itself as law, the make believe that calls itself religion. His attitude to all of these things is the attitude of the eternal protestant. It was not for nothing that he admired, most of all the English poets, Milton; for Milton too is the eternal protestant among poets, perhaps the only great protestant poet except Blake himself. It has been said that Milton's Satan is Blake's God: perhaps it would be better to say that Milton's Satan is Blake's Los. For Los—an obvious anagram for the Latin *Sol,* meaning in his peculiar mythical system the light of the human imagination shining backwards upon and consequently reflecting the light of the sky—is the true hero of the Prophetic Books. As regards God, it is almost correct to say that Blake had no God except the God comprehensible to man, the divine spirit of humanity incarnated historically in Jesus, and capable of reincarnation in Everyman.

Nor does Blake's rebellion end here. Having systematically denied God, he must next deny Nature. It is all Satan, all negation. "I assert that for me the natural world does not exist." Undoubtedly this view did not represent Blake's view at the outset of his career. It is only in the later works that it becomes predominant. The early prophetic books are full of pleas for the utmost abandonment to nature. The basis of all Blake's early teaching is to be found in the phrase "Everything that lives is holy." *Visions of the Daughters of Albion* is a plea for free love. *Songs of Innocence* and *Songs of Experience* have the same theme. *The Marriage of Heaven and Hell* is an attack on conventional morality and piety, brilliantly anticipating Nietzsche in many of its conclusions. Only with the revised *Vala* and in *Jerusalem* and *Milton* does the new view present itself and become important.

And the denial of nature in Blake leads fundamentally to the denial of sexual love. Sexual love became, in Blake's last years, the fall of man. Not that therefore marriage was commendable as an attempt to repair the fall. On the contrary, "He confessed a practical notion, which would do him more injury than any other I have heard from him. He says that from the Bible he has learned that *eine Gemeinschaft der Frauen statt finden sollte*," or, to put this into plain English, that all women should be held in common. Nor is this idea in any way contradictory of Blake's nondenial of the senses. Sin was only error—the fall itself was only error, and all should be forgiven.

But it is in "The Everlasting Gospel" that Blake's mind takes the final step of rebellion. When he wrote this poem, he apparently realized that whatever the value of his message, no one of his day would greatly care for it. So he left it a series of fragments. The hero of this poem is not one of Blake's myths, but Jesus Himself; and Blake's problem is here, the same which has tortured so many other modern thinkers. Assuming that Jesus of Nazareth as presented in the Gospels (whether He actually existed historically or not, is of minor importance) is the most perfect type of man possible, then the churches which were established in His Name are not Christian, because they render unto God the things that are Cæsar's and to Cæsar the things that are God's; they enslave the soul, and degrade the body, whereas Jesus aimed at liberating both. Blake therefore asks a series of questions. Was Jesus gentle, was He humble, was He without sin, was He chaste? only to answer each one in the negative. If He was gentle, why did He deny Herod, God's high king, and Caiaphas, God's high priest? If He was humble, why did He attack the Pharisees? Blake even goes further and asserts

> This is the race that Jesus ran;
> Humble to God, haughty to man,
> Cursing the rulers before the people,
> Even to the temple's highest steeple,
> And when He humbled Himself to God
> Then descended the cruel rod.
> "If Thou humblest Thyself, Thou humblest Me;
> Thou also dwell'st in Eternity;
> Thou art a man: God is no more,
> Thy own humanity learn to adore."

This is daring enough, but worse is to follow. Jesus was not only not sinless; He committed every crime in the calendar. As regards Jesus's chastity, the last wonderful section of this poem confronts Jesus and the Magdalen. And Jesus utters these words which are the core of all Blake's thought:

> Good and evil are no more,
> Sinai's trumpets cease to roar!
> Cease, finger of God, to write,
> The heavens are not clean in thy sight.
> Thou art good, and Thou alone,
> Nor may the sinner cast one stone.
> To be good only is to be
> A God or else a Pharisee.
> Thou angel of the Presence Divine,
> That didst create this body of mine,
> Wherefore hast Thou writ these laws
> And created Hell's dark jaws?
> My presence I will take from Thee:
> A cold leper Thou shalt be.

Thou that wast so pure and bright
That Heaven was impure in Thy sight,
Tho' Thy oath turned Heaven pale,
Tho' Thy covenant built Hell's jail,
Tho' Thou didst all to chaos roll,
With the serpent for its soul,
Still the breath Divine does move,
And the breath Divine is love.

That the man who uttered these words declared himself a criminal, asserted that what are considered as crimes upon earth are the glories of heaven, and died singing and shouting for joy, need surprise no one. For the fact of the matter is that William Blake was either a madman or a saint, if we understand thereby that madmen and saints are the only people who succeed in getting the better of human life as the respectable and worthy, and infinitely dull and tedious, majority conceive it. Yes, Blake was a madman to declare that the vision of Christ which he saw was the most bitter enemy of the vision of Christ other people saw. Why did he go out of his way to collect enemies, if it were not to love them? But his madness, like Hamlet's, was not without method (while the sanity of most people is entirely so) as we shall shortly see.

Blake realized that any truths that he might utter were certain to be unpopular truths. The world in which he found himself was a world in which it was thought sinful to give free rein to sexual desire, though God had Himself planted the sexual instinct in man's body; in which it was sinful to love one's neighbor as oneself, for to do so might be covetous; in which it was sinful to be proud of one's own achievement, for pride was the sin whereby the angels fell (as if it were not equally easy to fall, Blake might have retorted, through humility). It was equally sinful in Blake's world—which in all its essentials has not changed today—to give freely to the poor, because to do so might only lead them to become discontented with their lot; or to hate war, tyranny and bloodshed, because the church which had been developed from St. Paul's doctrine had counselled obedience to the State.

For this reason, Blake chose to speak darkly and in parables—finding as usual his justification therefor in the Gospels themselves. He called his chief books in poetry "prophetic," meaning thereby that some future age would be able to decipher their plain meaning from the complex "allegory addressed to the intellectual powers" in which he had chosen to embody it. The basis of this allegory is that man is potentially perfect only when all sides of his nature are in harmony. These four dimensions of the perfect human spirit (for Blake was the first Einsteinian) were reason, emotion, animal life, and imagination. They were called the Zoas, a name obviously derived from the Greek word for "lives." To be able to exercise all four simultaneously was to be Albion, the Fourfold Ancient Man, who lived in Eden at the beginning and was destined to live in Jerusalem (or Paradise) at the end. But between these states of perfect human creation and redemption stretched for Blake, as for Jesus Christ, the story of the Fall. This according to Blake had come about through the exaggeration of one side of human nature at the expense of others. Luvah (derived from the Hebrew word meaning "heart"), the human emotion, had seized the chariot (power) of Urizen (from the Greek οὐρίζειν, meaning to limit, cramp, bound, imprison) the human reason, and as a result everything had fallen into disorder. The reason (Urizen) had become cold, heartless, selfish; emotion (Luvah) had then been thrown into the furnace of sex by his female counterpart, Vala—which I take to be an anagram of the Latin *Lava*, the spirit of animal life; Tharmas (an anagram of the Greek ἄσθμα, the "breath") had nothing to do but mourn; and Urthona, the all-transforming imagination (perhaps derived from the New Testament spelling ἄνθρουπος, "man") became bound to a female, Enitharmon (from ἐνάρίθμον, "reckoned, counted, numbered"), or in other words became mortal. As a mortal, he took on the form of Los, of which I have spoken above. Los was identified with Blake himself, the imaginative artist par excellence.

The mythological system briefly sketched above is fairly clear and consistent, and does not require for its understanding the very elaborate and misplaced ingenuity of Blake's most celebrated editors, Messrs. Ellis and Yeats. Unfortunately, however, Blake himself gave these editors every temptation to hazardous conjecture through the number of subsidiary figures he has brought into his myth, and the confusion in which—perhaps due to lack of education or pressure of other work, or too direct dependence of inspiration unchecked by reasoning—he saw fit to leave his *Outline of History*. The early prophetic books are admittedly fragmentary, and make few attempts to explain the elaborate symbolism which was always latent in his mind.

Believing as he did, that art consists in minute particulars and not in generalized form (a belief which is only a half-truth at best), he strove to give his system significance by creating a whole pantheon of subsidiary figures: Thel, Theotormon, Rintrah, Bromion, etc., etc. According to my friend, Mr. Edward O'Brien, to whom I am indebted for valuable suggestions, all those names are readily derivable as anagrams from Greek, Latin, or Hebrew. Blake may have possessed a polyglot New Testament and obtained them from its pages. But the difficulty with the earlier prophetic books is that they represent various independent sides of a complex reality that slowly developed in Blake's mind. *Vala* or *The Four Zoas,* the lack of a definitive and final edition of which is an outstanding disgrace to scholarship, is an attempt to give the cardinal myth in some final form, but it was never entirely completed. *Milton* and *Jerusalem* are only new elaborations, carried out with such bewildering multiplicity of detail that the mind is bewildered and lost. In *Jerusalem,* for example, we are given a complete symbolic geography of England, in which each town, according to whether it is in the north, east, south or west, is ruled over by some "emanation," or descendant of the Four Zoas. Here ingenuity triumphs over inspiration; and we are left in the position of a man having a bunch of some hundreds of keys in his hands and being required to know which lock each one fits at any given instant. Blake's mythological and symbolic system is in reality the greatest bar to the understanding of his fundamental thought, which was magnificently simple and required no such elaboration. For all his mythological heroes (and especially Los) are, in a sense, Blake himself or Everyman; just as all his female characters are phases of the eternal female he discovered in his wife. Had he not in the comparatively simple "Everlasting Gospel," and the still later *Ghost of Abel,* made return to a more reasonable mode of stating his message, there would be some excuse for those who consider him eccentric, or even insane. *Jerusalem,* for example, is one of the most obscure poems ever written, though it becomes clearer if it is read after reading all the preliminary prophetic books in order; and it becomes still clearer with every successive re-reading, though in it from beginning to end Blake's mind moves through chaos.

Another and a more serious defect in Blake's system arises from his denial of nature above mentioned. Being, as he was, a man of highly strung imagination, and believing as he did that "it is better to believe vision with all our might and strength, though we are fallen and lost," he made the profound mistake of supposing that nature provides no help to the visionary imagination. "I assert that for me the natural world does not exist"—this remark of his later years reveals exactly where Blake went wrong. He committed precisely the error of early mediæval and monastic Christianity, which, seeing too clearly the miseries of this world, attempted to substitute for human life a period of trial, leading to a better world. But he did not see the paradox which modern science, no less than the Apostle's Creed, teaches us; that in whatever world we are, we cannot exist without matter in some form, without limitation and embodiment. Whitman and Patmore, each in his own way, saw the flesh and spirit, as one, not as apart; and their attempt to transcend life leads to life ever more rich and abundant; whereas Blake's way, the way of the imagination unaided and unbounded by reality, leads, as he himself admitted, only to eternal annihilation of all selfhood.

Yet we can forgive Blake even this final heresy, because we know dimly what he suffered. He was born a full century, at least, before his time. The political revolutionaries whose energies he admired—"energy is eternal delight" is one of his finest sayings—were one and all materialists, without imagination, without God. And the religious people of his day were one and all living in a state of reactionary negation, worshipping either the "selfish, cold" Urizen as God, or bowing before the Cross and Tomb instead of looking for the living risen Christ among mankind. The naïve egotism of his various addresses and manifestoes to the public are one index to the state of his mind; another and not less clear is the profoundly unforgettable note that he was to leave behind in his papers: "Tuesday, Jan. 20, 1807, between two and seven in the evening, despair." When that note was made, Blake was nearly fifty years old.

That he triumphed over his despair we not only have the fragments of the "Everlasting Gospel" as well as the Dante and Job series of illustrations to remind us, but also we have the public interest in his work to account for, which, though Blake has not yet been a hundred years in his unmarked grave in London, is continually busy with new editions of his work, or new studies of its author. That interest is, I suggest, not merely motivated by curiosity in an extraordinary man.

We have arrived at a time in the world's history when scientific theory and religious faith have begun, not to oppose, but to give support to one another; though many of our scientists and religious leaders fail to observe the fact. We have therefore come to the junction of art (which reposes in faith) and science (which reposes in knowledge). The synthesis of these two contrasting ideas, the artistic and the scientific, might produce a great poem. But to put a poem of that sort into concrete form needs not only experiment with all kinds of new utterance, but a personality strong enough to see the abstract concretely, and to write it in the form of "allegory addressed to the intellectual powers." We must therefore re-adopt Homer's prerogative, and re-create a mythology. Hitherto Blake's attempt has been the sole one in the field. And his triumph in it might have been even greater had he been given a lifetime to devote solely to poetical work.

The Spirit of
Thomas Hardy   *1924*

The number of great writers that any century can produce is extremely small. To begin with, the great writer must have the supremely rare power of seeing the universal in the particular. He must also, by the fact of circumstances which are beyond anyone's control, have been dowered by fortune with a degree of experience—and consequently of suffering and the wisdom which comes only through suffering—to which most of mankind are necessarily strangers. Again, he must have the power to set down what he has experienced; and this demands the effort of long and toilsome application, and a physique capable of bearing its stress. Lastly, he must instinctively foresee, grasp, and exhaust the particular moment of human history which has produced him; he must stand at the culmination of some special moment of human affairs, and point the way to the future development of man's ideas about his own fortune and destiny. For so gigantic a task the great writer must be prepared, and he must also be able to continue his striving towards the goal, even though—as in the case of Melville, for example—the less intelligent spirits of his day are unable to recognize his supreme ability and to appreciate it at its proper value.

Thomas Hardy is, by all the tests set out above, a great writer. Moreover, he has been singularly fortunate in having obtained, throughout his long career as a creative artist, an increasing measure of admiration and appreciation by his successors. It is universally agreed by those most qualified to judge, that he is the greatest writer in the English-speaking world of the present day; but it is not so clear wherein his greatness consists. Coming as the culmination of the Victorian era in English literature, with characteristics that recall

Thackeray, Dickens, George Eliot, Matthew Arnold, as well as tendencies towards the earlier period of abortive revolt of which Shelley, Byron, Wordsworth, and Keats were the spokesmen, it is not to be wondered at that so complex a figure is difficult to grasp in perspective. And when we have recorded the further fact that this man's life-span and mind-span have covered the downfall of the Victorian compromise in art, ideas, and life, and have pointed the way tentatively to new fields for creative activity in all three, it becomes apparent that to say the last word on him at this early date is practically impossible.

Recently several attempts have been made to estimate Hardy's achievement; of these I should like to say a few words before attempting briefly the definition of that achievement for myself. Of the books that have been written on him, I put first Professor Joseph Warren Beach's detailed and valuable monograph on the novels, entitled *The Technique of Thomas Hardy,* because it does not shrink from what to many is the invidious task of sorting out what is best in Hardy's fiction from what is least interesting. The study (*Thomas Hardy*) by Mr. H. C. Duffin is almost entirely worthless, being marred by faults of exuberance on every page, and by the sort of perverted sentimentality that is able to rate FitzGerald's third-rate *Omar Khayyam* above Hardy's own sterner, if more roughly ordered, verses. Professor Chew's handbook, *Thomas Hardy, Poet and Novelist,* is exceptionally well informed, and in small compass covers the entire field of both Hardy's prose and poetry. Finally, I would like to draw attention to the recent reprinting of Mr. Lionel Johnson's essay on "The Art of Thomas Hardy," still worth reading for the sake of its scholarly style and balanced enthusiasm, and remarkable for the date when it first appeared.

From all these books it becomes clear that as regards Hardy's novels, a wide distinction must be drawn between those which are first-rate, those which are distinctive but less satisfactory, and those which are comparatively worthless. Seldom has any literary artist been so consistently unequal in novel production; almost never has any writer beloved of the moderns seemed to be so much enamored of outworn devices of technique. As Professor Beach points out, Hardy has shown himself in the greater part of his fiction unduly concerned with the mechanics of plot, the stock elements of surprise, coincidence, overheard conversation, intercepted letters, and the like, being accepted by him almost unaltered from the novel of adventure of the eighteenth century and from its revival in the nineteenth by such writers as Wilkie Collins and Charles Reade. It is only in two or three instances, and then almost as it were by accident, that he has foreshadowed the modern type of novel with its interest in situation rather than plot, its psychological development of character, its perhaps undue concern with the dramatization of social theory. What has driven him almost unconsciously to modify the novel from its eighteenth-century proto-type, is his supreme sense of the truth of character.

Professor Beach ranks the novels in three classes thus: novels in which art and craft are one, consisting of *Tess of the D'Urbervilles, Jude the Obscure,* and *The Return of the Native;* novels which are in some de-gree overburdened with mechanical craftsmanship, but in which the truth and beauty of character and setting give an air of distinction to somewhat manufactured plot—in this group belong *Far from the Mad-ding Crowd, The Mayor of Casterbridge, The Woodlanders;* and novels of sheer ingenuity and decidedly inferior interest, comprising all the rest. I agree in general with this judgment, but I am by no means pre-pared to follow Professor Beach in his condemnation of *The Mayor of Casterbridge* as a mere moving-picture scenario. One might as well condemn Stendhal's novels as moving pictures; yet Stendhal is one of the world's greatest psychologists. More just would it be to say that in *The Mayor of Casterbridge* Hardy has written a romance of adventure of the older type, with this difference that in Henchard he has created a character whose astonishing truth proves him to be seen and studied from within, as Shakespeare's or Stendhal's characters were seen and studied. The sincerity and truth to life of such a character make the reader forget the whole apparatus of artifice and coincidence whereby he is presented.

As regards the poems, a complete difference of opinion makes it-self manifest. Professor Beach does not deal with them; Mr. Duffin, with his undisguised liking for what Whitman would have contemptu-ously called "piano-tunes," is scarcely prepared to admit that they can be called poetry at all, though he is obliged to concede that they are necessary reading for anyone interested in Hardy's philosophy of life; Professor Chew puts in a strong plea for *The Dynasts* and a less strong plea for many of the individual poems, and especially for the group of lyrics of travel written in 1887. Meanwhile it must be noted that any future critic of Hardy's poetry must somewhat enlarge the perspective of his standpoint to take into account the recently published *Late Lyrics and Earlier* in which the veteran author—in foreword and conclusion—reluctantly bids adieu to his audience.

What none of these critics has sufficiently considered is the close connection that subsists between Hardy's poetry and his prose. Professor Beach hints at this when he describes *The Return of the Native* as a five-act drama (the last book entitled "Aftercourses" being a mere sop to the public that will have a happy ending at all costs). He does not, however, sufficiently stress the fact that the real protagonist of this drama is no single human figure, but the vast inhuman influence of a natural scene: Egdon Heath, subduing all the human puppets that live upon it and walk about it to its own purposes. This dominant motive of a landscape background against which certain inferior human specimens work out the counterpoint of their lives, makes of *The Return of the Native* something more than an ordinary novel, and lifts it into the category of a poem: if one cares to call it so, a tone-poem. Similarly, the extreme simplicity of the plot structure of *Tess* recalls in its alternations between Alec D'Urberville and Angel Clare as the center of Tess's experience, as well as in its fitting of scene to situation and in its unforced pathos, the technique of many old ballads. *Jude the Obscure,* where the interest in "Wessex" as a background is absent, finds kinship in its severe massing of irony, to some of Crabbe's narratives, or to Hardy's own "Satires of Circumstance"; and in a great many scenes in the other novels the same poetic imagination is at work, transmitting character and scene from the particular to the universal. No one can do complete justice to either his novels or his poetry who is not ready to admit that, by right of this imagination displayed in the best of both, Hardy is essentially a poet.

Furthermore, the work he has produced is not only a unified whole, but it could never have come into being without the support of a definite philosophy, a way of looking at things which its author has made his own. What that way of looking at things is, and what its value may be to future generations must be the next subject for inquiry.

At bottom, Hardy is a fatalist; that is to say, he sees all phenomena (including the phenomena of nature, supposedly indifferent to man) as controlled and ordered by a single Immanent Will, unmoral and impersonal in essence, unlogical and unconscious as regards its own aims, forever weaving and unweaving the web of life in its creatures.

Or as the Prelude to *The Dynasts*, embodying his most mature philosophy, states it:

> It works unconsciously, as heretofore,
> Eternal artistries in circumstance,
> Whose patterns, wrought by rapt aesthetic rote,
> Seem in themselves Its single listless aim,
> And not their consequence.

But like Schopenhauer, and other philosophers who have held a similar view on the universe, Hardy seeks some means of escape from the logical consequences of it. Though the Will that guides the universe may be at bottom without logic, reason, or meaning, yet we, who are the mere pawns It shoves across Its chessboard, desire It to be otherwise, in so far as we feel pity and exercise charity to others. If the views of the impersonal Demiurge are to prevail in every instance over ours, then there is no reason at all for living, and the sooner we, like little Father Time in *Jude the Obscure*, commit suicide, the better. If, on the other hand, our better feelings with which we are endowed, are in any small measure to prevail, then there is a dim purpose to this "thwarted purposing," then life does not—despite Hardy's own assertion to the contrary—always "offer to deny," then, at times, there is a wrong "dying as of self-slaughter."

It speaks volumes for Hardy's integrity as a poet that he has at least faced this problem, that he has admitted some loophole of doubt in his own skepticism, that he has not only noted the "intolerable antilogy of making figments feel" but has found in that paradox some basis for melioristic faith. The reader who is unfamiliar with his poetry, may, however, be almost pardoned if he accepts the conventional average view of Hardy as a complete pessimist. In *The Return of the Native*, passionless Egdon works out its doom upon Eustacia and Wildeve, on Clym and his mother; in *Jude the Obscure*, the force of unchecked sexual passion in Jude and Arabella, makes havoc of every hope; in *The Mayor of Casterbridge*, Henchard's unreasonable, unreflecting, impetuous greed and vanity end in disaster for him and for all those with whom he comes into contact. Only in *Tess*, of all the greater novels, are we allowed, through the lavish beauty and pathos with which the author invests that character, to suspend slightly our judgment on the "intolerable scheme of things." In spite of Hardy's own fling at the "President of the Immortals" and his "sport with Tess," we feel in our bones that she owes her doom not so much to the workings of fate as to the shallow weakness and vanity of Angel Clare. As Professor Beach says: "We can almost forget the pain of the story in its loveliness. The rage and indignation pass; the tenderness remains. And if we say, how pitiful! it is to say, in the next breath, how beautiful!"

Above all, it is in the poems that this sense of the "tears of things" most often overpowers Hardy's own narrow fatalism, and leads him and his reader to accept the tragedy of life not so much as a ghastly mockery but almost as a triumph. In the scene of Nelson's death in *The Dynasts,* and in the closing pages of that drama; in the superb and unequalled elegies, "veteris vestigia flammae" of 1911–13, in the armistice poem, "And there was a great calm," in many and many a detached lyric, or narrative, the same thing is shown: the spectacle of a great artist so enrapt in the figments of his imagination as to forget the injustice of the world, to forget the impersonal horror of fate that weighs on us all, and to seek only the release of ecstatic joy through pity. And in this sense, whatever may be urged against his awkwardly prosaic vocabulary, his crudely hewn versification, Hardy proves himself the possessor of a mind that can only be called Shakespearean. When we read *Hamlet, Othello,* or *Lear,* we remain unaffected by the darkness of the outer tragedy, we see only the glory of the inner triumph. And so it is when we turn the last page of that enormous canvas, like a vast panorama of drifting shadows and intense lights painted by some Rembrandt, that Hardy has called *The Dynasts.*

The twentieth century is certain to be critical of the nineteenth, as the eighteenth was critical of the seventeenth and sixteenth, as the fourteenth was critical of the thirteenth, as the third century B.C. was critical of the whole effort that had expressed itself in ancient Greece.

We stand still too near to the enormous welter and chaos of the nineteenth century to see all its issues clearly; but this we may say, that of its latter cause—the four leading literary figures in Europe have been Tolstoy, Dostoyevsky, Ibsen, and Nietzsche. And this may also be added: that Hardy's achievement, even though we acknowledge its lesser magnitude, is yet so important that it can only be profitably compared with theirs.

It will be seen at the outset, when we attempt such comparison, that

Hardy stands closer to Ibsen and to Tolstoy than to Dostoyevsky and Nietzsche. He has none of the hopeless and boundless desire to create a personal faith in the abyss of skepticism that drove Dostoyevsky to explore to the bottom of every human soul, and forced him to expand the bounds of fiction in the direction of myth and allegory; none of the self-torturing contradiction that spurred the ascetic, Puritan Nietzsche to topple from the heights of Dionysiac ecstasy into the gulf of megalomaniac vulgarity. In other words, Hardy is not a Slav; he does not drive things to their ultimate conclusions; he does not attempt the impossible; at bottom his view of life is like every Anglo-Saxon view—a compromise, a bowing to circumstances.

The affinities between his work and Ibsen's are much more manifest. He has something of the ironic cold satire which Ibsen displayed in his later prose dramas, though little of that author's desire to preach, and perhaps even less of the sheer energy which culminated in the astounding dramas of *Peer Gynt* and *Brand*. Compared to such a man, Hardy's outlook appears weaker, grayer. It is not for nothing that he has so steeped himself in "Wessex" that his sense of background frequently becomes more important than the characters he sets against it. Ibsen, on the other hand, created always, even in his attempts to make a thesis, types that are universal.

It is perhaps Tolstoy, however, that Hardy most clearly resembles—the earlier Tolstoy up to and including *Anna Karenina*. The hay-mowing scene in the latter novel, for instance, recalls in its absolute truth of scenic presentation, the rick-burning of *Far from the Madding Crowd,* or Tess's dairying. *The Dynasts* is not inferior as a battle-panorama to the crowded canvas of *War and Peace*. It is even in some respects superior; for Hardy's Napoleon is much more plausible as a human being and nearer, I somehow feel, to the actual man than Tolstoy's maliciously distorted caricature. Nor is the philosophy of both works dissimilar. In *War and Peace,* Napoleon is made to break his too self-seeking will against the fatalistic inertia of Russia, symbolized in Kutuzov; in *The Dynasts,* the same will is broken against the heroic endurance, the quiet acceptance of self-sacrifice symbolized in the English of Nelson and Hardy, of Pitt and Moore and Wellington. One can acknowledge Tolstoy's priority here without in the least detracting from the magnitude of Hardy's achievement.

But with the unresolved Slav in Tolstoy, the later Tolstoy who sought ever to deny his own heritage as an artist, who tried to abolish even his own place and station in life for the sake of social theory, Hardy has nothing whatever in common. In a sense, his humility forbids him to be anything else but a recorder of his world, and never could he desire to be ranked as a teacher or prophet. In a recent poem, he goes so far as to reproach himself that he has never "taught that which he set about." Tolstoy could not have been modest enough to make this admission.

Nor could Tolstoy, even in his earlier work, despite his knowledge of the soil, have written a whole novel so saturated with the spirit of a single landscape as *The Return of the Native.* Here we have, if anywhere in Hardy's work, the sense of man subdued to nature that we find in the poetry of the Chinese, or of recent years in the short stories of Chekhov. As I have already said, a vein of poetry runs through this entire novel, a vein that is deeper, and stronger than the somewhat too ethical pantheism of Wordsworth and Meredith. Especially in the night scenes on Egdon Heath does the author seem to revel in the sense of the blackness of untamed nature, fiercely somber and luxuriant in dumb life under the stars, as contrasted with the feeble but pathetic human faces and souls that attempt to subdue it with their ineffectual lanterns. Here, as in *The Dynasts,* he seems to have learned a secret of intensification by means of contrast which only one other Western artist has fully fathomed; and that artist is Rembrandt.

On the other hand, in one respect at least, Tolstoy in his earlier works is far more normal than Hardy. Professor Chew has pointed out that although Hardy's portrait gallery of women is justly famous, he has never drawn convincingly the portrait of a child in any of them. The one exception to this rule, the sole child who figures prominently, little Father Time in *Jude the Obscure,* is horribly overdrawn. The scene of his suicide and the note he leaves behind, is one of the places where Hardy overweights his pessimism; a serious artistic blot on an otherwise fine novel. None of Hardy's women seems to be normally maternal, or to take any joy in maternity. This is unquestionably a limitation in his art.

We live in an age of rapid shift and disintegration; an age wherein— as regards Central Europe at least—most of the finer traditions and feelings of the past are either dead or dying; an age of tragic disillusionment elsewhere; an age marked by the emergence of new powers, economic and political, in Russia, the Far East, America. An age, above all, not so much of democracy, as of steady vulgarization in science, life, and art.

To such an age—the age of post-war conditions—Thomas Hardy may fail to appeal. His recent breaking of silence with yet another— probably the last of his volumes of verse—appears almost an anachronism. The whole ultra-modern school of novelists owe far less to him than to such writers as Nietzsche and Dostoyevsky, and above all to the Viennese school of psychology founded by Freud. Such writers as Duhamel in France, D. H. Lawrence in England, Waldo Frank in America, are more interested in man's newfound power to analyze his own subconscious self than in the older Greek view, which Hardy upholds, that man can never be more than an unconscious plaything of some jealous destiny.

Whether the psychoanalytic type of novel has reached its term in the recent work of James Joyce, or whether Joyce's work is in itself only the most complete parody of the psychoanalytic method possible, it is as yet too early to say. It is possible that we may have to wait another fifty or a hundred years in order to be able to compare confidently Hardy's work with the work of those that it most resembles: Sophocles and Shakespeare.

This much may be said: that this work, though based on conventions of art which many modern novelists and poets have discarded, yet points resolutely into the future. In novel-writing it has given us a far richer sense of integral character, persisting in some of the most humble and despised denizens of this earth's surface, than either Dickens or Balzac could command. In verse it has consistently upheld the highly unpopular view that poetry does not exist for the sake of slurring over the disagreeable things of life, or to blind anyone's eyes to its meanings; but rather as an instrument to test the validity of our highest ideas, our most profound speculations concerning mankind. Hardy is indeed entirely a metaphysical and a philosophical poet; as much so as Lucretius or Donne, though he may not subscribe to their particular creed. The only modern poet whom he recalls is, strangely enough, Shelley; and a curious parallel might be drawn between the ethereal Shelley and Hardy's rude, rough-hewn verses.

As for his own private standpoint on the perplexing problems of modernity, readers of *Late Lyrics and Earlier* may find it expressed with

characteristic stoicism and irony in some stanzas headed "An Ancient
to Ancients":

> Where once we danced, where once we sang,
> > Gentlemen,
> The floors are sunken, cobwebs hang,
> And cracks creep; worms have fed upon
> The doors. Yea, sprightlier times were then
> Than now, with harps and tabrets gone,
> > Gentlemen! . . .
>
> We have lost somewhat, afar and near,
> > Gentlemen,
> The thinning of our ranks each year
> Affords a hint we are nigh undone,
> That we shall not be ever again
> The marked of many, loved of one,
> > Gentlemen. . . .
>
> We who met sunrise sanguine-souled,
> > Gentlemen,
> Are wearing weary. We are old;
> These younger press, we feel our rout
> Is imminent to Aïdes' den,—
> That evening's shades are stretching out,
> > Gentlemen! . . .
>
> And ye, red-lipped and smooth-browed; list,
> > Gentlemen;
> Much is there waits you we have missed;
> Much lore we leave you worth the knowing,
> Much, much has lain outside our ken:
> Nay, rush not: time serves: we are going,
> > Gentlemen.

So we take leave of him, in the late evening of life, "still nursing the
unconquerable hope" that man may somehow inform the blind destiny of the world with a higher consciousness of its aims, cheerfully
resigned himself to death, but looking forward not unconfidently to
the future.

Walt Whitman   *1924*

I

In the summer of 1920 I was standing on an uptown corner of Fifth Avenue in New York City, waiting for a bus to carry me to my lodging in the lower part of the town. It was a stifling hot June day, and as I mounted the bus, I decided to go on top, in order to get the benefit of whatever fresh air might be available. It was the noon hour, and as I went down the crowded street, I was interested to see the crowds of workmen—most of them Jewish garment operatives, truck-men, and the like—standing on the pavement in the side streets enjoying their one moment of repose from the daily slavery of their existences. Groups of them were reading papers, arguing and discussing; some standing idle; others buying fruit or candy from some stall. At that moment, as I was borne past them, it seemed that time had somehow ceased to exist: all these lives, all these faces, became mine; I felt bowed down in worship to the unseen life-force that was pressing in and through them to some unknown end; and I understood in a flash of perception, greater than any I have ever enjoyed, the meaning of the poet who had walked these same pavements years before; the one unique, authentically great American poet: Walt Whitman.

Whitman was the supreme, the only democratic poet the world has ever possessed. In the hierarchy of art he stands alone in denying that art has a hierarchy. One need only read a page of his writings, and to institute a comparison with the technique displayed therein with the technique shown by any other competent writer, in order to see that in reality Whitman had no technique. To a writer whose aim is distinction in utterance, it is not so much the substance of what he says that is offensive, as his way of saying it. To the cultivated mid-Victorians of England, who were, far more than his rather ridiculous American disciples, the only discoverers and upholders of his genius, he appeared as a pure elementary savage, without knowledge, taste, or culture of any kind. Carlyle is reported to have said: "He writes as if the town bull held the pen." Swinburne, after a brief period of ecstatic devotion, recanted and declared that his muse was "a drunken apple-woman rolling in the gutter." The splenetic Patmore, after a bitter denunciation of democratic vulgarity, concludes: "That such a writer as Walt Whitman should have attained to be thought a distinguished poet by many persons generally believed to have themselves claims to distinction, surely more than justifies my forecast of what will happen." And in a sense all these judgments were, so far as superficial appearance goes, perfectly correct. Whitman had, more than any other great writer, no taste and no judgment. His poems are for the most part agglomerations of sheer native observation and second-hand ideas. *Leaves of Grass,* as we possess it, is only the rough blocking-out of a plan so vast that it could never be completed. Nor did the author, despite all his tinkerings and revisions, himself complete it. As late as 1876, after his final breakdown, we find him commenting, apropos of "Passage to India":

> It was originally my intention, after chanting in *Leaves of Grass* the songs of the body and existence, to compose a further, equally needed volume, based on those convictions of perpetuity and conservation which, enveloping all precedents, make the unseen soul govern absolutely at last. I meant, while in a sort continuing the theme of my first chants, to shift the slides, and exhibit the problem and paradox of the same personality . . . estimating death, not at all as the cessation, but as I somehow feel it must be, the entrance upon by far the greatest part of existence, and something that life is at least as much for, as it is for itself. But the full construction of such a work is beyond my powers. . . . Meanwhile, not entirely to give the go-by to my original plan, and far more to avoid a marked hiatus in it, than to entirely fulfil it, I end my books with thoughts, or radiations from thoughts, on death, immortality, and a free entrance into the spiritual world.

In so far as this is clear, it appears that *Leaves of Grass* was originally to have been two books, instead of one, the first ending presumably at the poem entitled "By Blue Ontario's Shore," and to deal with all sides of life, objectively, without introspection; the second to be more introspective and personal, and to deal solely with death and immortality. These two were telescoped into one, but the last half of the scheme was never fully completed. And we may likewise question whether the first half was fully completed either when we discover that "By Blue Ontario's Shore" is merely, in its essentials, a weaker recapitulation, eked out in the first stages of Whitman's collapse, of the superb preface to the original *Leaves of Grass*.

Let us, however, return to the remark that Whitman's poems are mere agglomerations. Consider the structure of such a work as "Song of Myself." Is there in fact any unifying idea to this poem? "I, Walt Whitman, am boundless"—is that not in effect all that it says? But, it may be objected, why attempt to state boundlessness in fifty-two sections? Why stop there? Why not fifty-three or five hundred? And—a more serious objection—does not boundlessness, in any case, imply contradiction?

The answer to that is complete, when it comes on the next to the last page of the poem:

> Do I contradict myself?
> Very well, I contradict myself;
> (I am large, I contain multitudes.)

Even this tremendous assertion may, however, leave us still unconvinced. Maybe it is a good thing to contain multitudes, but what do these multitudes themselves contain? Do not these same multitudes, such as I saw in New York in the summer of 1920, contain rubbish, contain even voids? Is it necessary after all to contain them?

The answer to that is: Yes, it is necessary to contain multitudes (and consequently contradictions, and agglomerations), for the reason that the multitudes exist. They exist in Fifth Avenue, New York; in Piccadilly or the Strand in London; in Tokyo, Peking, Berlin, Paris, Rome, Constantinople, everywhere. Whitman is the one voice, the one soul, who has been among them, lived their life, has felt them so much a part of himself that he has been able to tell us anything at all. Therefore we have to listen to Whitman.

II

Criticism has made more than its usual number of mistakes about Whitman: this is due, not, as in Blake's case, to the neglect of those who ought to have admired him, but were repelled by the obscurity of his thought, but, rather, to the enthusiasm of his early disciples, too ready to reduce his thought to its lowest common denominator of terms. These disciples hailed him above all as the prophet not only of democracy, but of the "divine average" inherent in democracy; a term implying no more, in his case, than a general commendation of life.

It would have been more to the purpose if the critics had insisted upon Whitman's position as the poet of personality, rather than of individuality. These terms are commonly confused in the minds of most people, and even held to be interchangeable. In reality a maximum of individuality implies a minimum of personality and *vice versa*. The individual, as such, is necessarily isolated and therefore devoid of personal ability to share in the lives and fortunes of others; the truly strong personality is he who is able most fully to share and understand the nature of those with whom he is in contact, and who correspondingly subordinates his individuality to theirs. And the same is true of crowds, as of individuals. A crowd has personality; it has little or no individuality. It is a fact that crowds in different countries reveal individual differences; thus an English crowd is less excitable, restless, noisy, than an American crowd; and a Chinese crowd may be even more reserved, for aught I know; yet, despite these accidents, each crowd expresses certain fundamental reactions, possesses certain elementary desires common to all humanity. Each crowd is at bottom a vast reservoir of blind desire, vague faith, dumb suffering; each crowd is composed of units that breathe, hope, die; each crowd is uncoordinated personality in conflict with individual differentiation; each crowd is at once Everyman and Noman.

Whitman felt himself to be a member of the crowd, and in this sense he was democratic; but primarily he knew that his function to the crowd was to be their poet, their interpreter; to be toward them in the position of "the child that went forth every day, and the first object he looked upon, that object he became." In short, because his personality responded readily to theirs, Whitman regarded himself as the spokesman of their aims. He did not notice, perhaps was incapable of noticing, that the individualists of democratic society are often supremely able to delude the unformed crowd-mind into an acceptance of their own falsely-coined values; and that the crowd, at bottom, will always look suspiciously on every man who strives to inform its ranks with a clear perception of his own personality. In other words, Whitman failed to take account of the forces of inertia and of individuality inherent in democracy. Nevertheless he persisted in his attempt to be at once democratic and a personality, though he was in reality unable to find anyone with the same aim and perception, except Lincoln.

That few critics have seen this is scarcely, perhaps, strange; for most of the critics favorable to Whitman have affected to think well of democracy on their own account, while those opposed have, naturally, regarded the great artist as a being immensely superior to the crowd of undistinguished individuals among which he was born. But neither group is altogether right. Neither is able to see that the core of Whitman's message is precisely "Produce great persons. The rest follows." And neither is capable of understanding that at bottom he had no use for either aristocracy or democracy as political systems except in so far as they responded to that final test of "producing persons."

In this respect, it is clear that Whitman as a poet stands at the antipodes to such a poet as Shakespeare. The Elizabethan poet gave us a great host of individuals, undominated by a single personality. He subordinated or sublimated his personal aims to the aims of his characters; there is no single character we can identify with Shakespeare himself, unless indeed it is Hamlet or Prospero—both sceptics, both in a sense men of the world who are acted upon rather than act for themselves. Whitman, on the other hand, wished the vast spectacle of life which he, too, aimed to present, to be entirely subordinated to himself. He regarded the poet as a man with a mission beyond that of irritating or amusing others: his mission was to save democracy by exalting personality.

It must be frankly admitted that Whitman's precept here runs counter to the practice of most modern poets since his time. Their aim has been, not the increase of the poet's personality, but the ever-sharper definition of his individuality. To test every possible mode of writing, to seek originality at all costs, is their aim.

Whitman's aim was at once wider, and more broadly generalized, than theirs. He was far too interested in society as a mass of vital, if undeveloped, sensations and ideas to care much for purely intellectual or individual revolt. Revolt there must be, certainly; but it must be revolt that is satisfying to the emotional and physical as well as the intellectual needs of man. However transcendental its aim, it must be grounded in the firm reality of the flesh, as Whitman was grounded:

My foothold is tenoned and mortised in granite;
I laugh at what you call dissolution,
And I enjoy the continuance of time.

And have the later modern poets, for all their restless experiment and originality, produced any greater person than Whitman? I think not. The beauty of his work does not spring from exquisite use of phrase or brilliance of method, so much as from the fact that in reading it we realize the author to have been at every moment entirely himself: that is to say, a man, a fluid, attractive personality.

III

That we live at all is, according to the most advanced school of philosophy, a pure unreasoned hypothesis or assumption: we live because we suppose that we live, and this supposition has to be continually tested by the trial-and-error method of experience. It follows, therefore, that every life, in so far as it survives this crude and empirical test, is equally vital and valuable; that life which is called evil as well as that which is called good. According to this view, ethics and æsthetics are both alike transcendental; neither is fully reducible to fixed terms, and both are in reality the same thing, which can only be described as that which remains above and beyond experience; in other words, God. Such at least, if I understand it correctly, is the view to which the chief modern schools, the neo-Kantian as well as the logico-mathematical, are tending.[3]

It is astounding to note that Whitman, by sheer poetic intuition, anticipated these views some sixty years ago. The whole purport of his poems is to show us that life *is*, without aiming to represent what life tends to become. From "The Song of the Open Road" to "Passage to India," his desire is simply to make of living an unlimited adventure. It is this sense of adventure, this sense of life continually transcending itself, and not the sense of the "divine average" inherent in democracy, that makes him continually a superbly intoxicated poet:

Allons! to that which is endless as it was beginningless,
To undergo much, tramps of days, rests of nights,

To weigh all in the travel they tend to, and the days and nights they
    tend to,
Again to merge them in the start of superior journeys,
To see nothing anywhere but what you may reach it and pass it,
To conceive no time, however distant, but what you may reach it and
    pass it,
To look up or down no road but it stretches and waits for you,
    however long, but it stretches and waits for you,
To see no being not God's, or any, but you go thither.

    .   .   .

Greater than stars or suns,
Bounding, O soul, thou journeyest forth.
What love than thine and ours could wider amplify?
What aspirations, wishes, outvie thine and ours, O soul?
What dreams of the ideal? What plans of purity, perfection, strength?
What cheerful willingness for others' sake to give up all?
For others' sake to suffer all?

Sail forth, steer for the deep waters only,
Reckless, O soul, exploring, I with thee and thou with me,
For we are bound where mariner has never dared to go,
And we will risk the ship, ourselves, and all.

Twenty-one years separate the writing of the first passage quoted
from that of the second, yet the thought is the same, though in the
first it was expressed with the full tide of Whitmanian energy and in
the second spoken with the rolling organ-notes of old age, after heavy
sufferings and losses.

It is obvious, however, that if we regard life thus, there is something that still needs explaining. This is the interruption in the stream
of consciousness caused by death. To anyone who regards endless
evolution as being the final law of the universe, death is the stumbling
block, the "last enemy to be overcome." There may be a material scientific explanation why the energy of the organism, striving to reach
higher levels continually, should only run down; but there is no spiritual explanation, and the efforts of the greatest thinkers have been
directed, since the arrival of man upon the planet, upon this unique
and appalling problem which contains and obscures all others.

Whitman was attracted to death partly because of its democratic character, but more because he believed in life as an endless adventure, an endless quest, an endless evolution to be accomplished. *Leaves of Grass* is one long pæan to evolution, and its genesis, be it noted, antedates Darwin. What place had death in such a scheme? Must we say that death was a mere accident, a flaw somewhere in the universe? Or must we deny the desire of our own hearts and the evidences of evolution, and think, as Lucretius thought, of matter alone as being triumphant and living? Whitman did neither. He strove to accept death as the purport of life, without being able to explain in the least why it should be so. The birth of this conviction in him that death is the clue, the key to life, "the word of the sweetest song and of all songs," is described in that marvellous poem "Out of the Cradle Endlessly Rocking." And over and over again, in the very finest poems he was to write: "When Lilacs Last in the Dooryard Bloomed," "As I Ebb'd with the Ocean of Time," "Passage to India," "Tears," the sense of death broods and lingers as the final overtone to his thought.

Yet as we have seen from the passage quoted in the first section of this essay, Whitman himself considered that he had failed to achieve the final purport of his life, which was to produce "poems bridging the way from life to death." But as a matter of fact, he judged himself in this respect far too severely. He is not only one of the supreme death-poets of the world, but probably the only death-poet who attempted such a feat as accepting death on the same terms as life. That he failed is due not to his weakness or inability, but to the impossibility of the task itself. We cannot accept death fully without dying ourselves; perhaps it is only in the death-moment, supposing that we are fully conscious of the death-moment, that we can at once live and die eternally, and that moment rests beyond all human arts or utterances. The nearest we can come to such a moment in life is some such experience as rests at the bottom of such a poem as "Out of the Cradle Endlessly Rocking," or Emily Brontë's "Last Lives." Such an experience, however, is necessarily relative; it can never be, in the nature of things, entirely final.

Yet throughout Whitman's poetry we do seem to perceive a latent and unexpressed idea, that the man who wrote these poems was in a sense mystically dedicated to death from childhood, or, if one prefers another way of stating the same truth, he was one who had discovered that "to lose one's life is to save it." The core of his achievement rests on personality, doubtless; but it is a personality which has gained its greatness by diffusing itself among other personalities, by completely abandoning itself to them, by renouncing the world that it might gain the world. Heroic such a personality must have been—and Whitman's war service in the military hospitals is there to notify us of the fact—but its heroism is of a totally different nature from the heroism acclaimed as such throughout the world. It is the heroism of Lee rather than of Napoleon, of Lincoln rather than of Wilson: a heroism completely grounded and held firm in self-devotion, in utter disinterestedness of effort.

For this reason Whitman was right in declaring that all his poetry rested on a religious basis, and proposed as part of the task of the poet that he should supply the world with something to take the place of what had been taught in the churches. Nor can we say precisely that Whitman failed, for we stand in a sense too near to him to know what some other century—especially if, as seems likely now, Western civilization should disappear—may make of him. To men of the thirtieth century he may quite possibly appear as a new marvellous gospel in a dead tongue. It is worth noting that the two most intelligent men of his day in America thought not only that he would go far, but strove in their own way to overcome what then and now has proved the only obstacle to his acceptance, the frank glorification of sexuality in "Children of Adam." Emerson spent an afternoon, as Whitman records, on Boston Common, striving to persuade the poet to withdraw or tone down this part of his book, but in vain. Thoreau was more farsighted. He says in his journal that he does not so much regret Whitman's grossness of utterance, as the fact that we are unable to read it and keep our minds pure; in other words, the impurity is in ourselves, not in Whitman. And, indeed, this is true. The only difficulty with "Children of Adam" is that it contains so little of the beauty and mysterious attraction of sex. It is as plain and ugly and forbidding as a biological tract. And we read it, hankering in our minds that it may be otherwise.

Whitman's significance, then, is that he gave a new sanction to democracy, and an entirely mystical one. We do not know, in fact, that all men are free and equal; we know, on the contrary, that most, if not all, men are sheer slaves to certain prejudices and are unequally shaped by circumstances. We merely suppose that all men are perhaps free and equal in the sight of God—a vastly different thing, and one of which little account is taken in the ordinary transactions of life.

In short, the idea of democracy is pure hypothesis, pure dogma, un-proved assumption, as unprovable as evidence as the first chapter of Genesis. But, as I have tried to point out in this essay, nothing in life is really logically provable, it is all miracle; and democracy is perhaps only the final miracle of an interlinked series of wonderful events. Whitman, in any case, showed that it might be made the basis for faith; it is for us to show that it can be made the basis of works, and life also. For Whitman's programme is so vast that it can never be carried out until plutocracy, mechanical civilization, mob law, rule of the dull, dead, dismal majority, and all the other crimes that now pose in the mask of democracy, are swept away and every man becomes "a king and a master in his own house." It is for this reason that we may call him not only religious, but Christian; for the aim of Christianity—though it may not be avowed in the churches—is to bring all men under Christ, so that they become Christ; to substitute for the repres-sions and tyrannies of our times the sublime spectacle, not of a univer-sal anarchy, but rather of a universal panarchism.[4] "A new order shall arise; and they shall be the Priests of man; and every man shall be his own Priest."

IV

The world may yet produce great poets: the most recent discov-eries of science and philosophy surely demand great poetry for their most profound and free expression; but it seems very unlikely that the world will ever again produce a Walt Whitman. More than almost any other great poet, he was the product of special conditions and cir-cumstances. In his young manhood, and up to his middle years, America was only emerging from the pastoral and agricultural age; long before he died it had rushed headlong into the welter of modern industrial civilization. To the evils and criminal blunders of mod-ern industry he was almost completely blind. In some of his later poems he gives his blessing to modern machinery, not realizing that modern machinery creates the mob-mind and the type of man who profits by the mob-mind—that is to say, the plutocratic demagogue. His finest work, therefore, seems to be "modern" only in the same sense that the Bible or Homer are modern; it rests so deeply on the perennially simple reactions of humanity as to appear eternally fresh and new.

Whether modern industrial civilization is an utterly incurable disease or not, we cannot accurately tell at the moment; what is more important for us to know is that it is a disease that must run its course. America will not again produce another Whitman, and if another is born, he can only come from the East. The poets who have succeeded him in America are one and all intellectually sophisticated, emotionally unstable, prematurely disillusioned people. They are, consequently, of less interest as persons, but of more interest as individuals than he. Where he moves freely through all the varied scenes and shows of existence, they are like prisoners chained to their self-inhibitions and vainly struggling to overcome them. What they gain, therefore, in tragic intensity they necessarily must lose in scope, breadth, and inclusiveness. The rebelliousness of Blake or the grim pessimism of Dante are more akin to the modern poet's temperament than Whitman's unwavering serenity.

It will only be, if ever, when the world turns from the profound spiritual weariness and disillusion that the industrial era has now created, and seeks again a more rational and vital organization of society, that we shall be able to estimate what we owe to Walt Whitman. What is already certain is that it is not the mob and its leaders, but precisely the intellectuals, who most enjoy and appreciate best his poetry. Unfortunately, these intellectuals are one and all unable to create a civilization resting on the values which he considered the sole permanent ones; for the reason that creation must rest on certain foundations; and Whitman's values are no longer the values now of the mob. International finance, common greed, machine-mania, have corrupted society from top to bottom. Whitman has sketched out a plan of a society which he himself could not realize, and which before his death would have been regarded with the utmost contempt by most of his fellow countrymen. But, as he himself might have said, a few centuries or so make little difference; and for my part, I cannot believe that Whitman's philosophy of life will be considered childish forever, by a world which cannot refrain from admiring, despite itself, the best specimens of his poetry.

Ezra Pound [5]   *1929*

I

The task of the poet in our day, or in any day, does not differ, except in degree, from the task of the novelist, the biographer, the historian, or anyone else whose life is spent in dealing with words. In any case, the writer makes an attempt to transmit, by means of words, an ordered judgment on the age he lives in, through the medium of his own personality. That is to say, the writer ineluctably expresses himself in relation to his surroundings, even when he is writing about the past. The result is that the completed work, if we take it apart from the accidental circumstances of the author's own life, represents something both greater and lesser than the combination of time, place, and talent that produced the writer in question. It is greater in so far as the writer has succeeded in recreating through the medium of his own experience the experience of others; it is lesser in so far as no writer (not even Shakespeare) has given us the full range of his age. We are therefore, whether we like it or not, obliged to rank authors by means of a very rough-and-ready calculation as to their approximation, or failure to approximate, to what appears to us to have been the central impulse of the particular period they lived in—and this calculation has to be usually performed long after the event. It is for the sake of establishing this approximation—indeed for the sake of establishing reputations that have already clearly established themselves—that histories of literature are written.

The judgment of a contemporary by a contemporary carries very little weight with the literary critic who is attempting to assess dispassionately the value of any particular work or writer. It is a well-known fact that Byron, for instance, preferred Moore, Campbell, and Rogers

to Wordsworth; that Coleridge acknowledges a debt to the Sonnets of
the Reverend Mr. Bowles; that Landor thought Southey important;
that Shelley was quite possibly almost as much in debt to Mrs. Ratcliffe
as to Æschylus; and that Blake enjoyed Ossian as much as the Bible.
This list, taken from the writers of a single period, ought to be enough
to convince us that every writer has to some extent, his own æsthetic;
the question whether that æsthetic remains valuable to a later age depends upon whether the later age can find in it a sympathetic reflec-
tion of their own peculiar experience. It is for this reason that literary
tradition is, as Rèmy de Gourmont has said, "a choice and not a fact";
tradition as a fact being "merely a mass of contradictory tendencies."

One may go even further and say that tradition as a choice is essentially a moral choice; one has instinctively given one's allegiance to this
or that side of literary achievement, and one must logically abide the
outcome of that choice. And this fact applies not only to great writers,
but to minor writers and even bad writers. Perhaps it applies most of
all to the minor writers and bad writers. For the great writer gives us
the illusion at least of almost complete freedom from traditional
bonds. He *is* his tradition at a certain high point in its development;
and that being the case, his tradition has had time to assimilate much
that was at first foreign to it (as the scholastic tradition of the thirteenth century assimilated Aristotle, or the humanistic tradition of the
best writers of the sixteenth century found a place for much popular
mediævalism). The question whether such a writer is possible in our
age when tradition, as well as much else, seems to have largely broken
down, is one that I am not called upon to discuss.

Now no one with an open mind can possibly read Mr. Pound's poetry without realizing that he is above all, a traditionalist. This fact
about him has now been discovered by Mr. T. S. Eliot, and has been
argued by him in an introduction of great value and interest. It is a
paradoxical fact that, to most persons, Mr. Pound's name still represents tendencies covering the entire extreme left wing of literature.
How this mistake came about has been largely due to Mr. Pound himself. As Mr. Eliot very justly observes, "Poets may be divided into those
that develop technique, those who imitate technique, and those who
invent technique." Mr. Pound has always been on the side of those
who either develop or invent technique, and has so strenuously opposed those who imitate technique, that he has seen fit to rank himself

with the extremists (even the most banally imitative extremists) rather than accept the academically imitative. But in this respect, Mr. Pound has done himself a disservice. It is no part of a poet's business to see that other poets do not imitate; it is only for him to make his own work as good as he can make it.

If we were given the following poem to read, without knowing its author, and were asked to set down the work of the poet whom it most resembled, what would our answer be? Here is the first poem in Mr. Pound's selection:

> I stood still and was a tree amid the wood,
> Knowing the truth of things unseen before;
> Of Daphne and the laurel bow,
> And that god-feasting couple old
> That grew elm-oak amid the wold.
> 'Twas not until the gods had been
> Kindly entreated, and been brought within
> Unto the hearth of their heart's home
> That they might do this wonder thing;
> Natheless I have been a tree amid the wood
> And many a new thing understood
> That was rank folly to my head before.

The answer to that is clearly, William Morris. And the careful reader of the poems here culled from Mr. Pound's two first volumes (*Personæ* and *Exultations*) will find many an echo, not alone of Morris but of Rossetti, and of the entire "æsthetic school" of the close of the nineteenth century. As Mr. Eliot remarks very justly, "In the background are the nineties in general, and behind the nineties of course, Swinburne and William Morris" . . . "the shades of Dowson, Lionel Johnson, and Fiona flit about." The poet, accordingly, that Mr. Pound in this early period resembles most is largely the early Yeats of "The Wind Among the Reeds"; not the later and less easy Yeats of "The Wild Swans at Coole." But where Yeats was able to refer his alchemical and astrological speculations back to their sources in folk lore and poetry, Mr. Pound took his materials mostly direct from the books in which he found them.

This however, does not exhaust the tale of early influences upon Mr. Pound. There still remains to be accounted for Robert Browning.

Had this influence persisted, I cannot help feeling that Mr. Pound would have been a better poet. For Browning—whatever the young of the present generation may say—was by all odds the most many-sided and intelligent of all the Victorians. Unfortunately, it seems to me that the tale of Browning's influence upon Mr. Pound stopped short at "Paracelsus" and "Sordello" and other of Browning's diploma pieces, and did not go on to the mature artistry of the "Ring and the Book" and "Parleings," which raise the ultimate questions of God's justice and man's, and the success of failure. But, in any case, Browning gave Pound the ability to see and depict people like Guido Cavalcanti, Bertram de Born, and Arnaut Daniel as living and breathing—the only unfortunate circumstance being that these were precisely the sort of people with whom Pound was most likely to identify his youthful self.

So far we need not deny Mr. Eliot's contention that "Pound's originality is genuine in that his versification was a *logical* development of the verse of his English predecessors." But, it must be added, that those predecessors were, except for Browning, poets of the nineties. The result is, that Pound merely further refined upon what had already been refined to the point of becoming tenuous. Moreover, at the time when he started to write, the "tradition of choice" that the English poets of the day followed, had already altered. A return to the romantic naturalism of Wordsworth, Crabbe, Clare, Cowper, and the early Romantics in general was beginning to be felt. This return was due possibly to the influence of Housman and Mr. Thomas Hardy; even more certainly it was due to the general breakdown of the "art for art's sake" attitude as a way of looking at the world. The new group of poets which it stimulated in England, were determined to cultivate not the "ivory tower" attitude of Lionel Johnson, but the fresher contact with the local soil which they thought they found in pure lyrists like Herrick. At the same time, the American poets began to cultivate their own local acres, under the influence, now for the first time completely realized, of Browning, Wordsworth, and Whitman.

With neither of these groups did Mr. Pound completely identify himself. Instead of combining more closely with his fellow-Georgians in England in their effort to develop further the tradition of rural naturalism, and instead of uniting with his American fellows in the effort to make poetry about their own local subject matter, he only burrowed a little more deeply into the past of his Provençal "personæ." And in this respect, he was following a side branch, rather than the main stream, of the European tradition. It is all very well to say that the Troubadours influenced the early Italian poets before Dante, and that therefore to understand Dante we have to study both the Troubadours and the early Italian poets. The fact remains that Dante acquired nothing from the Troubadours but a technique; into that technique he put a range of experience which had very little to do with the world as the Troubadours saw it. The fact that Dante could not have been the poet he was without that technique, is obvious; but the fact that Dante realized that the technique could be used for means which his predecessors would never have recognized as theirs is equally obvious. By confining his range of experience to what Arnaut Daniel might have felt and thought under the given circumstances, Mr. Pound became what he has remained, even in his latest verses: the most perfect type in our time of a purely "æsthetic" poet.

II

The attempt to classify writers by means of their conformity to certain clearly defined psychological types, is one that our age has only just begun to make; but some such classification is necessary, in so far as the old distinction between "classic" and "romantic" has to a great extent broken down. It is somewhat easier to define poets in this way, than prose-writers; inasmuch as the poets are more directly dependent on the effect of words. And it is through the examination of the vocabulary of writers—as well as their subject matter—that any fruitful investigations in the direction of the psychology of authorship will be finally made.

In the first forty pages of Mr. Eliot's selection from Mr. Pound's poetry one finds the following verbal forms: *syne, luth, torse, limning, everychone, fleet, foison, lutany, mnemonic, aspen, seneschal, jongleur, emprise, strath, garth, guerdon, terrene, email,* as well as numberless old verb forms such as: *playeth, knoweth, boweth, cometh, holdeth, bestoweth.* There are also compound verbal forms such as *wayfare, swordplay,* and such archaisms as *us-toward* and *we twain.* And the metrical forms are no less complex: canzone, ballade, sestina, alternate through these pages.

The argument that Mr. Eliot brings forward here in Mr. Pound's defense is worth quoting. He says: "Pound is often most 'original' in the right sense when he is most 'archæological' in the ordinary sense. It is almost too platitudinous to say that one is not modern by writing about chimney-pots, or archaic by writing about oriflammes. If one can really penetrate the life of another age, one is penetrating one's own." This statement is quite true, so far as it goes, but we still have to ask ourselves whether Mr. Pound has really penetrated the life of the remote age he has written about, by the means he has chosen, of heaping up archaic diction. We have only to compare Coleridge's vocabulary in "The Ancient Mariner" and "Christabel" with the vocabulary of "Personæ," to find the answer. In these two poems, Coleridge did penetrate the past by means far more sure, economical, and direct. We do not ask whether his diction is precisely that of the old ballads, because we feel all along that Coleridge sees the past that he has chosen to write about and his own life in *relation;* he has a *moral* sense of their points of contact. This moral sense is lacking in Mr. Pound.

Let us turn to the later poems selected from *Ripostes* and *Lustra.* Here we have a considerable clarification of technique, accompanied by a definite loss of power. Some of the poems in *Ripostes* are, nevertheless, perhaps the finest things that Pound has written: "Portrait d'une Femme," "Phasellus Ille," "Apparuit," "A Virginal," "The Return"—it is by such things that his reputation as an original poet will finally stand or fall. But over *Ripostes* as a whole, and still more over *Lustra,* there broods the atmosphere of a curious detachment. Pound is growing less interested in Provence, and he has not been able to interest himself profoundly in his own age. This detachment expresses itself throughout the series of short poems which, following Mr. Eliot, I call the Epigrams. Whether these are derived from Martial or Catullus, or simply evolved by Pound himself out of his own inner consciousness, I do not know. But one can say that they have neither the tigerish fury of Catullus nor the wasp-like wit of Martial. They are a detached comment, always from some safe point outside the lives with which they deal, on some of the minor follies of the age. And it is this attitude that gives them their agreeable sparkle, as well as their disagreeable air of pretentious flippancy. One has only to compare them with Blake's private epigrams, or Marston's "Scourge of Villainy," or the "Dunciad," to see the difference between this sort of thing and real satire.

So we pass, by way of the brilliant paraphrase of the Anglo-Saxon

Seafarer, or the even more brilliant paraphrase of *Cathay,* to *Hugh Selwyn Mauberly* (1920), in which, as Mr. Eliot notes, a fusion between Pound's archæological interests and his more personal feelings finally takes place. And this fusion took place because the war had made the "ivory tower" attitude finally untenable. *Mauberly* is—as the Epigrams are not—serious modern work; a document of intense interest for its time.

To say, however, as Mr. Eliot has done, that it is "a great poem," is a slight—if pardonable—exaggeration. When read as a whole, *Mauberly* has no cumulative effect. The first five sections of the book, numbered consecutively, are a single poem. Then we drift off at a tangent through a series of contemporary portraits to a discussion of quite a different theme; the relation of the writer to the age he lives in. Here the book halts half-way to interpose an Envoi in an entirely different key and mood from anything preceding. Progress is interrupted, and when we resume again, it is through a sort of coda on personal as opposed to general themes, that we pass to a final "portrait of a lady" that has very little to do with the mood in which the book started. The experience that began so promisingly has somehow been frittered away.

If we compare this book with *The Seafarer* or the poems in *Cathay,* we will find, I think, the key to Mr. Pound's failure as a poet. In these translations he not only had material that was congenial to work upon, but a structure already laid down from which his mind could not go astray. With the limits of form already marked off in his mind, he could happily transmute detail into something that was his and yet not entirely his. But when he has been obliged to set up limits for himself, in his own experience, the deficiencies of his purely æsthetic and non-moral sensibility immediately betray themselves. He cannot do so because of

> A consciousness disjunct
> Being but the overblotted
> Series
> Of intermittences.

And further:

> Thus, if her colour
> Came against his gaze,

Tempered as if
It were through a perfect glaze,
He made no immediate application
Of this to relation of the state
To the individual, the month was more temperate
Because this beauty had been.

But surely we have to relate beauty to something, even if it is only to the weather, the food, the traffic, or the day-to-day striving of this disappointing but highly necessary planet?

III

It is only by means of an intensive study of Mr. Pound's "disjunct consciousness" that we can attain to any understanding and appreciation of his "Homage to Sextus Propertius" and his "Cantos."

These poems are of the utmost importance as critical touchstones for whatever estimate the future will make of Mr. Pound's powers. The "Propertius" is omitted by Mr. Eliot from his selection, because, as he says, "if the uninstructed reader is not a classical scholar, he will make nothing of it; if he be a classical scholar, he will wonder why this does not conform to his notions of what translation should be. It is not a translation, it is a paraphrase, or still more truly (for the instructed) a *persona*."

The reader who has followed my argument about Mr. Pound so far, will here recall that I began by asserting that he was a traditionalist, a statement that I immediately qualified by noting that the tradition he has always followed is a purely æsthetic one, without reference to moral consciousness, leading inevitably to an expressed preference for the side branch, rather than the main stream. This tendency becomes acute in "Homage to Propertius." The fact is that to a poet of Mr. Pound's type, the academic classicist is as deeply anathema as the revolutionary innovator. The one takes for granted the substance of the classics, as seen through the perspective of generations of scholars; the other, starting from some illogically personal (hence "romantic"?) standpoint, gradually approaches the classic author, without ever completely identifying the text of that author with himself. Both are therefore examples of imperfect assimilation. The perfect assimilation, Pound might argue, is to transpose yourself fully into the life and times of the author in question. This attempt, which was begun with the Provençal poets, is carried out fully in the "Homage to Propertius."

The difficulty with this poem is that it represents neither Propertius nor Mr. Pound, but only what Mr. Pound might have thought and felt had he *been* Propertius. In the case of the early translations, he had been content to paraphrase the text. But here he assumes that the text already exists in his own mind and the reader's, and that he is free to comment upon it as if he had written it. The result is an extended criticism of Propertius, written by a modern mind temporarily masquerading as Propertius. Technically, the form conveys as accurately as anything in English can, the effect of the elegiac meter:

> Nor at my funeral either will there be any long trail,
>> bearing ancestral lares and images;
> No trumpets filled with my emptiness,
> Nor shall it be on an Atalic bed;
>> The perfumed cloths shall be absent.
> A small, plebeian procession.
>> Enough, enough, and in plenty.
> There will be three books at my obsequies
> Which I take, my not unworthy gift, to Persephone.

The technical quality of these lines must not blind us to the drawbacks of the method of presentation. When anyone writes about a particular epoch of the past, the question always arises whether he has primarily envisaged himself as living that particular life, or has simply let that life be relived as far as possible, without reference to how he might have desired it to be, letting the imagination follow perfectly the accepted details. The latter method is sensational and dramatic; the former intellectualist and static. One finds an example of the intellectualist method in Pater's *Marius the Epicurean;* a perfect analysis of a period seen through Pater's temperament. The sensational method was carried to great heights in Browning.

Now Mr. Pound's *Propertius* is as purely an intellectualist reconstruction as was *Marius.* The difficulty is that the method is subjective throughout. In other words, it depends entirely upon personal accidents for its successful use. Pater's Romans speak as if they had been to Oxford in the nineties; Mr. Pound's Romans speak as if they had gravitated between modern New York and London. What we get, therefore, in either case is not an example of the poetic imagination at work within a given scheme of historical data, but merely a transposal of certain personal accidents of likeness from one period to another.

But this does not exhaust the dangers of Mr. Pound's method. The mind that tends to transpose itself continually into a series of deliberately chosen pasts, without reference to the needs and exigences of the present day, tends to become *temporalized,* and to adopt what Mr. Wyndham Lewis calls a "time-philosophy." That is to say, juxtaposition in point of times becomes the important element for such a mind, and not association in point of fact. Such a mind rapidly becomes dissociated from everything except time; it lives in a sort of "continuous present" formed of a number of bygone pasts; and Mr. Pound logically took this step towards the goal he had unconsciously been aiming at from the first, when he began writing his *Cantos.*

The *Cantos* as they stand are unquestionably the *selva oscura* of modern poetry. They are an anthology of all the passages in poetry of the past that Mr. Pound has been interested in (I might almost say that they are Mr. Pound's "Golden Treasury," but decency forbids); they are an extended history of Rimini under the Malatesta dynasty, they are a commentary on Venetian and other history in relation to the artist, they are a collection of highly recondite and private gibes and japes. But to say that they are a poem in any sense of the word is to say that calisthenics are essentially the same thing as the Russian ballet. There is an element of poetry in them, just as there is an element of the Russian ballet in calisthenics, but the element is not only unsifted out from its less vital context, it does not even affect—in many cases—its context. Let me take two examples. Here is Mr. Pound's portrait of Henry James, in a London club:

> The old men's voices, beneath the columns of false marble,
> And the walls tinted discreet, the modish darkish green-blue,
> Discreeter gilding, not present but suggested, for the leasehold is
> Touched with an imprecision—about three squares.

The house a shade too solid, and the art
A shade off action, paintings a shade too thick.

And the great domed head, *con gli occhi onesti et tardi*
Moves before me, phantom with weighted motion,
Grave incessu, drinking the tone of things,
And the old voice lifts itself
Weaving an endless sentence.
We also made ghostly visits, and the stair
That knew us found us again on the turn of it,
Knocking at empty rooms, seeking a buried beauty.

This has restraint and dignity, and a handling worthy its subject. But here is another passage chosen at random from Mr. Pound's researches into Italian mediæval history:

Letter received and in the matter of our Messire Gianzio,
One from him also, sent on in form and with all due dispatch,
Having added your wishes and memoranda.
As to arranging peace between you and the King of Ragona,
So far as I am concerned it wd.
Give me the greatest possible pleasure,
At any rate nothing wd. give me more pleasure
    or be more acceptable to me,
And I shd. like to be party to it, as was promised me,
        either as participant or adherent.
As for my service money,
Perhaps you and your father wd. draw it
And send it on to me as quickly as possible.

And so on for several more lines. All that one can say about this is that it is "merely work chucked away," to quote from Mr. Pound himself, a few lines lower down. Whether it is "poetical" or not matters little; the fact remains that we have a right to demand something better from a serious poet than the versification of fifteenth-century (or nineteenth-century) business letters.

The Modern
Southern Poets   *1935*

It has seemed very strange to me that no critic of discernment or capacity has yet arisen to say anything of importance concerning the present-day Southern poets, in regard either to the value of their achievement, or to the prospects for its continuance. It is still more strange if we reflect that, for New England at least, there is already a body of quite respectable critical writing about such contemporary figures as Frost and Robinson. In my belief, which I hope to substantiate, the poets dealt with in this essay are fully as important for the history of American poetry—if that ever comes to be written by some critic with no axes to grind—as either Robinson or Frost, or the Mid-Western movement (now apparently at an end) that centered about Masters, Sandburg, and Lindsay. And they are a hundred times more important than those inverted sentimentalists, Elinor Wylie and Edna Millay.

In the essay which follows, it is my purpose to take up the work of each of these poets in turn, to say something about it, and to conclude with some attempt at a statement of general tendency, and a discussion of the future prospects for poetry of this distinctively "Southern type." I would like to request the reader to remember that poetry, in this section, has already suffered from three major catastrophes. The first was when the Civil War swept away promising beginnings under Poe, Chivers, Timrod, and Hayne. The second was when, after the war, Sidney Lanier chose to lisp knightly and honeyed sentimentalities rather than voice the outrage done to justice by the North. The third was when the men of the "Nashville Group" emerged too late upon the scene to be talked about and discussed in the same serious terms as were the earlier poets of 1913–1920. If this essay can avert still a further disaster, its work will have been done.

I

John Crowe Ransom

John Crowe Ransom was born in Pulaski, Tennessee in 1888, and so is now, in 1934, just four years short of fifty. His father was a Methodist clergyman of high scholarly attainments, a traveled man, engaged in foreign mission work. Ransom, after an American college education, won a Rhodes scholarship and went to Oxford, completing his course there with high honors in 1913. He immediately took up teaching at Vanderbilt and has been there ever since, except for two years' service in France as First Lieutenant, Field Artillery, in 1917–18. In 1931–1932 he obtained leave of absence from his Vanderbilt post, and returned to England where he spent considerable time in a remote Devon village, also teaching and lecturing at Oxford.

Poems About God, his first volume, written as stated in its preface, before America entered the war in the spring of 1917, contains very little of the essential Ransom. It is written for the most part in a bald and prosaic style, possibly derived from Frost (though one poem, "Sunset," reveals that Ransom has pondered the Imagists) and notable only for its ruthless and outrageous abuse of rhyme. But though the technique of this book is inferior to the early work of almost any of the other Southern poets who have followed Ransom, the thought underlying it is peculiarly Ransom's own.

Ransom is, as he says in his preface, a man puzzled about God. He accepts the God of his forefathers, but that God seems to him both cruel, arbitrary, and profligate. So he lets himself go in a flood of juvenile blasphemies, of which the following may be taken for a specimen:

> My window looks upon a wood
> That stands as tangled as it stood
> When God was centuries too young
> To care how right he worked, or wrong,
> His patterns in obedient trees

Unprofited by the centuries;
He still plants on as crazily,
As in his driveling infancy.

Here is the germ of the Ransom irony, the oblique shaft which buries itself in the heart of its subject by asking the question, "Well, if this exists why does it exist in that particular way?", a question that no one has yet been able to answer. The attitude differs, be it noted, from that of Thomas Hardy (perhaps the poet most akin to Ransom) in that, to Hardy, the God of the Christian Revelation was effectively dead (Hardy hymned his funeral in one of the greatest poems he ever wrote) and the God of the Unconscious Will has definitely taken His place. Ransom does not invent any new explanation like this. He merely questions angrily the old explanation. Only occasionally, in "Under the Locusts" or in the stark little lyric, "Darkness," he shows what a poet he was to become.

Between the writing of *Poems About God* and the achievement of *Chills and Fever* in 1924, Ransom had gone a long way. For one thing, he had obviously read Hardy, and that poet had helped him to an attitude and style far beyond the shallow rattle of his own early verses. In *Chills and Fever* indeed, there are direct touches of Hardy, such as the poem "Night Voices" which opens thus:

By night and inky fog
Unseen they hoped of all the synagogue,
Two pale high-fronted youths withdrew apart
Upheaving each his bitterness of heart
In a dark dualogue.

This has even the Hardyesque rhythm and pulse. One might also cite this image from "Philomela":

There was no more villainous day to unfulfil;
The diuturnity was still.

What Ransom has added to the lesson he has learned from Hardy is a wild gallant sense of the sublime and the ridiculous mingled in irony, and unmatched, so far as I know by anything in either English or American literature. It is a sharper irony than anything in Eliot—if one omits "The Hippopotamus." One must go to Heinrich Heine for a parallel—and where Heine is deft and sauve, Ransom is savage and mercurial. Perhaps the great meeting of Christ and Antichrist in "Armageddon" will show the manner of its achievement as well as anything in the book:

> Christ wore a dusty cassock, and the knight
> Did him the honors of his tiring-hall;
> Whence Christ did not come forth too finical,
> But his egregious beauty richly dight.

> With feasting they concluded every day,
> But when the other shaped his phrases thicker,
> Christ, introducing water in the liquor,
> Made wine of more etherial boquet.

> At wassail, Antichrist would pitch the strain
> For unison of all the retinue;
> Christ beat the time, and hummed a stave or two,
> But did not say the words, which were profane.

> Perruquiers were privily presented,
> Till knowing his need extreme, and his heart pure,
> Christ let them dress him his thick chevelure,
> And soon his beard was glozed and sweetly scented.

"Finical"—"egregious"—"wassail"—"retinue"—"profane"—"perruquiers"—"chevelure"—"glozed": here is the Ransom vocabulary at full blow! And it is strange to observe how, underneath the light elegance of this elaborate phraseology, the sense of dark bitterness persists. Ransom is not an optimist—of that we may be certain. His jesting conceals tragic depths here and elsewhere in this volume. Sometimes it rises to a wild scream of mockery, underneath which the tragedy lies even more obvious, as in "Captain Carpenter." At other times, the mockery melts into nostalgic sentiment, as in "Old Mansion," to me the most beautiful thing Ransom has ever written.

Two Gentlemen in Bonds, which appeared in 1927, did not add very much to the reputation fully established by *Chills and Fever;* what it did add for the most part was, like "Our Two Worthies," and "In Mr. Minnit's House," taken from John Skelton *via* Robert Graves. The sonnet sequence at the close threatened, in fact, to lose itself in finical overelaboration—the fact that always threatens so scholarly a poet as this. Perhaps the only poem that stands out is the really splendid "Equilibrists"—Ransom's major performance on the theme of married love.

After this volume, Ransom gave up poetry to bury himself in the pure metaphysics of *God Without Thunder,* an extended and elaborate survey of the same theme that had so haunted him from the start. So far as I know, he returned to poetry only about a year and a half ago. Of the three poems of his latest phase I have seen since then, it is perhaps too early to speak. But in the case of two of them at least, it seems to me that the poet has attempted to borrow too many devices of ellipsis and intellectualized cross-reference from the poets of the Eliot following—and has pushed these devices into realms of abstract thinking far removed from the "simple, sensuous, passionate" thing that is poetry. The third of his recent poems I have seen, repeated in a lower key much of the charming nostalgia that sometimes, in the pages of his earlier books, swept away the defenses of his own sardonic sensibility.

II

Donald Davidson

If Ransom is by nature an intellectual, and in his work both scholarly and ironical, Donald Davidson is continually groping, exploring, experimenting both as writer and man. He has to his credit what (with one possible exception to be presently noted) is, so far, the only extended major poem written by an avowed Southerner: *The Tall Men.*

Davidson was born in Tennessee in 1893, and has spent his lifetime teaching in his native state. Like Ransom, he went overseas in the war; but otherwise he has had no contacts with Europe. Unlike Ransom, his temperament is not primarily abstract and metaphysical: he is interested in the concrete things of life, and has in him—despite doubts and hesitations—much of the simple, warm, joyous acceptance of the earth that has helped so many lyric poets to their songs and their reputations.

An Outland Piper, which appeared as his first volume in 1924, reveals Davidson as a belated lover of the great Romanticists. Many of the poems in the first section of this book derive directly from William Blake. For instance, "The Tiger Woman" and "Following the Tiger," both quite striking poems, and also "The House of the Sun":

> The doorways of the sun were closed,
> The muted bells gave forth no sound.
> But while the windy prophets dozed
> A child a little crevice found.
>
> He pushed with one small straining hand;
> The massy doors moved willingly.
> And he has wakened all the band
> Of singers. They rise eagerly.
>
> Who can sing the House of the Sun?
> Who can frame its dreadful art?
> His childhood never must be done.
> He must have a wondering heart.

Blakean or not, there is nothing to be ashamed of in such verses. Technically, they are superior to anything in Ransom's first volume.

The second and third sections reveal that Davidson had read not only Ransom but T. S. Eliot. The naive Romanticism of youth gives way to a disillusion that echoes pleasantly in "Corymba":

> Corymba has bound no snood
> Upon her yellow hair.
> But better so, no doubt,
> For the pale youths look elsewhere
> At sleek curves and proud glitter
> And flesh powdered and bare.—
>
> Corymba has not rejected
> Familiarities.
> It is past noon. She dozes
> With half drawn-up knees,
> Thinking of new stockings,
> And other such verities.

Others of these poems, like "Naiad," are almost pure Ransom:

> Bathers ashore were cultivating a tan,
> The fat and the lean were gauded cap-a-pie,
> She thought that jerseys were not Arethusean,
> And a gartered limb to her was a monstrosity.

But despite these light touches of irony, the tone of the whole volume is an impenitent Romanticism, repeated again in the last poem, "The Man Who Would Not Die":

> The hill-top was all blazed with noise of worlds,
> A whirling scroll of kingdoms, cities, islands,
> Seeded like fields with fates men might behold;
> Of rivers dredged that swift gray ships might bring
> Cargoes to lands that never knew the sea;
> Of marble buildings yet unreared, and streets
> Made newly splendid for such folk as hear
> Music yet to be thought and songs unwritten;
> Of islands fabulous at last disclosing
> Secrets of buried tongues, old monuments,
> Young heroes and fair women not yet won;
> Tales unhinted and ways of coming men
> Plying the tangled threads of world-desire
> To some dim ever far-off destiny.

It is easy to stigmatize such work as mere old-fashioned rhetoric, but there are not many poets capable either of writing it, or of endowing it with any fresh meaning.

The Tall Men appeared in 1927. It should have been given the Pulitzer prize, but once again the fact that Davidson was a Southerner got in the way. Who got the prize that year I do not recall: probably Robinson with one of his overpraised revampings of Arthurian legend.[6] The next year the prize was given to the dreadfully Hollywoodish and falsely theatrical "John Brown's Body." *The Tall Men* as a poem is not in this class. It is in a class to itself, as any honest critic must recognize, before he reads many pages.

The poem opens with a prologue in which we hear a voice not unakin to the voice of desolation that blows through the best poems of Eliot:

> Pacing the long street where is no summer
> But only burning summer—looking for spring

186

That is not, spring that will not be here
But with its blunt remembrancer and friend,
Its blunt friend Death—Pacing the long street
That ends with winter that will never be
Winter as men would say it—Thinking of autumn,
What but a few blown leaves and the biting smoke
That feeds on all of these till autumn is not
Autumn? The seasons, even the seasons wither,
And all is mingled with a chaff of time,
Till I must wonder, pacing the long street,
If anything in this vague inconscionable world
Can end, lie still, be set apart, be named?

That might be *Gerontion* except that it breathes a less obvious irony, and has in consequence a greater ground-swell of strong feeling behind it. From this prologue we leap straight into the epic measure of *The Tall Men:*

It was a hunter's tale that rolled like wind
Across the mountains once, and the tall men came
Whose words were bullets. They, by the Tennessee waters
Talked with their rifles bluntly and sang to the hills
With a whet of axes. Smoke arose where smoke
Never had been before. The red man's lodges
Darkened suddenly with a sound of mourning.
Bison, cropping the blue grass, raised their heads
To a strange wind that troubled them. The deer
Leaped in the thicket, vainly, loathing the death
That stung without arrows.

Louis Untermeyer, the one critic who has written with any intelligent appreciation of the Southerners (in this respect, anyone who takes the blithe mumblings of Alfred Kreymborg for criticism is making a huge mistake) says that *The Tall Men* combines Eliot and Masters—yes, Masters!—simply because Davidson ends this section weakly, with epitaphs obviously influenced by "Spoon River"! But it surely is clear, to anyone who has read American poetry carefully, that the blank verse here is entirely *sui generis:* no other American poet, unless it be Hart Crane, in the rare moments when the flame in him broke through his own inflated rhetoric, has so authentically sounded the heroic note.

There are whole pages that stride on with a power that defies such lesser men as Eliot and Masters. For example the magnificent concluding passage of "Geography of the Brain," on page 41. (I doubt if Mr. Untermeyer, for all his enthusiasm, ever got so far).

The fault of the poem is not that of a failure in aim, but the fault that probably only MacLeish has (in *Conquistador*) been able to steer clear of, the lack of singleness of purpose. The poem lacks climax and culmination, it does not exist as a single structure. But the same objection could be brought against Pound's *Cantos* and Crane's *The Bridge*. This poem deserves its place alongside them.

Since *The Tall Men,* Davidson has been silent, and has devoted himself mainly to criticism—a serious loss, for he has not, primarily, the temperament of the critic. But in *The American Review* for May this year, he returned to poetry, with another triumph, "Lee in the Mountains"—again an epic in little, and a poem of such majestic structural unity that the South might well be proud of it, provided there are left any people in the South who either read or care for poetry.

III

Allen Tate

John Orley Allen Tate was born in 1899 in Fairfax County, Virginia, was reared in Kentucky and in Tennessee, and was educated in both public and private schools, including a brief—but for him mentally important—period during which his education was directed by Jesuits at Georgetown, District of Columbia. Everything about Tate smacks of the *outré* and the unexpected: his roving life, his combination of precocity and ferocity, his education, and his poetry. He is the one poet of this group guaranteed to administer a major shock to those who still think all poetry should deal in pretty sentiment and pleasant phrase—his poetry having little of either. Indeed, it suffers from an introspection that is almost abnormal, and which is certainly remote from Davidson's lyric objectivity. Its nearest of kin are the poems of John Donne, Edgar Allan Poe, Charles Baudelaire, and T. S. Eliot.

One of the most startling things about Tate's genius—for genius he has without doubt—is his extreme dissatisfaction with his own work, as well as with that of his own contemporaries. As a friend, and a critic of some distinction, once expressed it, "Tate has the unfortunate trait of never wanting to write a bad poem." It is an unfortunate trait, and the one that made Ben Jonson, a better craftsman, inferior to Shakespeare. There are plenty of bad things in Shakespeare, but he is, for all that, the greatest poet in the English tongue (despite Ezra Pound, who prefers Chaucer), while Ben Jonson, who may have been a better craftsman, comes in a bad second.

Tate's art is that of the lapidary, polishing and repolishing his work till it literally, in many cases, has no life left. I myself have seen three or four different versions of some of his poems. Poets of this sort are unquestionably valuable, in that they usually invent new forms and magnificent original metaphors, and achieve fresh effects that startle and surprise; but most of them (perhaps Donne is the only exception) have poetic lives that are short, and they do not write a great deal. Tate's entire output so far has been two small volumes and a handful of recent sonnets and lyrics which appeared in various magazines about two years ago.

Like all the other Southern poets, Tate is metaphysical. But where Ransom's metaphysic attacks the problem of God, and Davidson's is forever brooding on the variations possible between the past and the present, Tate is primarily concerned with one thing: death. Poem after poem reveals this peculiar undertone. It is this kinship in mind that brings him close to Eliot, not the early Eliot of "Prufrock" and "Portrait of a Lady"—that Eliot is closer to Ransom; nor the more recent ecclesiastical Eliot of *The Rock*. The Eliot he recalls is the Eliot of "Ash-Wednesday" and *The Waste Land*.

Although he makes certain obeisances to classicism, he is the antitype of a classical poet. He may wish us to think his work classical, but there is nothing in him of the inspired commonplace that guided Cicero, Vergil, Horace, or Ovid. His imagination is baroque, and he is never, except perhaps in the very beautiful recent "The Mediterranean," straightforward in his approach to his subject. As he says himself, his mind continually circles around a subject. He catches always the uncommon pose, the unexpected angle of illumination. In this again he resembles the poets I have mentioned above: Baudelaire, Donne, and Poe.

Like these, he has not written a single long major poem: unless we take the whole of his work as being that poem. The nearest he has come to it is in the "Ode to the Confederate Dead." This, though it still owes much to the late Elizabethans *via* Eliot, is the one poem that could be matched with the noblest pages in Davidson. Whether it is superior or inferior, I do not know. But in its three or four pages exists, in fierce distillation, matter enough for a great epic. Here again, as so often in his case, we have to deal with a text rehandled and rewritten. The earlier version, printed in Mr. Untermeyer's *American Poetry* is, I think, in every way superior, except for the last line, one of those unexpected touches that he has so great a flair for:

> Sentinel of the grave who counts us all!

Whether Allen Tate will again write poetry such as this, I do not know. I do not think he is likely now to follow his mentor, Eliot, and write dramatic libretti on themes supplied him by the Church of England. It may be that he will not write again, or will not write for a considerable number of years. In his case, we have to make allowances for the intermittencies of genius.

IV

Robert Penn Warren

Of all the Southern poets that have not yet published a volume, Robert Penn Warren is the most promising, and this because of the fact that his work combines something of Tate's one-sided relentless probing of mortality with Davidson's many-sided facing-up to life. In his case, I have been permitted to see certain recent unpublished poems which confirm me in my suspicion that he is genuinely one of the finest younger poets of the South.

Robert Penn Warren was born in Kentucky in 1905, and had an extensive college education: at Vanderbilt, the University of California, the Yale Graduate School, and New College, Oxford, where I first met him in the summer of 1929. He has written, besides poetry, a biography of John Brown.

As far as I know the first poem of his to see print, was the "Kentucky Mountain Farm (At the Hour of the Breaking of the Rocks)" which appeared in the first *American Caravan* of 1927. Here is its concluding stanza:

> The hills are weary, the lean men have passed;
> The rocks are stricken and the frost has torn
> Away their ridged fundaments at last,
> So that the fractured atoms now are borne
> Down drifting waters to the tall, profound
> Shadow of the absolute deeps,
> Wherein the spirit moves and never sleeps
> That held the foot among the rocks, that bound
> The weary hand upon the stubborn plow,
> Knotted the flesh unto the hungry bone,
> The red-bud to the charred and broken bough,
> And strung the bitter tendons of the stone.

The language here is Saxon; the feeling for nature is also primevally English; the sense of time passing on and waste and ruin following upon human effort is Warren's own. He has often dealt with this theme of the futility of human effort—a theme by the way, peculiarly Southern—in his later poems.

The *Second American Caravan*, 1928, added two more of Warren's poems: "Grandfather Gabriel" which is not much more than a swaggering joke, and the famous "Pondy Woods" which betrays the influence of Ransom—an influence not always happy. Despite its famous phrase, now become almost classic, "Nigger, your breed ain't metaphysical," the poem as a whole is not highly important. But very beautiful in their lucid realism and thoroughly characteristic of Warren are the lines:

> At dawn unto the Sabbath wheat he came,
> That gave to the dew its faithless yellow flame
> From kindly loam in recollection of
> The fires that in the brutal rock once strove.
> To the ripe wheat-fields he came at dawn.
> Northward the painted smoke stood quiet above
> The distant cabins of Squiggtown.
> A train's far whistle blew and drifted away
> Coldly. Lucid and thin the morning lay

APPRECIATIONS OF INDIVIDUAL WRITERS

Along the farms, and here no sound
Touched the sweet earth miraculously stilled.
Then down the damp and sodden wood there belled
The musical white-throated hound.

"Tryst on Vinegar Hill" which appeared in the last of the *American Caravans,* rehandles the theme tackled in "Pondy Woods," and does the subject more justice, I think, though it does not contain any lines so splendidly complete in their unemphatic visualization as the ones I have just quoted.

"History Among the Rocks" which resumes the "Kentucky Mountain Farm" theme contains what is, along with the passage I have just quoted, Warren's finest portrait of a landscape:

Under the shadow of ripe wheat,
By flat limestone, will coil the copperhead,
Fanged as the sunlight, hearing the reapers' feet.
But there are other ways, the lean men said:
In these autumn orchards once young men lay dead—
Gray coats, blue coats. Young men on the mountainside
Clamored, fought. Heels muddied the rocky spring.
Their reason is hard to guess, remembering
Blood on their black mustaches in moonlight,
Cold musket-barrels glittering with frost.
Their reason is hard to guess and a long time past.
The apple falls, falling in the quiet night.

Whether Warren has ever carefully considered the Imagists, I do not know, but a piece of work such as this shows that he aims at exactly what they aimed at: to describe an incident or a scene along with its connotation of emotion, the connotation being *implicit in some part of the scene itself* (in this case "the apple falls" conveying the connotation).

"Letter of a Mother" again reveals the Ransom influence at work, but "Pro Vita Sua" is entirely Warren's own, and a very strong Saxon poem to boot. It might have almost been written by the young Thomas Hardy. I shall not quote it, but shall simply direct those who might care to read it to Mr. Untermeyer's anthology.

The last poems of Warren which I have seen are three that appeared in the May 1932 number of *Poetry,* of which both the "Owl" and the "Cardinal" again showed Warren's command over the moods

192

of nature, and the far more experimental "So Frost Astounds," also published in *Poetry* for July 1934, with "The Return; and Elegy" in the same magazine for November. I should like to compare the last with an unpublished poem, called "History" which is here on my desk as I write, in an effort to gauge Warren's direction, which I hope will be important for Southern poetry in the not far-off future.

Both "So Frost Astounds" and, still more, "The Return" are poems that by using the device of parallel commentary on the action as it unfolds (a device invented by Eliot in *The Waste Land* and imitated, not altogether happily, by Tate in the final version of "Ode to the Confederate Dead") aim at giving a choral effect. But unlike Eliot, Warren remains resolutely Saxon and plain-spoken in his approach to his subject—witness this passage from "The Return," an elegy to the memory of Warren's mother:

> Locked in the narrow cubicle
> Over the mountains through darkness hurled,
> I race the daylight's westward cycle
> Across the groaning roof-tree of the world
> The mist is furled.
>
> *a hundred years men took this road*
> *the lank hunters the men hardeyed with hope;*
> *ox-breath whitened the chill air the goad*
> *fell; here on this western slope*
> *the hungry people the lost ones took their abode.*
> *here they took their stand:*
> *alders bloomed on the road to the new land.*
>
> *here is the barn the broken door the shed*
> *the old fox is dead.*
>
> The wheels hum—
> The wheels. I come.
> Whirl out of space through time, O wheels!
> Pursue past culvert, cut, embankment, semaphore,
> Pursue down backward time the ghostly parallels
> Pursue down time. The pines, black, snore.

"History," as yet unpublished, and existing only in manuscript, shows an even greater maturity of handling in its steel-keen phrases:

Past crag and scarp,
At length way won;
And done
The chert's sharp
Incision;
The track-flint's bite,
Now done, the belly's lack.
Belt tight,
The shrunk sack.
Corn spent, meats foul,
The dry gut-growl.

I will not quote any more of this powerful poem, but it is surely obvious that the man who at thirty can write lines like these is no minor poet.

V

Minor "Fugitives"

With four such figures as Ransom, Davidson, Tate, and Warren as leaders, it is scarcely to be wondered at that most of the other modern Southern poets are obliged to stand far in the background. A certain number of them are included in the anthology published by Harcourt, Brace in 1928 under the title of *Fugitives*. Others have popped up in magazines here and there since. It is now time to say something about them.

If we take only those published in the original Fugitives anthology, omitting William Yandell Eliot as one who has ceased to be a Southerner, and Laura Riding as one who was never one, the name that immediately clamors for discussion is that of Merrill Moore. This is because Mr. Moore has already published a volume of his skilfully irregular sonnets and promises to give us another. As a matter of fact, this name need not detain us long because Mr. Moore suffers from a fault that is not peculiar to Southern poetry, but which is ineradicable wherever found.

The fault is that of a smart glibness, a superficially ironic outlook on life. Mr. Moore is in reality a maker of light verses, and is no more of a poet than were Dobson and Calverly before him (perhaps it is for this reason that he appeals to Mr. Untermeyer). He lacks fundamental seriousness. For my part, I prefer altogether the hobbledehoy rusticity of Jesse Stuart, the Kentucky hillbilly who last year stumbled into the ranks of the poets with his *Man With a Bull-Tongue Plow,* a book that contains a great deal of trash but also a very considerable amount of deeply-felt poetry.

Much more attractive to me are the contributions to *Fugitives* of Alec Brock Stevenson and Jesse Wills. Stevenson is still living and writing in Nashville; what has become of Wills I do not know. Wills has here two fine poems to his credit, "The Survivors" and "A Fundamentalist," both excellent in their balancing of age-old myth against the shallowness of modern science. Stevenson in his contributions reveals mostly a Gallic sort of romanticism that seems to come from Hilaire Belloc, and a love of long sinuous wreathing lines that seems definitely Irish. His best poem is, I think, "Icarus in November" which appeared in the January–March 1934 number of *Hound and Horn.* I must be allowed to quote two stanzas:

> There is a moment blind with light, split by the hum
> Of something struck and shaken otherwhere
> And if breath's pausing stills the heartbeat and the dumb
> Wet trees clutch every leaf, then on the air
> Will blow slow, small, and keen, and faster, greater, higher,
> The hissing whoop of wind through timeless wings,
> A thuttering drumbeat round a cold immortal fire,
> Half-muffling such a cruel cry as brings
> Fear to the lonely soul's imaginings.
> A crescent wailing—and the little heart inclined
> Hears Icarus, and how the chill gale mourns behind.
> O Icarus is fallen, alabaster foam
> Hangs stilly still, *Icare est chut ici,*
> White tangent to the green wave's arc he's shotten home;
> Man-bird, sky-arrow to the unriddling sea;
> Who was so questing, so unsated, lost to act,
> Quartered the zig-zag sky for beauty's use,
> Swooped, soared, sailed, wheeled, and sudden stopped on fact
> Or use's beauty, or the keen mind's loose

> Hot ions streaming in a fluent sluice,
> Heedless that Icarus must fall against the wind,
> Echoing, ever falling in the hollow mind.

The beauty of this is immense from every point of view: it has original rhythm, vivid and lithe vocabulary, a fire that only Chivers at his rarest moments has surpassed. If Stevenson had written but this one poem, he would have added much to American poetry. He has written others, but is averse to publication.

Among the younger men who did not enter the Fugitive ranks, the name of Gene de Bullet engages most my sympathy. I know little concerning him, and owe an acquaintance with his work largely to the persistence of the Editor of this magazine.[7] It is work touched with the lingering and hankering melancholy of lonely moonlit nights in remote country, and recalls—in a less emphatic and more emotional key—the work of Warren:

> We have known peace but more we cannot say
> Than that the secret of the hidden word
> Was lost upon the darkness as we came
> To this renewal of banalities.
>
> Also within our minds the peace grows dim
> And we remember only that we lay
> Quietly with deep silence and foreknew
> The world's heart broken in its breast of clay.
>
> Wherefore the flesh, how valiantly it strives,
> Can never salve the itch nor dull the ear
> These nights when wind is in the maple leaves
> With things we do not understand, speaking
> From leafy throats, and we are bound to earth
> No more than the hollow bones of gusty birds
> Blown in a twitter against a winter sky.

The most recent of all the Southern poets to appear before the public are Randall Jarrell of Nashville with a group in *The American Review* for May 1934, and Edwin Richardson Frost who has recently published a book, sponsored by Ransom, and entitled *Daemon In the Rock*. In dealing with either of these men, I must confess that I am somewhat at a loss. It is quite obvious that the creative aim of this, the most recent Southern poetry, has been to attempt to restore to English the dignity of the "grand style"; the special vocabulary and world-outlook that were common to English poetry from the Elizabethans to Milton. Ransom has swung the whole weight of his critical authority recently to special praise for John Milton (thus opposing Pound who detests Milton, and Eliot who avoids him) and has been followed by Tate. It is clear that both Jarrell and Frost are aiming at some such revival of the "grand style" in poetry.

The difficulty with their attempt lies at the root of the special problem of the survival of the poetic impulse in this present day. The background of religion, of culture, of economics, ethics, politics has so completely shifted since Milton wrote, that to restore the heroic style in English demands a complete poetic renovation of style, of imagery, of metric. One cannot go back to a set of symbols that once had validity, and imagine that we can extract from them the same overtones today. That was the mistake made as recently as the early years of this century by William Vaughan Moody. That the task of inventing a new heroic style is not altogether hopeless may be seen in MacLeish's *Conquistador,* and in Robinson Jeffers. But neither Jarrell nor Frost seem to me even to have attempted it.

In the only work of his which I have seen, Jarrell is both verbose and adjectival; nor are his adjectives especially well-chosen. Frost apparently wishes to revive all the old poetic language of the Victorian epoch, for some obscure mystic reason of his own that I cannot fathom, and so crams pages on pages with this sort of thing:

> Beclouded rest those mystic Grecian glades,
> The Ever-Living glyphed in noetic stone,
> Entombed the sharply-towered palisades
> Where Dzan vastated questless renegades,
> And stars invited meaning to charades
> In bone.
> What sword endures whose lethy blades
> Atone?

This has about as much relation to poetry as a crossword puzzle has to literature. I should respectfully suggest to Frost (and through him, also to Ransom) that though poetry does necessarily employ rhetoric (here Eliot is correct and Pound is wrong), rhetoric itself is not some formula handed down by professors in a university classroom, but is a vivid heightening of discourse that the poet himself must freshly discover and apply; and I would also suggest that the same remark applies to symbolism. Symbolism is not something invented once and for all by the Greeks or by "Dzan" (whoever he may have been) "vastating questless renegades" but it is something that essentially springs from the poetic (that is the myth-making, as *opposed to the noetic,* that is the abstraction-making) quest into reality. Wordsworth found effective symbolism in a leech-gatherer, Whitman in a brown bird heard singing at the edge of the sea, and Mr. Frost could find some doubtless in Nashville—if his head were not stuffed full of so many other notions.

VI

John Peale Bishop

John Peale Bishop was born, May 21, 1892, in Charlestown, West Virginia, of a family which, according to a poem ("Beyond Connecticut, Beyond the Sea") in his most recent volume, originated in Connecticut six generations before his birth, and which came South only after the Civil War. A grandmother of the poet was connected with Virginia, which may account for the move. Bishop graduated from Princeton in 1917, so he belongs undoubtedly to the "lost generation" of Scott Fitzgerald and Ernest Hemingway. At Princeton he presumably made the acquaintance of Edmund Wilson, and took part in *An Anthology of Princeton Verse* edited, under the auspices of Alfred Noyes, in that year. He published, immediately following his graduation, a book of juvenile verse *Green Fruit,* which I have not seen, and then went abroad, with the American Expeditionary Force, serving in France for twenty-six months in 1917–1919. After the war he was employed for a time, together with Edmund Wilson, as managing editor of *Vanity Fair.* Together with Wilson, he brought out in 1922 the volume of mingled prose and verse called *The Undertaker's Garland.*

The Undertaker's Garland is certainly an entertaining book, as I recall it. It contains a series of sketches of deaths, ranging all the way from the "Death of a Soldier," who, characteristically, is not killed by a shell, but by pneumonia, to the "Death of a Dandy" who dies—as I re-call it—fussing over details of his costume. It owes a great deal to Laforgue, to Eliot, to Scott Fitzgerald, to Anatole France, perhaps to the earliest Hemingway. The ideas it contains are not new, but the handling of them is highly brilliant. There is a statement at the begin-ning of the volume, disentangling the work of the two collaborators, but I have forgotten which did most of the work and which did the best. The book is a curiosity in respect not only to its theme, but in regard to the fact that each of its contributors wrote apparently equally well in prose and in verse. I should like to discuss it more fully, but find I cannot lay my hand on the one copy I possessed. Perhaps someone else has found it as entertaining—in the best sense—as I did, and has, accordingly, taken from my library my only copy.

Shortly after publishing this book, Bishop went abroad, to live in France, and did not return till 1932 or 1933. During the ten years he was abroad, he wrote mostly short stories, one of which won a Scribner prize for the best long short story in 1931.

Now With His Love, which appeared late in 1933, is Bishop's most ambitious claim to distinction as a poet. It represents a type of poetry which, though not distinctively Southern in theme (with one or two exceptions), nevertheless approaches the same problems that the Southern poets, dealt with above, have also handled, and in much the same manner. That is because Bishop, like most of these others, is concerned with a metaphysical problem; though unlike them, he has presumably read little in English poetry, and much in modern French. He has also unquestionably looked into Eliot; but the French influ-ence is the clearest and the most obvious, and brings him into contact with the Southern tradition through such a poet as Allen Tate, who also owes much to French models.

Arthur Rimbaud is probably the French poet who has taught Bishop the most. His influence is to be found in such verses as:

> Shrieks in dark leaves. The rumpled owl
> Disgorges undigested bones
> And feathered bits of lesser fowl.

> When black obese flies are few
> Starved spiders have been seen to drink
> Gold mornings in a round of dew.

199

There have been soldiers too, who drank
A yellow water from steel casques
Not minding how the sunlight stank.

This is like the earlier Rimbaud—that extraordinary combination of intense realism and visionary imagination—but this which follows is like the later, the poet of *Les Illuminations* who has also helped MacLeish to so much, in *Conquistador:*

Night and we heard heavy and cadenced hoofbeats
Of troops departing: the last cohorts left
By the north gate. That night some listened late
Leaning their eyelids towards Septentrion.
Morning flared and the young tore down the trophies
And warring ornaments; arches were strong
And in the sun but stone; no longer conquests
Circled our columns; all our state was down.

There are also echoes of Verlaine and certainly of Eliot to be found in Bishop's verses. Consider, for example, the following stanzas:

And in this street
Dawn begins not as light
But as the sound of ashmen's feet,
And the young man passes doors
That have the odor of sleep,

Down a descending
Perspective of grey houses.
If this is day it has
The complexion of a night-beggar's
Unshaven and disastrous face.

This is not to say that Bishop—though to achieve technical effects as clear and distinct as these is no mean feat—has not, when he chooses, accent of his own. One finds these accents, perhaps at their clearest, in four such poems as "Portrait of Mrs. C," "Ode," "Twelfth Night," and "Easter Day."

The first is a picture of an old Southern aristocrat dying amid the faded relics of her former splendor, and recalling the past:

You must not think me shiftless. I know this room;
Haircloth was once elegant. The rest is gone.

The portraits and the consoles; Lettice Buckworth
Whom we thought a Lely; Banister Owen
In the buff-satin waistcoat, three buttons undone,
And the brownish sheep in the background: all but one,
My great-aunt in the oval over your head.
Maria Boys, who took to her bed still young,
Who had her slaves brought to her side there
And whipped until they bled.

Although this poem owes something to Eliot, too, in its concluding irony—for the old woman dies calling for her daughter, Margaret, long since married to a Mr. Moskowitz: "From his name I think he must be a Pole"—yet it is as remarkable in its way as a picture of the Plantation South as Ransom's "Old Mansion." The "Ode" which might be set in contrast to it, cannot be quoted in fragments. Its subject is the Three Fates—again we have in Bishop a Southern poet concerned with past glory and present ruin. Finally in "Twelfth Night" and "Easter Day" we have Bishop's dealings with the Christian myth, again alluded to in a fine poem "A Defense" which appeared in *The New Republic* while this essay was being written.

Both of these two poems represent an acceptance of the Christian myth akin to that referred to earlier in this essay as being peculiar to Ransom alone. Bishop believes that the Christian myth can save the world; he cries in another poem that "the ritual must be found," but when he comes to discuss the evidence on which the ritual rests, he is angrily suspicious or doubtful of its validity. He pictures the skeptic, and unconvinced Magi, led to a stable, or Pilate washing his hands because

Youth is a sepulchre, dust is not justice.
Nor will the metaphysical toil of spiders
Conserve the shroud that hides decaying bones.

This attitude of skeptical reserve, of doubtful but honest disillusionment, of finical and ironic evasion, resembles Ransom's, but where Ransom approaches Christianity in the Protestant spirit, Bishop—perhaps thanks to the Latin clarity of his mind—has strong leanings towards Catholicism. His real *métier*, which he has been slow in finding, is to be a religious poet in the modern sense, as Ransom and Eliot are—and as Tate, despite his attempts at orthodoxy, is not. He can illuminate the position of orthodoxy by throwing a sidelight of heterodox irony on it, and through another heterodoxy, common to all these Southerners, the heterodoxy of disbelief in progress, can safely again reassume the position of orthodoxy.

Conclusion

The modern Southern poets with whom I have dealt in this essay have probably been, through their work and their influence, the outstanding phenomena in the course of American poetry during the past ten years. In dealing with them I have been obliged to set aside as not germane to my purpose the poetry of such a writer as Conrad Aiken, whose contact with the South was early, accidental, and largely superficial. I have also set aside my own work as representing perhaps a more Western tradition; I have not mentioned many excellent Southern Negro poets (their work being immensely different in approach), nor have I said anything about the stirrings of poetical effort as far afield as New Orleans and Charleston. I have confined myself mainly to what I believe has become now the central tradition of Southern poetry, the doctrine of the "Nashville school" and of its affiliates.

That doctrine has great virtues and also some startling defects. Perhaps its chief virtue is that in contrast to the earlier efforts of the Mid-Western, New England, and Imagist schools, it has always insisted that a poem should be well written, that there is a specific language to poetry other than the language of prose (despite Wordsworth to the contrary) and that poetry is closely akin, in its essence, to the metaphysical and ontological speculations which lie at the base of major religions. Ransom has, in particular, written very well on this theme, and there is no doubt that what he and others have said on it is having its effect in drawing American poetry away from its concern with the merely temporal and ephemeral aspects of reality into questions of more serious and unchanging import.

The position, however, assumed by these Southerners is not without its attendant dangers. The chief business of the poet is to communicate a heightened sense of pleasure, a more complete participation in his experience to his readers. It is difficult to find out just where this pleasure lies or what experience is intended to be communicated, in language such as this:

> So that the extravagant device of art
> Unhousing by abstraction this once head
> Was capital irony by a loving hand
> That knew the no treason of a head like this:
>
> Makes repentance in an unlovely head
> The vinegar disparagement of flesh,
> Till, the hurt flesh rescuing, the hard egg
> Is shrunken to its own deathlike surface.[8]

It will not do, however, to say with Max Eastman in America or the recent English critic, John Sparrow, that verses such as these are willfully obscure, or deliberately nonsensical, or representative of an experience so private to the poet as to be publicly negligible. If we believe that poetry has something to say to us which is important for our lives (and I, for one, believe this, or else I would not have written this essay) then it follows that even statements of experience so recondite as this must have *some* value (though surely not the value of statements of experience more inclusive and universal). The difficulty with poems of this particular type, which seem to create obstacles to their own comprehension as they go along, lies rather deeper. The modern poet, such as Mr. Ransom in the lines I have just quoted, supposes that in order to be philosophical about his subject it is necessary for him to detach himself, to analyze it thoroughly as he goes along, with the result that we get—and not from Mr. Ransom alone—a series of learned, but at bottom meaningless, essays *about the process of poetic creation*, rather than the clear resultant; or in other words, rather than the *poem for what it is worth*.

In other words, the "Southern type" of poem discussed in the above essay, does tend to become distorted, fragmentary, obscure, the more the poets I have discussed here find their stock of subjects running low, or the more they speculate on the *intellectual* content as opposed to the emotional, or *sensible*, content of their subject matter. What these Southerners need now is less of new technical devices, but rather more of subject matter. We have a right to demand from them poems that are not obviously patched together like the specimen I have just quoted, but which are so complete in themselves that none need ever analyze or ask how and why they were done: poems like "Lycidas" or "Ode on the Intimations of Immortality," to take two specimens of sharply divergent schools.

Since most of these poets are specifically concerned with ideas rather than things (the "thinginess" of the Imagists is foreign to them) let them, instead of giving us more and more remote abstract idealizations, take up poetry again where it can be both intellectual and "thingy": that is to say, in the drama. That drama has a religious root (even so secular a drama as Shakespeare's) should interest them with their rage for metaphysics; therefore let one of them write for us a great religious play. Eliot in his recent *The Rock* has already shown them the way. I do not recommend that they directly follow Eliot. But why not a great religious drama on the subject of conversion, a theme handled so far on the American stage (and that badly) only by O'Neill in his latest effort? Such a work would be of more value to future American literature than many of the metaphysical bowknots which some of these Southerners now take such pleasure in seeing tied; and moreover it would mark for Southern poetry a clear line of advance; and it would not lead—as I am convinced the stanzas I have quoted above only too clearly lead—into a complete critical cul-de-sac and the blackest of poetic blind alleys.

Herald of Imagism   *1936*

I

The public, or rather that part of it which is interested in modern poetry, may well feel that there is cause for congratulation in the fact that the chosen biographer of the late Amy Lowell is not only a poet and a scholar of established reputation, but also a New Englander. Mr. Foster Damon has appeared before, with carefully documented and painstakingly accurate studies of William Blake and Thomas Chivers. It is no derogation to his competence as a biographer to say that, in writing the life[9] of Amy Lowell, he had a subject still more congenial to him. For as he reveals in his opening chapter—as good a synthesis of the Bostonian spirit as I have ever read—he is himself steeped in the peculiar and paradoxical mixture of individual independence and Puritan conformity, of worldwide curiosity and rigid intolerance, of reformist zeal and of naive self-satisfaction, that have made New England what it is and has been ever since the days of its settlement.

The subject of his chronicle, Amy Lowell, was herself a New Englander of New Englanders—a fact which she tried desperately hard to conceal, and which, despite all her efforts, sticks out at every point in her life and poetry. I recall that when I first met her, in the summer of 1913, I was not made aware of the fact that she stemmed, in all her virtues and defects, from the longest-lasting and least-varying tradition of Anglo-Saxon origin we now possess upon this continent. Nor did I realize just what the New England tradition was, nor what was her relation to it, till I came, over a year later, to live in Boston and to see her frequently for well over a year. It is true that I had been prepared for the shock that the New England mind and conscience can administer to a Southerner such as myself, by previously attending Harvard; but I had gone through its portals as in a dream, guarded by the illusion (if illusion it was) that the Southern culture to which I had been born was dead, and that the only culture worth noting, since the South seemed unlikely to recover its lost heritage, existed in Europe. Later events have shown me just how much I was mistaken, both as regards the possibility of a Southern revival, and as regards the possibility that any day European culture worth mentioning might continue. In the case of New England, I still tend, since my association with the subject of this biography, to mingle my admiration with a certain amount of distrust, which the readers of this review will no doubt note, with satisfaction or the reverse, as they go on with this essay.

In nothing is the New Englander, and particularly the Bostonian, more immediately identifiable than in his ability to grumble at, to criticize, and privately to underrate New England. Mr. Damon notes this fact in his opening chapter, and it is as true of Amy Lowell as I suspect it was true before her of Channing and Alcott, Hawthorne and Emerson. Born on February 9, 1874, she inherited the momentous burden of a tradition which would have been an absolutely crippling handicap to any ordinary mortal, and unbearable even by such a dynamic nature as hers, had there not been added thereto also the possession of wealth more than is usually given to most of the children of this planet. Mr. Damon gives us full details concerning the background of her ancestry, and in doing this he is quite correct, for it may be said with perfect justice that her life corresponded at almost all points with theirs. They had, one and all, ever since the first of them appeared in Massachusetts in 1639, given lavishly of their lives, talents, fortunes, and offspring to the upbuilding of that Commonwealth of the Calvinist Saints they had erected on the shores of Massachusetts Bay. They had been, in turn, landed aristocrats, shrewd lawyers, and great builders of the industrial empire of the spinning-jenny and the power loom, which, after the Napoleonic Wars, cast its shadow over New England as it had already cast its shadow over England itself from the end of the eighteenth century onwards. They were wealthy, arrogant, autocratic—yet with a touch of erratic and capricious generosity. Several of them had been pamphleteers, all of them philanthropists, and a love of horticulture and gardening was also predominant. And—above all—they were trained, from infancy up, to belittle and despise the influence of women. The eldest of Miss Lowell's brothers, nearly nineteen years her senior, spoke of his father as follows: "Mentally he was the son of his father; as a matter of fancy as well as of fact, his mother's share in him being chiefly physical," and also declared his ancestry to be an outstanding example of "prepotence in the male line." All this was bound to have its effect on the fact that Amy was born, not a boy but a girl.

Not only was the fact that the child was of the female sex a handicap, as Mr. Damon abundantly shows, but also the fact that her nearest sister was already twelve years old at the time of her arrival. She was born so late as to be known as "The Postscript." Her mother was already a perpetual invalid; her father was immersed in the multifarious activities incidental to the life of a highly successful New England industrialist; he was busy with the Lowell Institute, the Massachusetts Institute of Technology, the Boston Athenaeum, and a host of other concerns—not to mention the fine estate in Brookline whereto he had moved in 1866. He was, at the time of Amy's birth, already forty-four years of age; yet his New England energy was in no wise diminished. One of his daughters later said of him that he rose in the winter mornings at 4:30 and in the summer at 4; walked the streets of Boston without an overcoat; and went in swimming every day in the summer, till the end of his life. His education had been eminently of the practical sort; but his wife had been carefully trained, spoke several languages, and was musical. The perpetual invalidism, to which she was already subject, left Amy the liberty to do what she liked.

The result was that she became at first completely the tomboy. Lacking as she did any predisposition toward the feminine in physique or temperament (Mr. Damon makes it plain that the later squareness, stoutness, and general masculinity began early), she was brought up, according to family legend, largely by the coachman, and to the end of her life kept her passion for horses and driving, despite the disastrous fire that destroyed the family stables—burning several fine horses to death—in 1909. Her education was, as far as schools went, practically nil. At ten she was finally sent to school, and emerged at seventeen, but as Mr. Damon's selections from her early writings abundantly demonstrate, never acquired any assurance in spelling, punctuation, or grammar. She was a failure in French, German, and Italian—and learned nothing of either Greek or Latin. What she lacked in education, however, she made up by the habit of omnivorous reading, in which she was encouraged by both parents, so that she began collecting books at an extremely early age. The first spate of juvenilia and fairy books—as Mr. Damon says, they were all books of adventure or fantasy, with not a single sentimental tale among them—were succeeded by hard book-learning. Shakespeare, who was undoubtedly spoiled for her by being presented as a dry-as-dust academic model; undoubtedly, her cousin, James Russell Lowell; Longfellow and Matthew Arnold; and presumably Tennyson. It was all pretty stiff, the correct stuff for a genteel Bostonian girl of the time to assimilate. But it lacked life. What wonder that she preferred sleigh riding or tomboy jokes, or devoured volume by volume the novels of Scott? But, still more remarkable is the fact that, despite the grind of schooling, she discovered in her father's library, at seventeen, Leigh Hunt's *Imagination and Fancy* and through its pages got an insight into what poetry was, as well as the knowledge that a great poet named John Keats had once existed. That fact stuck with her for over twenty years. She read Keats, now or later, but could not read Shelley, as her father—knowing Shelley to be an atheist—had refused to possess a volume of his poetry. She also, now or later, read the poet who, next to Keats, was most to influence her later, and whose work presumably replaced in her affection the icily correct image of Matthew Arnold: Robert Browning.

What is obvious, from a careful reading of Mr. Damon's account, is that as she grew to womanhood she felt that, despite the passion for reading, for driving horses, for dances and other social entertainments which she was able to indulge to the full, she was getting more and more maladjusted to the world in which she had been asked to exist. As early as 1897–8, she was sent away to Egypt for the entire winter, to live on a diet of tomatoes and asparagus, in order to overcome the distressing and increasing tendency to stoutness. Damon wisely prints many of the letters she wrote from there; and these, as well as her more juvenile fairy stories written at the age of eight, reveal the possession of a natural and vivid literary talent. But who, among her circle, had ever heard of a woman poet? It is true that Emily Dickinson had succeeded in being one, by letting no one know about it; but the only poet the Lowells had ever heard of was her cousin, James Russell Lowell, who had so nicely balanced the careers of writer and diplomat, and whose *Sir Launfal*, as well as his physical

presence, had overawed her girlhood. After her father's death in
1900, she had to take up a whole series of practical activities and duties which apparently were his sole legacy to her: she became a member of the Executive Committee of the Brookline Education Society,
Chairman of the Library Board in the same town, a member of the
Women's Municipal League, and a prominent participant in the affairs of the Boston Athenaeum. Meanwhile, as early as 1905, she was
satisfying, or attempting to satisfy, other hankerings by buying all the
Keats material she could lay her hands on, and by indulging in day-
dreams of becoming herself a writer.

Her physical disadvantages had already barred her from a happy
and successful marriage. Literally, she had nothing to expend her store
of energy—which was very great—upon, except upon her house, her
garden, her library, her horses and dogs, and the more or less meaningless round of philanthropic and social activities expected of one in
her position. The régime of diet which her doctors had prescribed for
the Egyptian trip left her already a prey to insomnia and to perpetual
attacks of nerves. What wonder if, under the circumstances, she fell
under the spell of the life of the theatre, with its elaborate artifice, its
stressed emotions, its nocturnal brilliance? She began to cultivate
actresses, and soon learned that she herself might easily—but for the
fact of her physical shape—be as good an actress as any one of them.
Duse enthralled her, and while still under the spell, she found that
she could write verse. Why not cultivate this gift? So from 1902 onwards, the ten years preparation began which was to launch her on
the world in 1912 as the author of a book, a contributor to the *Atlantic
Monthly*, translator of poetic plays, and friend of Josephine Preston
Peabody, who was all that the good Bostonians of that day expected
from a woman poet.

II

Amy Lowell was already thirty-eight when her first poetic venture
thus timidly appeared; she was to die a little over twelve years later,
while at the height of a public career which had already achieved
more notoriety than that of any other poet on this continent, and
which was well on its way to the achievement of permanent fame; she

left behind her seven volumes of poetry, one of poetic translation, three of literary criticism, and the vast two-volume study of John Keats, not to mention the enormous hoax of "A Critical Fable"— surely no small output for twelve years! She had already become a legendary figure, and her name had been carried from England to Japan. Yet it is obvious and it cannot be gainsaid that whatever qualities her work showed later must have been implicit somehow in the efforts of those thirty-eight years when she grew up in Brookline, unknown to the world without, and yet preparing for her attack upon it.

What is to be found, I think, in her earliest efforts, which Mr. Damon wisely prints, is the possession of a vivid but undisciplined imagination. The earliest of all, the fairy stories collected by her mother under the title of *Dream-Drops,* show her full of love of such fantastic and incredible adventures as are normal to a child who is bursting with vitality. There is, however, nothing particularly domestic nor feminine about these stories. Neither is there anything domestic or feminine about the later letters from Egypt, which reveal her as already possessing a singularly vivid, direct, sensuous apprehension of reality; much the same kind of apprehension as reveals itself in the early work of her mentor, John Keats.

It is interesting to compare these early literary exercises with the poems contained in *A Dome of Many-Colored Glass,* the volume with which she first made a bid for the suffrages of the public in 1912. The former leave behind just as clear an impression of bouyant high spirits as the latter exhale the atmosphere of repression, mufflement, feeling gone stale and conventional, thought cramped into unyielding forms. Mr. Damon makes a valiant effort to prove that, for a first book, *A Dome of Many-Colored Glass* is not so bad, quoting Miss Lowell's own statement to the effect that it contained at least three good poems; "Before the Altar," "Behind a Wall," and "The Road to Avignon." It is true that these three poems are probably better than anything in the entire collected works of that idol of the Bostonian public of the day, Josephine Preston Peabody; but the tone of the whole book is not echoed by them, but by such verses as these, which the author herself, with merciless clarity, called "Fatigue":

> Stupefy my heart to every day's monotony,
> Seal up my eyes, I would not look so far;
> Chasten my steps to peaceful regularity,
> Bow down my head, lest I behold a star.

Let each day pass, well ordered in its usefulness,
Unlit by sunshine, unscarred by storm;
Dower me with strength, and curb all foolish eagerness.
The law exacts obedience. Instruct, I will conform.

And these lines were printed when their author was already past thirty-eight!

The conclusion is inescapable that the writer of these lines was growing increasingly baffled and unhappy; a soul divided between the claims of the wealthy but tame society in which she lived, and other more urgent claims of the imagination which pictured other possibilities, but which had not yet found a clear means to release. This means was found when, in June, 1913, she arrived in London with a letter of introduction from Miss Harriet Monroe to Ezra Pound, and there first heard of the school of poets who called themselves the Imagists. Within the space of two brief months, as I can testify, her entire being was transformed, and she became overnight, as it were, the Amy Lowell which the public later knew.

The event had been preparing in her for many years. She had, without cavil or doubt, considerably more literary talent than almost anyone that I have ever been able to discover living in Boston at that time; but it was a talent that had lain fallow, neglected, a plant that had been pruned and lopped to a stunted and dessicated shape. The Imagists, with Pound at the head, poured out for her all their headiest goblets of poetry distilled from the Anglo-Saxon, the Greek, the Chinese; Flint and the author of this essay were ready with news of the doings of the Symbolists in France; the Russian Ballet, with Diaghileff and Bakst, Nijinsky and Stravinsky, was giving forth to London an unsurpassable display of free, intoxicating rhythms wedded to great music. So that which was in Amy Lowell grew monstrously, and became an enormous tree, overshadowing the landscape. At thirty-eight she was set headlong on that course of endless experimentation, restless and omnivorous adaptation of other poets, unlimited—and, alas, often inchoate and disordered—creation which only ended on the day of her death. The Imagists: Pound no less than Aldington, Flint no less than Fletcher, H. D. no less than the humblest scribbler who hung on the outskirts of the movement looking for a nod of approval, had provided her at last with a key to unlock everything, good and bad, noble and base, in her imagination. Having achieved so much, after years of frustration, she felt she had a right to throw the key away.

Whether she ever was, or could be, an Imagist; whether she ever actually understood Imagism, is a point not worth discussing. Imagism at least taught her that poetry need not be written in the style of Tennyson or Matthew Arnold to be good as poetry. It taught her to avoid clichés, inversions, sentimental flourishes, metrical monotony. It taught her that much of the French poetry which she had read before embarking for London was better than the corresponding poetic product in England. It taught her to avoid the sentimental preciousness, the false simplicity, of its chief rival, the Georgian school. It taught her not to be ashamed of herself. And it taught her to boast of her "externality" as a poet; an "externality" derived from the use of the so-called "unrelated method."

Since I was the chief inventor and experimenter with this "external" method, and since my own association with Imagism has often been called in question by various critics, it behooves me here to say something on this subject. Although I was far from subscribing to Aldington's or H. D.'s elaborate Atticism, or even to Pound's early blend of Provençal and Browning, I had already met the chief protagonists of the movement before meeting Miss Lowell, and had been especially impressed with the theories of Hulme, Pound, and Flint— then the best brains that the movement possessed. Especially, I had been fascinated by Hulme's ideas, with their sharp concreteness and exact definition. Such sentences as those Mr. Damon prints, to the effect that "thought is prior to language, and consists in the simultaneous presentation to the mind of two different images"; "that style is short, being forced by the coming together of many different thoughts, and generated by their contact"; that "the form of a poem is shaped by the intention," had struck a completely responsive chord in my mind, which had already been stirred by the intellectual ferments of William James and of Bergson—thinkers on parallel lines to those set up by Hulme.

It seemed to me that, if the basis of Imagism resided in such ideas as these, then I was indeed an Imagist. Although I disliked intensely the public logrolling and back-slapping in which the group generally indulged, I felt that, at least, I entirely subscribed to their theories. As Mr. Damon is at pains to point out (and his account is the most complete and exact of the years 1913–1914 I have ever read, years of as great import to my own development as to Miss Lowell's), I tried to support the Imagist movement and group in every way possible. My chief concern at the time—and for years later—was to write a poem of considerable length and scope about the life of some great modern cosmopolitan city, preferably London. I had already attempted this back in 1909–1910 in Whitmanian form. In my "Dominant City," published in the spring of 1913, I had attempted another solution, in forms dictated largely by Baudelaire and Verhaeren. I was now already feeling my way to a third tentative solution of this problem, when I met Miss Lowell.

This solution was to leave the poet's mind entirely blank, like the *tabula rasa* which, as Locke had said, we all are endowed with at birth; and to make the resultant poem entirely reside in the simultaneous presentation to the consciousness of as many contrasting images as possible, derived openly from, say, one's association with them as one walked through the crowded streets of the city which one happened to be inhabiting. Thus was to be accomplished, in perfectly pure form, that passage of analogies "from the eye to the voice" which Hulme had described as of the very essence of Imagism. This method described, as Mr. Damon points out, to Miss Lowell as early as June, 1913, was displayed finally in three experimental poems, each called "London Excursion," of which only one ever saw the light of print. These were written the following spring, of 1914, and represented each a day spent in London, and a return to an adjoining suburb. In the first, the protagonist came into London by train; in the second (the sole one published) on the top of a bus; in the third, he travelled afoot. I have forgotten what became of the other two, but the readers of the first of the anthologies published under the title of *Some Imagist Poets* may still read the bus top version of "London Excursion" as an example, at full bloom, of my "unrelated method."

This method so interested Miss Lowell that she promptly adopted it as her own henceforth, and called it the "external method." Personally, I was in doubt then, and am still more in doubt now, as to whether to call such a means of writing "external," is entirely correct. It is true that the whole content of such writing resides in the fleeting impressions the external world makes upon the eye. But the identity, the self-awareness of the poet, observer himself under such circumstances, is far from being annihilated by contact with dead objects, as Keats thought. It is rather heightened, brought to an extreme pitch of intense subjectivity, ready to receive still further and further revelations from them. So much so, that the state in which such poems can be written is not far from the state of mystic illumination as described in the lives of many of the saints.

Unfortunately, it seems to me, Miss Lowell's personal dislike of mysticism (of which Mr. Damon makes something, but not really enough) operated so strongly that she never fully understood what the "unrelated method," as developed by me in 1913–1914, actually had as its object. Nevertheless, out of that method, and out of the tenets of the Imagists, and out of her own general adaptability and unlimited energy, she pretty soon had made up a new kind of poetry that left everybody gasping and which carried her on from triumph to triumph till death closed her career in 1925.

III

What sort of poet was Miss Lowell? Here Mr. Damon's book—though its later chapters are no less fully and exactly documented than the earlier ones—will no longer serve to tell us. He calls his book, appropriately enough, a chronicle; and a chronicle is absolved, by the very nature of the case, from exercising too elaborate a critical judgment. He is, furthermore, perfectly correct in saying that, when Miss Lowell died, she was still at the height of her powers. Nevertheless, had she been granted another dozen years of life to add to what she had already accomplished between thirty-eight and fifty, I do not believe that she could have done much more beyond stressing, clarifying, and further exemplifying what had been, all along, her original intentions.

Few poets enter the lists with a body of critical theories concerning their art ready-made, and waiting to be broached, whenever called upon. Of all the poets of the period between Edwin Arlington Robinson and the present day, I can recall only one who was able, from the beginning, perfectly to double in both rôles, as poet and critic of poetry. That one was T. S. Eliot. Thanks to various accidents of transplanting, Eliot's criticism, if not his poetry, has had more effect on England than on the poetical development of this country. Miss Lowell was not, primarily, a critic of her own accomplishment. She was not primarily a critic at all, as anyone reading straight through her life of Keats can testify. Her researches into Keats' life and background are as thorough as the critical opinions she derives from Keats' own writings are superficial and perfunctory.

What she was is best described by saying that she corresponded exactly to the view of America once taken in my presence by an extremely cultivated Englishman, who remarked, "You Americans have a genius for improvisation." Alike in her own work, and in the organization of the forces that fought the battles of the "New Poetry," she displayed the immense quickness and resourcefulness of the Yankee ancestry. Frankly she pillaged and imitated others, only to give to each borrowing and imitation some native energy of her own. As for the public—that was her audience, come to listen to her, and to applaud; or to be scolded if unprepared to do so. Her career presents some curious parallels to that of Vachel Lindsay. Each had a bad education. Each suffered from the narrowness and insularity of his environment. Each escaped by means of collecting the largest audience possible and by holding these spellbound. And each died in the midst of the fight. Some of Lindsay's poetry will doubtless survive all changes and variations in fashion, and so will some of hers. Mr. Damon need not have exercised so much painstaking care in making out a case for all her volumes.

But even this does not describe her talent fully. Had she, like Lindsay, one type of poem which she could write so perfectly as to make everything else she did seem utterly unimportant? The answer here must be in the negative, to anyone who, like myself, has read and enjoyed a great deal of her work. Nothing is so immediately perceptible in it as her ability to assimilate all kinds of form. There was scarcely a poetic school with which she did not flirt, from the Anglo-Saxons down to the present day, except possibly the metaphysical, beloved of Eliot and his followers. Nor was there a form in which she did not write, from the sonnet to "polyphonic prose," except possibly dramatic blank verse (and had she lived longer, she might have attempted even that). Her work is an encyclopedia of poetic modes rather than a mode in its own right.

Is this a defect? The consensus of critical opinion, not of this generation alone, seems to leave established that it is. With the solitary possible exception of Shakespeare, there is not a single major poet in the English language who does not bear upon the surface of his verses the impress of an obvious and highly individual style. And the same is also true of the French poets, with the exception of Victor Hugo, to whom, as Mr. Damon points out, Miss Lowell had herself given early and uncritical admiration. The reason, indeed, why such minor and less comprehensive poets as Baudelaire and Verlaine make a greater appeal, in the long run, than Hugo, is that we know better where to place them. Their talent, such as it is, is sustained from first page to last; it is not, as in Hugo's case, a matter of random flashes of genius imbedded in a great mass of absurdity.

Miss Lowell's talent was largely of the Hugo order. It was a strange rôle for a woman poet to fulfill, to write the kind of poems she did; but everything about her poetic career was highly paradoxical, and one has only to compare the work with, say, Edna St. Vincent Millay's or Elinor Wylie's, to have such paradoxes fairly leap into the eye. She gallantly set herself an almost impossible task, and may be said to have succeeded to her own satisfaction, at any rate. Whether she has succeeded or can succeed in passing the challenge of posterity, is another matter.

Since her day, the question which the Imagists, as well as every poet of that day, totally ignored has come up again in an aggravated form. The question is, "What position—political, moral, social—should the poet take up in regard to the modern state?" This question, as I say, Miss Lowell found no reason at all for answering. To her, the mere fact that one could write good and original poetry was a guarantee enough that he had something of value to offer to mankind. It was on this basis that she championed other poets; and it was on this basis that she wrote poetry herself.

Nevertheless, the question has come up, and there have been at least two attempts to answer it. The first of these has been supplied by the Southern Agrarians, who were linked together for poetic purposes under the name of "The Fugitives." These argue that, since their political, moral, social views point towards the restoration of property in land, the checking of industrialism, and the creation of a body of independent settled landowners, that poetry should also reflect the types of mind common to such a landed society; and should therefore return to the material upon which the metaphysicals worked in the seventeenth century, and on which Milton, Dryden, and later classicists worked in the seventeenth and eighteenth. The Communists, on the other hand, argue that all poetry hitherto has, with rare exceptions, postulated the political, social, and moral viewpoint of the bourgeoisie. They propose a drastic alteration in viewpoint, rather than any specific new revolution in form. The poet may be free, under them, to choose any form he likes, so long as he uses it definitely in the interests of the proletariat.

Between the Agrarians' following of Donne, Herbert, Vaughan, and Marvell—largely as seen through the eyes of Eliot—and the Communists' insistence that the Agrarians are all disguised fascists, and that it does not matter in the least how a poet writes, so long as he writes on behalf of the working class—between these two contending parties, the case for the "new poetry" so gallantly championed by Miss Lowell and others years ago, seems now definitely to have gone by the board. But there is no real reason or cause for despair. Poetry, and especially American poetry, which at the time of the Great War and for a few years after, seemed in so flourishing a state, has now lost favor with the public—and without public favor, what art can flourish? The poets of the present day must simply bide their time, till the moment when the public chooses to become interested again in what they are doing.

At the same time, it is perhaps not altogether futile to warn several of the younger generation of poets (in this country, a generation lasts only about five years, as Mr. Tate has wittily remarked) that by insisting upon the propaganda value of their verses, or upon their conformity to a given tradition, they are doing poetry itself, as well as all critical standards, a disservice. A good poem, whether the poet in question happens to have heard of Marx or not, or whether he happens to have read Donne or Marvell or not (Blake, admittedly a great poet, had presumably read neither), is simply a good poem through the possession of inherent merit. One can only judge poetry by poetry, just as one can only preserve a tradition by adding something to it. We know pretty clearly now who were the best poets up to the Victorian era; but after that, everything is doubtful battleground. Particularly in this country, the youngest generation seem peculiarly to delight in smashing all the standards set up by their immediate elders. By no such means is a literary advance possible. American poetry cannot survive, cannot achieve anything but an endless series of creative blind alleys, unless the present generation takes into account what was being said, thought and done, back in 1913, when—after years of suspended animation—new voices were heard again in the land. The moment has now come when through understanding analysis and critical appraisal the precursors of that generation—Robinson, Frost, Sandburg, Masters, Lindsay, and Miss Lowell—again must take the places that are rightfully theirs in the sight of the present day.

Mr. Damon has brought that moment appreciably nearer by the publication of this carefully documented and sympathetically understanding study. As I have already pointed out, he has not attempted a final critical estimate of his subject. I am possibly even less capable of making such an estimate than is Mr. Damon, having known Miss Lowell at first hand even earlier, and having had—at least for three years—an even closer association with her work. Yet it may be that I looked on her from a greater aesthetic distance, inasmuch as I was then, and am still, a Southerner; and though her family had been, as Mr. Damon quite correctly states, Cotton Whigs, yet they certainly were not Southerners. It seems to me that those poems of hers which will bear the longest and the sternest test of continuance and survival will not be her showy bravura pieces, but rather those works in which she deals most frankly and directly with the material nearest her hand, to wit, New England. To take but two examples: both "Lilacs" and "Meeting House Hill" are admittedly among her finest poems, and both presuppose considerable knowledge of, and sympathy with, the New England background. Her New England is one entirely different from the New England of Robert Frost's backwoodsmen, or the New England of Robinson's decaying gentility; yet it is not less authentic, being in fact the New England of the opulent merchant princes, the progressive industrialists. Perhaps the finest and most culminating examples of the culture of that class (now in decay) are to be found in some of her works. This surely is distinction enough, as distinctions go nowadays. A judicious selection from her output (Professor Lowes made one, but I have not seen it) would, I am convinced, become an exhibit that none who cares at all for the future of American poetic expression need ever disown, or leave unread.

PART III

*Essays on Art
and Philosophy*

The Secret of
Far Eastern Painting   *1917*

Since Admiral Perry's fleet definitely opened Japan to the West, barely sixty years have elapsed; but during that time scholars and men of science have discovered that in all the arts of civilization—music, poetry, painting, sculpture, architecture, religion, philosophy—China and Japan can boast of a record as long and as fruitful as any in the West. Particularly has this been noteworthy up to the present in matters of painting. Chinese and Japanese painting in this country can boast of its enthusiastic collectors like Fenollosa and Freer, its admirers and followers like La Farge and Whistler, its students like Ross and Cram. In the great Freer collection at Detroit, which will some day become part of the national collection at Washington, and in the Boston Museum of Fine Arts collection, we have materials for estimating the value and importance of Chinese painting (of which Japanese is only an offshoot) which can only be equalled, if equalled at all, in the Far East itself. A few bold spirits even now are beginning to declare that they are able to draw more pleasure and inspiration from the masterpieces of Far Eastern painting than from the best Western efforts of today and yesterday. What, then, is this charm—wherein lies the secret of Chinese and Japanese painting?

A great mistake is made by the Western nations in supposing that education is a matter of the development of purely intellectual faculties. Education is not of the mind only, but of the body also. To fill the memory with immense quantities of uncorrelated, misinterpreted, and undigested facts is far more noxious than to remain in sheer ignorance. A true education is that which trains the senses to investigate for themselves, the brain to observe and correlate sensation, the spirit to receive it and give it out to the world.

Now the extraordinary point about Chinese and Japanese painters is that, although they were trained to observe nature and life, their work looks to us altogether artificial and conventional. How deep that training went may be shown when I say that in the later Sung period, about 1200 A.D., when Chinese landscape art reached its high water mark, the artists who achieved this summit were trained in the Zen Buddhist doctrine, a natural pantheism, the cardinal point of which was that everything in nature has, not only its outer form, but its inner state of feeling, with which the artist must be in sympathy before he can properly paint it. If the aim of the Chinese landscapists of the Sung period was to get as far as possible into sympathy with their subjects, why is it that they painted in such a conventional manner? It is because the act of receiving inspiration from nature and the art of rendering it again, are altogether different processes.

In nature everything exists in a state of diffusion. You look at a figure or a landscape, and you come away with a feeling of peace; at another, and you have a shrinking of horror; at another, and you have a feeling of conflict, of battle. To make plain all these underlying emotions and feelings is the aim of art—of any art. If one sits down and attempts to absorb all the various detail that made up this feeling, one simply absorbs the illusion and not the underlying reality. Everything remains diffused, unsynthetized, uncoördinated. Mental effort of this sort is only the absorption of a certain number of curious statistics. If one tries merely to put these statistics down on canvas again, one produces a sort of statistical analysis, drier and less interesting than the reality, which not only contained these statistics but something which appealed to normal universal emotion as well. If one proceeds by the Oriental method, one does not necessarily seek to put down any of the statistics of the reality. One selects from the whole object or series of objects before one a few features which contain all the emotional import of that object, and strives to render these in such a way as to suggest all the rest. One art is an art of statement; the other, an art of selection and restatement in another medium. One is uncreative; the other is creative.

The first secret of Oriental art is therefore that, unlike Western art of today, it does not rest on the doctrine that the eye transmits certain things to the brain, and the brain, through the medium of the hand, tries to transmit them unaltered to the picture; but that the brain constantly uses the eye to grasp the meaning of what is set before it, and the hand renders again this meaning in a different way. The Western artist uses nature as an end, and painting as a *means* to that end; the Oriental uses painting as an end, and nature as a means. Western art is a worship of external form; Eastern art is a rendering of internal mood.

In no ways are Western and Chinese art more contrasted than in their ideas of composition, perspective, and color. Let us take up composition and perspective first, and try to grasp what the Oriental means by them.

Of the famous six canons of Chinese painting formulated about fifteen hundred years ago, the first is life rhythm, and the last composition and finish. Perspective is not mentioned. This is instructive, but more instructive still is the old anecdote of some Chinese artist who became famous for his ability to render a hundred miles of landscape on a fan.

The Western artist always conceives of his picture as fitting into a frame. He literally grows into the habit of looking at nature through the medium of a round or square or oblong hole. To fill this blank space is his object. The habit of squaring off one's drawing, or measuring the proportion of objects with the stump of a pencil extended at arm's length, finishing a painting after it has been framed, is altogether Western. The Western picture is evidently a well-filled, but limited cross section of space.

To the Oriental nothing seems more absurd. He conceives of a piece of silk or of paper as capable of infinite extension. He does not work inward from the frame; he does not stand mentally outside his picture and look into it; he works outward from the center, and standing at ease there looks about him on every side and sees the dignity and beauty of infinite space. Thus many Chinese and Japanese works look empty to our untrained eyes. The objects therein are simply space boundaries which are enclosed by emptiness. When a Chinese speaks of composition, he means the spacing of his objects. He arranges his spaces in such a way that the material or filled element becomes merely a boundary of line or tone to restrain the extent of the immaterial or unfilled space. This is done, first, by lines tending to the horizontal, expressive of breadth; by lines tending to the vertical, expressing height and depth; by gradation of tone, expressing the infinite variations of materiality; and, finally, by spotting, which is perhaps the most important of all, since every touch in this art tends to become a spot of interest on which the eye can rest for a moment before traversing another free space. It is this conception of composition as arrangement of subject matter diverging into space, rather than as filling a square or oblong or circle with converging shapes, that makes the actually smaller Chinese and Japanese *kakemonos* more decorative and bigger in effect than the enormous walls of European and American public buildings, crowded with figures. It is also this which enabled the Oriental artists to give us the *makimono*, or roll picture, of which only one section could be seen at a time, but which had the continuity of a frieze, as well as an infinite variety of movement and arrangement. Beside many of the *makimonos*, the Parthenon frieze looks conventional—the mere repetition of a pattern. Finally, it was this constant freedom from space limitations which enabled the Chinese and Japanese to give us different and unrelated aspects of a scene or landscape in one work; as, for instance, the painting of all four seasons on a single screen, or of a hundred miles of landscape on a fan, or the telling of an entire story in one picture.

As for perspective, the idea that Chinese artists knew nothing about perspective still persists as the popular view. Now, it may be true that far objects do appear smaller than near ones. But a thing may be true to fact without being true in art. When one seeks to interpret nature, not merely to state her, one may discover that a tiny speck of distant mountain overpowers all the foreground. The real perspective is the mental perspective, not the ocular. It is bad art to try to paint objects at their relative depth for the eye, because, in the first place, it denies the most obvious fact about painting, namely, that painting is something on a flat space of paper, silk, or canvas; and, secondly, because thereby we are merely parroting nature, without thought, without attaining any nearer to nature's meaning. It is enough to see things in perspective; why should we trouble to paint them in that way?

The last, the greatest, the most difficult secret of Chinese painters is their science of color. There has been a great deal of talk about the beauty of color in Oriental art. Incidentally, a goodly portion of this refers to the later realistic work of the color-print school, which, as every student of Oriental art knows, represents the decadence. The astounding, paradoxical fact about Chinese color is that the great Chinese artists avoided color as much as possible. Their highest art was simple monochrome in black and white; their science of color was not a science of color at all but the relations of tone. To appreciate the highest Chinese art an eye trained to distinguish the most subtle gradations is necessary, just as to appreciate Chinese music the ear must catch the subtlest dissonances and variations of rhythm.

It is a fact that black in painting does not necessarily represent darkness, nor does white represent light. The Occidental painter—particularly if he be of an academic cast—appears to think that he need only paint in dark colors to represent shade and in light colors to represent sunlight. He even goes further and talks of hot and cold coloring. All this would appear sheer nonsense to the subtle Oriental. There can be glossy warm blacks or dull dirty blacks, just as there can be dull lifeless whites or singing dazzling ones. It is this play of illuminated or of unlit surfaces, this grading of tone, not according to its color, but its value as light or the reverse, that is the great secret of Oriental art. The Japanese call it *notan*.

The reason for this astonishing diversity between the East and West, is after all, less a divergence of conception than a divergence of technical means. The Chinese and Japanese never employed oil painting. All their work is done in washes of watercolor on silk or paper. The surface of the silk or paper represents, in this case, light. The washes permit certain amounts of light to filter through, or block these out, as the case may be. Oil painting is not capable of such translucency. All the light in an oil painting must fall directly on the canvas. Hence the old convention—so puzzling to an outsider—which leads Western painters to paint in a deeper range of tone than that which nature offers them, is justified. Take an old Chinese picture and hang it alongside an old oil painting. In the Chinese picture the silk has gone brown, but the colors have not altered; in the Western picture the colors have grown dark and clogged with age, but the canvas underneath remains the same. It is an interesting problem to settle: has oil painting given us the most satisfactory, the highest form of painting possible?

I do not pretend to answer this question. *Notan*—the gradation of tone harmonies—is possible to a certain extent even in oil painting, though not to such a subtle extent as the Chinese offer us. Although the Oriental mind accepts monochrome as the highest form of art, again and again the great Chinese and Japanese have put color into their work. This is especially true of religious paintings, which were especially meant to give richness of effect among the gorgeous splendor of temple decoration. But even then color was used in a restrained way, and always in combination with *notan*.

Among Western artists the quarrel still persists whether art should or should not have a moral purpose. This quarrel has never existed in the East. To the Oriental, education is just as much of the body as of the soul. A beautiful material thing is the outer envelope of a beautiful spiritual thing. The Oriental shuns vulgar coarseness as he shuns narrow didacticism. And here again he is right. Anything that is so presented to us as to impress us with its dignity is not only beautiful but also morally uplifting and cleansing. Little does it matter whether Michelangelo has preached for us a sermon on the Sistine ceiling; the dignity of the presentation is in itself better than any sermon, while in the case of the "Last Judgment," the want of dignity makes the sermon fail. When Ma Yuan in one of his landscapes gives us a fisherman's hut, a few sprays of bamboo, and the outlines of immense distant mountains, the subject matters very little, the treatment becomes everything.

Style, therefore, becomes the secret of art. Style is artistic morality; it is more—it is the means by which our consciousness of man's mission asserts and expresses itself. Man differs from the rest of the animal kingdom precisely because he is concerned with the purposes of things rather than their effects. To explain and investigate his vague and hesitating notions of the purpose of creation, he has invented speech, music, drawing, arts, and sciences. To draw anything is to describe it, to fix the consciousness steadfastly upon it. It is to write its meaning in a hieroglyphic freer and less conventional than that the author uses, but at the same time more comprehensive. Hence the stress laid upon line by the Oriental artists. Hence the long and earnest study of style, which to their eyes is always inherent in line. Hence the analysis of every form of brush stroke that it is possible to make, for a brush stroke is only a line. Hence the alliance between good writing and good painting—the joining together of drawing and calligraphy. The superiority of a great Oriental painter over a great Occidental is a purely moral superiority. The Western artist may have spent all his life trying to drive home moral teachings. He may be richer in color, more diverse in range, more skilled in science of form, capable of bolder conceptions. But all this avails him nothing against the dignity with which the Oriental has invested a spray of simple bamboo. The dignity was not in the plant itself, but solely in the painter's eye, mind, and hand, as these worked together to render it in line, tone, and feeling.

Let no one suppose that I am advocating a slavish submission on the part of Western artists to Oriental doctrines and precepts. To create a tribe of imitators is not my aim. High as Chinese and Japanese art was at its zenith, it, too, suffered complete decadence through a facile and feeble eclecticism which went on producing copies of copies of copies until nothing was left. There is no painting worthy the name now in China; and in Japan we have nothing but a feeble and meaningless compromise between realism and the weakened dregs of stylistic training, or an even more preposterous aping of European methods. Great Chinese and Japanese art is gone—as completely, as utterly as Greek, Florentine, or Venetian. But while it is gone, there have been signs that a new development of Western art was coming.

The movement labelled loosely Post-Impressionism has proved at least one thing—that there is a genuine revolt against the shallow pseudo-scientific training of Western artists and art schools. Men like Cézanne, Gauguin, Van Gogh, were undoubtedly men who were honestly seeking to bring about a greater conception of painting, based on primitive impulse and feeling rather than on scientific perspective or analysis of light. Whether their work was successful or not, it was right in its aim, in that it combated the stifling realism and super-culture of the nineteenth century. Unfortunately, the mannerisms and not the aims of these great men have borne their fruit in the cubist's and the futurist's efforts—work which agitates the brain to no end, as Okakura pointed out, work devoid of anything but surface sensation. The war has ended this craze for novelty at any cost. And now art, if it survives at all in Europe, will probably revert to the sterile academic formulas of the Salon schools and the Royal Academies,—the shadow of a shadow of a shadow,—or it will have to start again from the very beginning.

America is more fortunate. We are escaping the war at a period when it is more necessary than ever before that we cease taking in elements from without and begin to create something like a homogeneous national development. Paris has nothing more to teach our artists. We have at least twenty men who can beat anything in Paris (except the work of a few veterans) on its own ground. But China and Japan can teach us these great lessons: Natural form is necessary to a picture, but natural form that is not felt is unnecessary. Realism is bad art, but reality that is interpreted and made lofty and dignified by its interpretation, is great art. In a picture nature must appeal to our emotions just as much as she does in a scene, and not to our knowledge of cast shadows, or brushwork, or perspective, or a dozen-and-one other interesting matters for scientific—not artistic—investigation. Finally we must understand style but never degrade it, for style is the universal morality of art.

The Future of Art [10]   *1925*

The completion of Elie Faure's *History of Art* in its English version is an enterprise of which the publisher, the author, and his faithful translator, Mr. Pach, have every reason to be proud. It will enable many who have hitherto been almost totally ignorant of art, or of its message, to acquire an enormous amount of information—scrupulously and carefully illustrated—concerning the activities of man in the direction of plastic creation. M. Faure throughout has retained the enthusiasm of a pioneer, of an explorer, of a naturalist collecting rare specimens. But the coldly dispassionate thinker will not be content with this author's unflagging enthusiasm or his breadth of mind; all through the first three volumes he will look forward—as I did—to the final volume, wherein an attempt is made, not only to discuss the development of modern art, but to forecast its eventual future.

M. Faure is possibly not unaware of the fact that artists have been asking themselves for the past three or four years the question: Is art still possible? For we live in a world in which the unit of the family, of the nation, of the race, and of religion have all successively broken down and proven impossible as supporters of the strain of the growing complexity of life. The only force of cohesion that mankind at present has, over the whole area of Western civilization, is the force of material expansion, of purely scientific development. We already have scientific capitalism; scientific industry; scientific research; and scientific living (prohibition, inoculation against disease, vitamins, diet, and regulated exercise). We shall shortly have scientific organization of time: we shall live, read, sleep and make love by time table, and tomorrow there will doubtless come scientific religion, acceptable by all

229

except those desperate moderns who deny the existence of a soul. This prospect does not seem to appall M. Faure. He thinks that art will survive it. He believes that Europe is about to assimilate the traditions of Asiatic art and to incorporate them into its own. In fact, he sees a movement in that direction in the painting of Matisse, Picasso, and Derain. Finally he believes in a new architecture: ferro-concrete, and the development of classic types of apartment house, cinema, and factory. And he thinks that the artist, whose business is to create according to his feelings, his impulses, will survive all this chilling and regimentation. He thinks scientific art to be possible. He believes in man's effort which he says increasingly tends to approximate to the life of bees in a hive, without ever attaining it. And his history ends with a paean to France, which he thinks will give a direction to the art of the future.

To this theory, set forth with all the grasp of detail of which M. Faure is an acknowledged master, there are a considerable number of objections to be made. In the first place, art—as Professor Perry has shown in two eminently stimulating and suggestive books, *The Origin of Civilization* and *The Growth of Magic and Religion*—is essentially bound up with man's religious observances, with his attempts to ensure for himself a life beyond the grave. What religion does the present age possess in the Occident? We have Christianity, which is a marvellous ethical system, skilfully blended with pre-Christian ritual, to produce a creative force which has in our days largely lost the creative energy it possessed. Sixty years ago it was no longer considered possible to reconcile the mythical and poetical truth of Christianity with the biologic facts of science: men were obliged to take sides; we had Darwin and Huxley on the one hand, Newman and Patmore on the other. Nowadays it is even more doubtful if we can reconcile the myths of religion with the new myths of science—after Einstein and Niels Bohr it is impossible to say that science possesses any facts. At the utmost all that we possess is a theory, made to fit certain facts, which is past its prime, as opposed to a theory made to fit other facts, which is just being born. We stand at the threshold of scientific religion, and the "ethereal age," foreshadowed by Henry Adams, is already upon us.

Are there any signs that modern city life is spontaneously evolving in the direction of religious ritual? The question is important, for the city is the final development of Western industrial science. I think there are many signs of such a development, but they are not to be found in France, but in America. Those who have seen the interior of, let us say, the Woolworth Building, the Western Union Telegraph Building, and the Cunard Building in New York will realize that the architect in each case deliberately planned the ground floor to resemble a temple, and was told to spare neither money nor space so long as this result could be arrived at. In such buildings as these, we cannot buy a ticket, send a telegram, or go to an office without surrounding these seemingly unimportant acts with a great deal of the apparatus of awe and religious mystery. And the effect of the Pennsylvania Railroad Station is even greater. The mere going to find one's train in such circumstances becomes a poetic mystery. Here in America man has already learned to surround the machinery he himself has created with an atmosphere of worship; it is our native tradition to do so; and the engineers take their places in our American Walhalla a long way before the poets or the painters. In Europe, generally, the effect is likely to be different; engineering and the arts, science and religion, are always likely to be more or less opposed to each other. Perhaps their perpetual conflict will result in a finer harmony, according to M. Faure; but he does not specifically say so. In fact he seems to be definitely opposed to the expressionistic revival in Germany; a movement that aims at restoring a definite religious meaning to painting, sculpture, and architecture.

A second question that must be settled is the question of the rôle that painting and sculpture are going to play in the art of the future. Already the moving-picture camera has conquered a dimension of reality entirely beyond the range of the painters of the past; it is useless to blink this fact, and to deplore the cinema as an institution likely to destroy civilization, when all that we mean is that the cinema has destroyed tradition. The question of whether the painter has any business to paint at all, and if so, what he should paint, is a question that is still unsettled. And the same remark applies to sculpture. Apparently the most advanced sculptors of the present day are aiming at a kind of free sculpture: a development of architecture within the sculptural block that will make that block an entity in and for itself. But what all this has to do with ferro-concrete architecture remains to be seen.

Another question here arises: Is the art of the future, more complex than the art of the past, to be essentially romantic or classical in its adaptation of form to impulse? Is our aim to be static or dynamic? We cannot avoid this question; it is the question of the day. M. Faure, despite some remarks derogatory to the Greeks, seems to think that the future of art lies in its development along lines of classic restraint and balance. I cannot agree with him. If we have to be modern and scientific and industrial, then the more modern we are the better.

Russia, by way of communism, has crawled back to the status of a mediaeval peasant community; she will sleep there undisturbed for at least several generations further. The Western world, with America in the van, has refused to follow her example. Then why hesitate at classicism, which is nothing more or less than the old eclectic academicism of the late sixteenth century in new form? Why not deliberately, once and for all, embody our entire aspirations—our whole tragic human longings to create something more great than has ever existed—into the machines which may hurl us into dissolution or live on to supplant us?

The Key to
Modernist Painting[11]   *1928*

In his recent *History of Modern Painting,* Mr. Frank Jewett Mather has remarked "Cézanne is the key to modernist painting." And, further, "Is he just an interesting character, and a stalwart experimentalist, or a great artist? The answer to these questions is crucial." These sentences are perfectly just. Anyone who accepts the advanced painting of the present day accepts it ultimately through Cézanne alone. Compared to his enormous influence the influence of Van Gogh and Gauguin, who also regarded themselves as pioneers, is a vain and petty affair. The old recluse of Aix is the acknowledged father of a school, or rather of half a dozen schools. Cubism, Expressionism, Constructivism, Vorticism, even Futurism—all start from Cézanne.

It is therefore a good sign that there should now appear in English, not one, but two books on this artist. And it is interesting to note that one of these books is produced for a popular, while the other is obviously intended for a small and select, audience. For the great masters of art belong not only to the cultured minority, but to all mankind. If Cézanne is such a master, it is right that his work and influence should be as widely spread as possible. If he is not, it is for those whose views on art are opposed to his to speak out openly. The publication of these two books will force everyone to make up his mind concerning a life and work of peculiar, even of unique importance.

The life of Cézanne is generally supposed to have been uneventful. In reality it was a tragedy of the utmost complexity and obscurity. Compared to his career, the more picturesque careers of Gauguin and Van Gogh are comparatively simple and easy to understand. But what are we to make of the son of the bourgeois banker of a small provincial town, who becomes fired with the ambition to paint, goes up to Paris at twenty-one, returns home disillusioned, continues to paint in a style that shocks everybody, returns to Paris, quarrels alike with official art and with the advanced guard of the day, returns home in disgust, completely alters his style and subject matter at thirty-three, exhibits with the Impressionists at the height of their fame, makes no effect on anyone, and retires to complete solitude for the remainder of his life? And when one considers that all this record of outward failure—for it was only at sixty-three that Cézanne had any acclaim—was complicated with a temperament of such a sensitive order that, in old age, this man could never endure even the touch of a friendly hand upon his shoulder, that he destroyed canvasses in ruthless fury at the slightest suspicion of a derogatory remark, and yet continued to struggle, one is faced with a problem of enormous dimensions.

Cézanne's art was the exact counterpart of his career—as has been the case with every great artist (and most small artists) the world over. That it was made more difficult to understand by the fact that Cézanne, like every good modern artist, had to struggle against the current of popular art in his time is merely a side issue, of which Meier-Graefe makes far too much. Yet this conception of a man battling against a whole epoch for a more dignified, honorable and responsible role than either the Salon artists or the Impressionists were ready to grant him, is a better one than the conception of Mr. Roger Fry, who almost asserts, in his dislike of his hero's violent early romanticism, that Cézanne had no right to have an imagination at all. Both Meier-Graefe and Mr. Fry suggest a psychologic comparison with another great suppressed Romantic, Flaubert, but there the likeness between them stops.

Mr. Fry goes on to analyze minutely the technique of various pictures, dropping meanwhile such remarks as "the earthly paradises of the romantic school had ceased to be convincing"; "Cézanne could not create masterpieces while he persisted in struggling against the current of his genius" (apropos of the period from 1861 to 1873); "Every artist who is destined to arrive at the profounder truths requires an exceptional humility" (what about Michaelangelo, El Greco, or Blake?); or, apropos of *The Cardplayers*, "There is here no appeal to any poetical association of ideas or sentiments—it is a triumph of that pictorial probity which it is the glory of modern art in France to have asserted." Mr. Fry's assertion that pictorial probity forbids the artist to have any poetical sentiments at all—not alone the sentiments of Puvis, Chasseriau and Watts, who are here rated inferior in monumental quality to Cézanne, but even the sentiment of Giotto, if you like, or Rembrandt, Daumier, or Hogarth—is surely a sweeping one. All that we have to do, then, is to burn the Metropolitan, destroy the Louvre, and paint nothing but apples on a plate for the rest of our lives. And indeed this prospect seems to delight Mr. Fry, inasmuch as he declares elsewhere that it is a pity we do not possess a series of still lifes painted by Raphael!

In distinction to this unimaginative and academic treatment of the anti-academic Cézanne, Herr Meier-Graefe tends to stress the Gothic and romantic qualities of his subject's temperament. That he does not altogether succeed in making his account clear is due partly to errors by his translator and partly to faulty proofreading. His thesis, as I have indicated, is that Cézanne was born when great painting, in the Renaissance sense, was no longer possible. Delacroix had already exhausted the tradition, and the future was for realists like Courbet, intelligent *pasticheurs* of taste like Manet, or crude and simple impressionists like Monet. Cézanne unfortunately fitted into none of these categories. He was, if one may allow the paradox, a romanticist with strongly classical leanings. His ideals were Virgil and later Delacroix. But some remote northern strain in him warped this tendency, and made of him a sort of monster, always poised between Rembrandt and Grünewald on the one hand, and Poussin and Chardin on the other. Thus he became, not an eclectic, but a primitive—"the sole primitive of the way I have discovered", as he calls himself in one of his later letters. Meier-Graefe rightly emphasizes the great importance of the early Cézanne, the Cézanne of before 1872, in this development. In pictures like *The Pasha*, or the *Landscape with Sail*, or the *Dinner on the Grass* we have already all the qualities of the mature artist plus a self-confident fury of assertion which is later totally lacking. All that the study of Impressionism and the influence of Pissarro could add was a heightened palette, and a substitution, for the free sweep of baroque brush-work, of niggling thin touches of paint. The early Cézanne is eloquent, the later Cézanne stammers. For the early Cézanne one might say, in the words of Fuseli, "Nature puts me out"; the other is fettered and bound and cannot get free from nature. And yet all through his life, this painter strove, as even Mr. Fry will admit, to produce a great imaginative canvas: an Earthly Paradise, a Temptation of Anthony, a Don Quixote alternating with apples on the plate and Montagne San Victoires.

Even Meier-Graefe therefore, in his eagerness to make Cézanne greater than the ages which fathered him, fails to bring out the strange duality of this man's temperament. For the duality was not altogether between Gothic romanticism and chastened classicism, nor was it altogether between an unbridled and intractable temperament and a sort of inner humility, as Mr. Fry insists. The fact of the matter is that Cézanne was singularly great and petty at the same time. Great in that he persisted; in that he went on painting despite contempt and neglect; in that he made his own path, showed us that even nature and natural fact cannot be painted simply by trusting to the eye, but must be absorbed, transmuted, built into architectural form; so that every work of art, even a still life, or a study of a tree, has to recreate through the mind a whole range of facts, and shape them in rhythmic and ordered sequence. Petty, because he was afraid of others, and after his first failure at Paris afraid even of himself; because he was, as Mr. Fry says, a man without a skin; because he shrank from life instead of transcending it.

He was bourgeois in everything but his painting, and his own painting he affected to despise. Perhaps, Meier-Graefe adds, he despised all painting; and after 1880 would have been glad to have seen the Louvre destroyed and the works of others treated as he treated his own; abandoned in the fields or given to his young son, with orders to cut out doors and windows from the buildings in the picture. But that, too, is petty, and however great Cézanne's approach through patient assimilation of means to a synthetic and ordered conception of reality may be, no artist has the right to despise his own lifework on which he has launched all the intelligence he possesses. Least of all in our own day, when every artist with a conscience has to undergo martyrdom to do anything. The key to Cézanne's blend of truculence and timidity is to be found in his own self-portraits, with their aggressive beards and chins and suspicious, sneering eyes. Why this expression was never charmed away and a happier one substituted we can perhaps also surmise. Perhaps Zola's early defection from friendship was in part to blame; but more certainly Madame Cézanne was also responsible. That bovine and perfectly uncomprehending face, painted so often, must have duly served to doubly irritate the splendid misogynist's rage against the whole world of womankind.

Yes, Cézanne was great and petty; a failure and a genius at the same time. And his temperamental peculiarity has resulted in all that is really questionable in modern art. For the trouble with modern art is not that it is incompetent, or barbaric, or childish, or mad, as the Academicians assert: the trouble with it is that like everything else in our unfortunate age it lacks altogether any scale of values. If a well-painted plate of apples is as great as Delacroix's *Medea Sacrificing her Children,* and is as great also as Michaelangelo's Sybils or Rembrandt or Picasso in any one of his phases, then chaos is come again. "There is nothing so like a daub as a masterpiece," said Gauguin—precisely, but do we want daubs or masterpieces, or do we want painting at all? That is the question Cézanne has left us to settle, and he has given us no answer to it except this: that he neither signed nor dated any of his pictures except some of the earliest, and one of the latest, for posterity.

East and West   *1928*

> "From being forever in action, forever in contention, and for excelling in them all other mortals, what advantage derive we? The insects have more activity than ourselves, the beasts more strength, even inert matter more firmness and stability, the gods alone more goodness. To the exercise of this every country lies open; and neither I Eastward nor you Westward have found any exhausted by contests for it."
>
> Walter Savage Landor
> *Imaginary Conversations*

I

The present moment in the world's history is significant in human development for one outstanding reason that has not yet been fully discussed or estimated in the public press of English-speaking countries. It has produced the first complete confrontation of East and West known to history. For the first time since human history began, we are able to see beyond the charmed circle of the Mediterranean and North Sea basins; and to discover counterparts and contrasts to Spain, France, England, Italy, Germany, Greece, in Arabia, Persia, India, Cambodia, China, and Japan. At every step we are now able to read our own historical record in the light of other civilizations, which display a complete contrast to ours. Nor is this all. The conclusion of the European war revealed to us an Orient rapidly altering, assuming the right to dispute the primacy of civilization with ourselves, and prepared to adopt our machinery, armaments, diplomacy, business methods, and general efficiency (which none can deny, alas, that *we* have invented) in order to defeat our aspirations to be masters of the world.

This state of affairs has come about through the operation of three factors. In the first place the East was completely opened up to trade and influence of the West, thanks to Commodore Perry's expedition to Japan in 1859, and England's great countermoves of the purchase

238

of the Suez Canal, the establishment of foreign settlements at Singapore, Hong Kong, Shanghai. Second, the European war itself revealed the complete disunion of Europe and the lack of common cause among the Allies, to every intelligent Oriental. Third, the Russian Revolution, which was the outstanding result of the war, made it clear to the world that Russia was not racially or socially able to take part in the European tradition, that Russia was not occidental in essence; and it also left open to doubt whether the United States of America could be regarded as occidental and European in essence either.[12] The result of all these three factors of influence was that for the first time since the downfall of the Roman Empire, Europeans, especially in defeated Germany, began to ask themselves the question whether, after all, European culture, highly specialized and limited as it is, was so vastly superior in outlook, and whether there was not a good deal to be said for the Oriental attitude towards it.

There are those who see in the raising of this question a threat to civilization itself. These are the scholars and politicians to whom the Greco-Roman tradition is something sacred in itself. This tradition accepts largely, as the basis for values, the institutions of codified law, ecclesiasticism, the plastic arts, logic, and the Agora. In Anglo-Saxon and Scandinavian countries there are probably others to whom the Teutonic-Norman tradition of common law, anticlerical independence, the arts of literature and music, metaphysics, and the free parliament are sacred things. The former class have found able spokesmen in France in Messieurs Massis, Maurras, and Maritain. The latter class needs a champion still; when he comes, I do not doubt that he will be able to put up as good a case for his side, the Protestant side of the West, as these champions have for theirs. But as a matter of fact, all these discussions of the primacy of Western Culture over Oriental, or of one half of the West over the other part, are highly artificial and sentimental. If we cannot adopt Spengler's fine suggestion, and use the word "civilization" to mean only the last stage of every great culture, let us at least be sensible enough to admit that India, China, Japan have as much right to be called highly civilized peoples as England, France, or Italy. If we do not admit this, we run the risk of adopting a narrow rationalist academicism that would make all creative talent, all new subject matter alike impossible. Such academicism—as France can witness—tends to eclecticism on one hand and to naked barbarism on the other. It promotes a revolt from below, by limiting the concept of order to traditionally fixed forms of art and thought. In France today one must be either Racinian or Surrealist, either an out-and-out defender of Descartes, or more Bergsonian than Bergson himself in the contempt one pours on the intellect. Let us not accept such crippling views of either tradition or civilization. The world will be both better, truer, and more interesting if we admit that both Orientals and Occidentals, in all their richness and variety, have full right to their respective modes of existence.

Yet this does not settle, after all, the primary question which is: Whether the Oriental mind does not work differently, perhaps better: whether the present state of Europe, decadent and anarchic, will be further marred or improved by study and contact with Oriental forms of culture and life?

II

I am by birth, upbringing, and experience an Occidental. That is to say, I have a specifically "Western" view of life derived from personal experience, environment, and the traditions of my race handed down through centuries. This accumulation of acts, observations and attitudes in which I move choosing and rejecting is my native atmosphere; it has grown up about and within me unconsciously; but when I consciously examine it, I can discover a single thread of continuity running through it all. I regard the most valuable aspect in life, that which in me and my fellows has primacy over the rest, as the will that extends itself in the conquest of external circumstances: my favorite heroes are those who have willed to be "masters of the world" in the Nietzschean sense; Napoleon, Julius Caesar, Goethe, Beethoven are examples which recur to my mind constantly. Even Jesus of Nazareth, so far as I look on Him as being man, appeals to me because He willed to be the Messiah, because He willed His life and His end. Life seems to me to be a fundamentally dynamic activity, a life-force, a Heracleitean fire, a conquest of inertia and shapelessness. In this attitude of mind, which I achieve by an act of faith, my work seems worth the effort and intensity I put into it. This faith in work and activity for its own sake, Goethe's "*Arbeiten und nicht beklagen*" has been fortified by the evolutionary philosophy of the last century, with its insistence upon "struggle for life" and "survival of the fittest." I regard nature and natural forces, therefore, as things which I must overcome. If, therefore, I had been brought up in, or shown any aptitude towards what is known among the English-speaking peoples with whom I have lived, as "a successful business career," I might have regarded any devotion to the arts or to learning as harmful to the accomplishment of material success; but in devotion to poetry, arts, religion, science, I find some hints and indications of a harmony between man and the universe, between nature and ethical striving, between knowledge and desire, between beauty and truth, that insinuate doubts and hesitations whether after all I have been on the right path. It is for this reason that those people are particularly dear to me who have some other basis for faith than this limitless belief in activity for its own sake; who without destroying liberty still insist that man is not free to overcome nature altogether, and who maintain that the human will and the world will must strike a balance, if humanity is to survive.

Now, in the Orientals, so far as I understand them, I find an altogether different basis for faith. To the Oriental the triumph of the naked life-force in which most of my kind believe, is the triumph of Shiva the destroyer; to the Oriental, the activity of the will so long as it is directed outwards towards the conquest of life, and not inwards to the conquest of self, is altogether perverse and evil. The harmony that the Oriental seeks is the harmony of stability, even of inertia, rather than this ceaseless Occidental going forward with the flow of things. It is for this reason that the Oriental above all honors his ancestors, whereas we tend to deny ours; it is for this reason that the Golden Age lies for him in the remote past, whereas we tend to envisage it as coming in the immediate future. The great teachers for the Oriental are Confucius, whose teaching laid stress on observance of old rites and ceremonies, Buddha, who conquered nature and the world by simply sitting still, Lao-tzu, who said "do nothing and all things shall be done," Mohammed, whose leading idea was submission to incomprehensible fate. All these men would seem to be failures from the point of view of such representative "Westerners" as Edison, Marconi, Ford.[13] They are all lacking in some quality of the will that is particularly dear to the Western spirit.

The reason why the West regards these men and their like as failures, is because they inculcate passivity, submission, precisely where the West inculcates activity and rebellion. When the Oriental becomes converted to Christianity what appeals to him in the figure of Jesus is probably the attitude of mind expressed in the words, "take no thought for the morrow," "if thine enemy smite thee on the right cheek, turn to him the left," "they that take up the sword shall perish by the sword": words which we of the West continually disregard or neglect. Non-resistance to nature, letting things take their own course, is the first precept of Oriental morality; social agitation, making things better is the first precept of Occidental morality. There can be no two attitudes of mind more distinct, more divided in essence than the Western and Eastern. Yet the Oriental has exactly what the Occidental lacks, or finds difficult; resignation, humility, endurance of evils that cannot be mended or cured.

Now the question that uprises in me and presses for a solution is this: Which attitude of mind, which point of view is better? Must I, as a Western, go on imposing my will on the order of nature, or must I, as an Eastern, submit my will to whatever nature demands? One or the other point of view must prevail in the long run, because neither the Oriental nor I can escape from the hope and faith that humanity does after all possess some principle of unitary harmony which can be found and followed. This unitary harmony can be called whatever you like: God, the knowledge of perfect truth, absolute beauty, universal charity, the brotherhood of man, the goal of evolution; it still exists and the Oriental and I incessantly tend towards it. So the question arises and demands an answer: which of us has done the most towards achieving that final absolute of human perfection we both desire? Which of us has chosen "the better part"? This last phrase reminds me of the fact that there is something on the subject in the Gospels. When I look up the passage in question, I am confounded. For there it is said of Mary who waited for the Lord's coming and of Martha whose "soul was cumbered with many things," that Mary had chosen the better part. And it seems to me that the East, with its stress on inward contemplation, has played the part of Mary, while the West with its insistence on outward activity, has only too often been akin to poor, foolish, blundering Martha.

242

III

The conflict which I have just been describing as personal to myself, between the Occidental ideal of dynamic vitality and the Oriental ideal of contemplative stability, has in the East, as well as the West, become today the leading problem of the world. Lacking the ordered religious faith of our forefathers, and in danger of losing completely the social structures that gave that faith force and coherence, we have to create a scheme of inner self-control out of the best that has been said and thought for the past two thousand years, or else to yield ourselves to a new mysticism of purely material forces, which will sweep us unthinkingly onwards to a completely unknown goal. When a Sir Arthur Keith, at the opening of the Congress of the British Association, is allowed to say that we do not know what makes man's mind so superior to that of other animals, but that we must nevertheless hold the belief that the superiority is due to biological factors that can be tested and measured, we can see how dangerously near such a pseudo-scientific mysticism really is. The understanding and measuring of such forces need not impose upon us any ethical scheme of self-control or demand any conscious contact with the culture of the past at all. The "superiority of the human mind," once it becomes the prey of impersonal and external laws that regulate every other kind of organic matter, need not assert itself in the construction and preservation of a race memory, or in the control of its own inner impulses, or in the achievement of an artistic style at all. We need only better and more accurate standards of measurement to live correctly under such a faith; in other words, more and better mechanisms to explore life. And while the East seems about to abandon its stability of the past, and to become ready to accept wholesale the machinery and chronic political disorder in which the industrial system of the West finds its proper expression of Sir Arthur Keith's creed, we of the West who retain respect for the pre-industrial triumphs of the human consciousness, labor at a disadvantage. We have to choose the position of carrying on a war of outposts, largely leaderless, and lacking in cohesion, while the mechanical and scientific dynamism of our time goes on from conquest to conquest. We have no political presentation or defense of our case. We are in the proper sense of the term, individualist reactionaries, and as such, outlaws in every modern Western state. Even a Mussolini has hinted that he prefers Italy to produce aviators rather than philosophers and artists.

This state of affairs brings up the question whether the West, or any part of it, has a right to assume the philosophic attitude that has been familiar to the older East for thousands of years. And this question brings me to the chief point of my essay, which is to examine and controvert if possible the doctrines put forward by M. Henri Massis, in his *Defense of the West*. Now the gist of M. Massis' argument is that in Russia and in Germany, since the War, there has been a growing tendency to "orientalize"; and against this tendency M. Massis brings forward the authority of Latin Mediterranean civilization, controlled and directed by the Catholic Church.

In examining this argument I am struck by the fact that M. Massis, despite his expressed passion for order, has fallen into some characteristic confusions. For example, he confuses the India of today, of Ghandi and Tagore, with the India of the remote past, before the Western influence had set to work upon it; he repeats the same error with regard to Japan; and he confuses also the doctrines of the Bolshevik leaders, who are Western materialists of an advanced type, with the atavistic Mongolian yearnings of the Slav race. These details I gladly pass over in order to concentrate on what seems to me M. Massis' main problem: the question of the Oriental tendency that the chief leaders of thought and culture have recognized as existing in Germany since the end of the War.

Since the conclusion of the barbarian invasions, that is to say from about the eighth century of our era, Europe has been roughly divisible into two halves: the Northern and the Southern. These divisions have been largely psychological and racial, rather than political and social, though as M. Massis himself admits, they correspond closely to the limits that the Roman Empire set up in extending its conquests. On the one side, you get the Latin Mediterranean civilization of Italy, Spain, Southern and Central France, Bavaria, Austria, a civilization largely Catholic, Classical and concrete in tendency and thought. On the other side, in Northern Germany, the "Low Countries," and in Central France and Scandinavia, you get a civilization largely Nordic, Gothic,[14] and abstract. This division persisted, with fluctuations, throughout the Middle Ages and the Renaissance, up to the twentieth century. Despite a Thirty Years War, despite a Napoleon, the Latin-Mediterranean civilization has never brought the Teutonic mind under its sway, except in a few places such as England and North-Western France, where, largely through Norman influence, something was borrowed from both Teutonic and Latin cultures and fused into permanent form. But the Great War itself, or rather the peace that was imposed on Germany, thanks to the defection of both America and Russia, left Germany politically, socially, and morally bankrupt. Uncorrupted Teutonism of thought, life, art, was henceforth no longer possible; but the German leaders of thought themselves, unable to accept the Latin-Mediterranean political triumph which they had never shared, were able to find in the passionless wisdom of the East some respite from their own despair. This is the explanation of the Oriental tendency in present-day Germany, which has so mightily agitated M. Massis.

The question arises whether the Germans were right in turning to the East as a relief from their own political and cultural bankruptcy. As a matter of fact this change of mental attitude on the part of a whole people must be examined in the light of European politics as a whole, and is not to be taken as M. Massis seems disposed to take it, as a move towards Bolshevik Russia at all. Rather is it a protest against Republicanism in its present-day form and in favor of aristocracy. The Mediterranean mind, despite anything that M. Massis may say, is now, and has been ever since the French Revolution, in favor of a republic or a dictatorship as the best political state. The Teutonic mind, on the contrary, has been largely aristocratic and stable in its outlook. Germany is not now, and never will be republican in feeling, any more than England. The Prussian monarchy having failed in its first duty, to wisely guard the country against combined Latin-Mediterranean and Anglo-Russian aggression, the Germans nevertheless instinctively sought the one philosophy of monarchy left in the world to protect them from the Latin-Mediterranean principle of dictatorship which the victorious Allies wished to force upon them. This philosophy they found in the words of Confucius, of Buddha, of Lao-tzu: all thinkers whose life-work and impulse derived completely from an aristocratic, stable monarchial society. Thus, as German philosophy and music triumphed over the political chaos that followed from Napoleon's downfall, so it was hoped that Teutonic mysticism in alliance with

Oriental disciplined thought might again be victorious over Latin-Mediterranean "political realism" of the type with which M. Clemenceau has made us familiar.

This prospect now alarms M. Massis. As champion of Mediterranean culture, he has nothing to oppose it except the tradition of the Catholic Church, and the figure of the active saint as opposed to the contemplative sage. Whether the Mediterranean world of today is capable of producing a very high grade of active saints (compare for example, Saint Thérèse of Lisieux with Saint Theresa of Avila) may be doubted; but I must follow M. Massis' argument step by step in order to show him how much he is mistaken. Let us therefore see whether this Mediterranean world of his has the cohesion and stability he says it possesses.

IV

It is generally assumed among European historians that there was a period when Western society achieved a balance between stable faith and unstable reason; this period is usually placed in the thirteenth century. It was then, we must assume, that those ideas which M. Massis calls "the maternal ideas of the Occident: personality, unity, stability, authority, continuity," reached their highest development. And the only difference between a Catholic writer, like M. Massis, and any defender of Protestantism in this respect, is that the former is prone to assert that this beautiful harmony was broken by the diabolical heresy of the Reformation, while the latter insists that the harmony was already broken, and that Christianity was in danger of losing sight of its goal when the Reformation recalled it to itself. A question of detail, which is not yet settled, and which at bottom obscures the main issue.

For the fact of the matter is, that this fine harmony between faith and reason in the West did not get beyond the stage of purely intellectual theory in which Thomas Aquinas and the other schoolmen left it. It never succeeded in embodying itself in practical politics. According to M. Massis, in the age of Louis IX, all of Christianity was submissive to the papal tiara. He may be right so far as the secular clergy, the bishops, priests, cardinals were concerned; so far as the regular clergy, the monastic orders, were concerned, he is wrong. Witness the struggles between the successors of St. Francis in the Franciscan order itself, and the Popes. As for the various kings, emperors, free cities, and feudal lords of the time, there was no order, no harmony in their relations to the central seat of Christian authority at Rome, nor did the Popes make any attempt to create one.

During the period of the early Crusades, it is true that, thanks to the preaching of the monks, all Western Christianity shared, for the moment, in a single political and spiritual aim. This aim was the winning of the Holy Sepulchre from the hands of the Infidel. But once this aim began to be successful, and the leaders of the Crusades began squabbling among themselves for political precedence, or for some share of the spoils, the Papacy could not and did not interpose. And the reason is, that from the days of Constantine the Great down to the present, the policy of the Papacy has been to support any government that guarantees freedom for worship and that does not meddle with the prerogatives of the clergy. Whatever individual Catholics may think or wish, the Papacy itself has always been an extra-political power, concerned only with abstract faith and morals and not with any earthly political principle, purely opportunistic in its outlook, ready to uphold any strong government that will not interfere with the practice of the cult, or touch Church property.

Such an organization—ready to trim the sails of its policy to whatever wind is blowing—would be anathema to any Oriental, as it was to the early Protestants. If there is to be only one God and one Divine Law for the whole of Christianity, and the Pope is His Vicar, then the Pope should have the power of deposing and appointing monarchs; nay, he should be monarch, emperor and high-priest in one person. Up to 1910, the Emperor of China was primarily the Son of Heaven and the offerer of the great annual sacrifices on Earth; the Emperor of Japan, to this day, holds quasi-divine descent and authority; up to the end of the War, the Khalif of Islam was spokesman for the whole Mohammedan world; the British Government owes its sway over large portions of India to the fact that if the native Rajahs consent, their people will consent. To say that there can be one order within religion and another order without in the secular state, that the state must support religion, not religion create the state, is the great heresy of the West, in which both Catholics and Protestants equally share; it denies the facts of historical development (witness the part religion played in the upbuilding of Egypt, Greece, India, the Mayan Confederation, Persia, Judea, or China), and tends to uphold bargaining hypocrisy between church and state with all its concomitant symptoms of anarchy, disunion, instability. The most logical Christians from this point of view were the English Puritans and Covenanters of the seventeenth century with their demand for a kingdom of saints on earth to correspond with the divine order of heaven. So an Oriental might fairly argue, and it seems to me there should be some attempt on the part of M. Massis and other Catholic apologists to fairly meet this argument, and to answer it.

But this is not all. If we look at the Middle Ages closely enough, we will see that there was a feeling on the part of many, though perhaps only a minority, that if the Pope was to limit his power to being only a spiritual ruler, there must then be somewhere in European Christendom one great secular ruler, consecrated to the task of keeping the nations together. Since the Pope had declared that his kingdom "was not of this world," then let him bestow the world on someone strong enough to hold and unify it. And the only person that this designation fitted was the head of the Holy Roman Empire, who since Charlemagne, had been the chief vassal of the Papacy in Europe. It was for this reason that Dante, who was the complete heir of Thomas Aquinas' thought in every respect, logically took the single step that Aquinas had refused to take, became a partisan of the Empire in its struggle with the Papacy, and devoted his life and his great poem to the defence of the Ghibelline cause which demanded a single secular ruler for Italy and the world.

But the papacy, embroiled in local politics and desirous of keeping Lombardy and the two Sicilies as pawns in its hands, paid no heed to the clear warning of events that either the Empire must be wholeheartedly preponderant, or the rising power of France would soon stifle the very existence of the Church itself; and it was Phillip IV, the successor of that St. Louis under whom M. Massis sees the whole Christian world "submissive to the tiara" who showed the world that if the Pope, through private avarice and narrow-mindedness would have no single ruler over Christendom, any of the nationalist rulers could be strong enough to make and unmake popes. France, orthodox France, taught the world this lesson in 1309. The Pope of the day, a French bishop and the creature of Phillip, took the road to Avignon, and there the Papacy stayed as pawn of France, to 1379. When it returned to Rome, the opportunity had been lost, the impulse of the Middle Ages was spending itself in the dreary Hundred Years War between France and England (in which the Holy Roman Emperor took the side of England), the Black Death had swept over the world, the Church was split in twain by the Great Schism, and the Renaissance and Reformation were inevitable. And the world owes this not to Luther and Henry VIII, but to the ancestors of those very Frenchmen who today assert their Catholic fervor, and who are ready to reassure all and sundry that it was Protestantism, wicked Protestantism, that wrecked the "great historic possibility of the Middle Ages."[15] And the world, in the long run, was right in following their teaching. No one can believe for long in a "commander of the faithful" who will not command, or in a "*pontifex maximus*" who instead of building bridges to tie his forces together, counts on dividing his supporters by resting the weight of his authority now on the one side and now on the other. Dante had been a true prophet. He had condemned the Middle Ages in its most exalted representative, the Pope himself. And the Middle Ages had perished, finally and ultimately, as he had foreseen.

M. Massis, in his *Defense of the West,* does not see that Catholicism and Nationalism began as incompatible forces; he does not understand that the sole power which could have saved the Middle Ages from shipwreck and kept the principles of "unity, stability, authority, continuity" intact, was the Holy Roman Empire in alliance with the Church. He is in the pathetic and impossible position of trying to uphold at once the Catholic policy, which has itself betrayed its sole historic mission of being the great unifying force of Europe, and the policy of French nationalism which historically helped the Church to consummate that betrayal. Moreover, by his insistence that European culture can only exist under the direct influence of Greco-Roman ideas, he reveals the real cause for his falsification of history. The Holy Roman Emperors were, after all, Germans; and to men of M. Massis' stamp naught save sweetness and light ever came from the Mediterranean, naught save demoniac darkness from Germany. Very well, then. Let M. Massis be honest with us and admit that he does not care a button for "unity, stability, authority, continuity." Let him declare frankly that all he, as homo Mediterranius, cares about is "gloire" in the good French sense of military anarchy and class-war. And, above all, let him stick to his conception of "personality"—"*le culte de moi.*" We who uphold the old Teutonic conception that the state is more than the individuals who comprise it, who believe that religion and art have a higher sanction than personality, may then respect him more as our open enemy than in his Jesuit disguise as our friend. His attempt to defend the Papal policy without defending the sole secular instrument that could have maintained the unity of Christendom in its highest aspect, becomes what it is: a secret plea, not for stable, imperial and ecclesiastical order, but for internal intrigue and underhand Bolshevist tactics.[16]

V

But, after all, we have higher game to hunt than such "propagandists of faith" as M. Massis. Let us, in the light of such knowledge as we possess concerning East and West, Teutonic and Mediterranean culture, look at Europe and the world today.

The Great War left Europe economically crippled, politically shaken, internally threatened with collapse. But it did not change Europe's internal character, nor make that character more consistent, more refined, more exalted. It did not convert Europe to any higher aim than the local and petty politics the preceding eighteen centuries had exhibited. It still left Frenchmen declaring, with Jacques Rivière, that the "French intelligence was the sole intelligence in the world" (and this after the Ruhr fiasco); Germans asserting that the Teutonic spirit was the Holy Spirit of Europe; Englishmen insisting that the practical commonsense of their island would soon reestablish stability, Italians vaunting their bravery and adventurous resource. Nationalism in this sense is not dead, it is more alive than ever, it has only been intensified by the recent conflict. And we, who are either Europeans or nothing, can only laugh bitterly at the tragic comedy that is being played out before our eyes. We laugh, but inwardly we are sick of it all. Europe in the eyes of anyone who has self-respect, respect for the highest human values, knowledge of tradition, and desire to see some other form of politics flourish than bargaining diplomacy and unprincipled truckling to the basest instincts of the mob, appears today like an old drunken woman staggering in the filth of the gutter-press, and the infamy of the popular franchise. She has long since mortgaged house and home, has driven off her best children into exile, has let others starve, has sold herself to the highest bidder, has set fire to the roof over her head, and at last is driven to pawn her wedding ring in order to buy drink and repeat to the bystanders: "You see how pretty I was once." Yes, Europe was once pretty. That is all we can say about her.

We who aspire to create things of lasting worth for the future, who aim to achieve a better world out of the chaos in which we must needs live, can no longer keep faith in Europe. With much regret, but with a sense of secret relief, we turn to wider horizons. There are two great powers in the world today. These are Russia and the United States of America. These two powers are the most active creators of the present-day world. Neither of them is entirely European by race or tradition. Neither is entirely Eastern nor Western in outlook. Their colossal extent, their geographical location, make of them immense land-bridges between Orient and Occident, between Atlantic and Pacific, between Caspian and Chinese seas. The "new capitalism" of the one, as the "nationalist communism" of the other make of them synthetic forces, undermining the last remnants of stability in Europe for the sake of a future world-unity they dimly foresee and seek along parallel but divided lines to create. Both fight with the weapons of the present day, which are not armaments and spiritual ideals, but economic aims and propaganda. Meanwhile Europe is economically mortgaged to America, is faced with the specter of Red Army revolts at home. What resistance can be expected from that quarter?

Even the Catholic Church which is still the spiritual head of Europe and Europe's greatest betrayer, plots to betray Europe again. Instead of defending the nationalist monarchy which represents the ideal of Messrs. Massis and Maritain, she is all for the new bourgeois republics of anti-clerical origin (except in proletarian Mexico). Those who believed Catholicism indissolubly wedded to royalism, those who taught a Catholicism synonymous with the union of the altar and the throne, the Joseph de Maistres, the Gobineaus, the Daudets, were simply mistaken. The recent condemnation of the *Action Française* and the almost completely passive attitude that the Vatican has taken up towards Fascism (as contrasted with its attitude towards Mexico) can scarcely leave room for doubt on this point. They are now faced with a proclamation of nullity from the Vatican itself. The Church is thoroughly republican, indissolubly bourgeois, unmistakably democratic. Her chief enemies are no longer the satanic radicals of the Garibaldi and Mazzini type, but the mildly prophylactic advocates of birth control. For the rest Cork and Chicago matter more to her than the Tuilleries or the Quirinal. Thus Rome consummates her descent into the abysmal vulgarity of our age.

Meanwhile, between the two great forces of America and Russia, a third power is slowly coming into being and seeking a common point of coalescence. This is the power of the British Empire, or rather of the British Commonwealth of Nations. This power also is neither Eastern nor Western, but it lacks so far a common focus and a common cause. It is scattered over the face of the globe, and entirely dependent on sea communications for its life. One thing is certain, that it is neither entirely European nor entirely against Europe. So long as Europe will keep the peace, she may have whatever form of government she likes, in England's view. Thus England turns her back upon European problems and strives to create sovereignty out of insularity. But the question still arises, how far is England's culture Catholic and how far non-Catholic in the modern sense as defined above? Is she essentially Teutonic and Imperialist, Gallic and Nationalist, or Neo-Catholic and Fascist in outlook? And arising from this, comes the last, most tremendous question of all: If England opposes Russia's programme in the Far East, must she not equally oppose America's programme in the Far West? An answer to these questions will probably be given by history before the close of the present century.

In the meanwhile, let us not suppose that in struggling to restore order to a chaotic and disintegrating world, we can achieve the order we seek by closing our minds to such manifestations of the human spirit as appear to be hostile to us. A faith that is achieved, like that of M. Massis, by excluding from its mental survey everything that was not accepted by Pius IX in his Syllabus, is a faith that is not worth having. To condemn everything Oriental, from Confucius to Ghandi, and tacitly to accept such manifestations of Occidental sanctity and wisdom as Marguerite-Marie Alacoque, Bernadette Soubirous, Benoit Labre, Therèse of Lisieux, is surely a poor victory for "personality." It may be that the East, like the West, will shortly have to undergo the mechanization and consequent democratic decay under which we of the West now suffer. But let us not suppose that the creed which M. Massis professes can save the Orient from this fate, or do anything except to hasten this consummation. Only the best minds of the East and the West, working together, can now save some fragments and remnants of humanity from the worst evils of the machine-age in which we live. The task that is before us, that of revaluing all the values of the past, demands the utmost vigilance and intelligence; such a task can never be accomplished by accepting the method M. Massis seems to have chosen; i.e., by seeking for scapegoats in the East and among the Protestant sects, and fixing upon them all responsibility.

Notes

1. Mr. Waldo Frank has argued that folk music is bad, because jazz is folk music. The use of folk rhythms and color in jazz no more makes it "folk" than the use of Greek motifs in a skyscraper makes it a Greek building.

2. I have omitted *Canzone, 1911*, and also *Sonnets and Ballate of Guido Cavalcante*, both of which seem to me to be slighter work—Pound trying to fit himself into the Victorian order of Rossetti or Yeats.

3. Cf. *Tractatus Logico-Philosophicus*, by L. Wittgenstein. *The Philosophy of As If*, by H. Vaihinger.

4. Miguel de Unamuno: *The Tragic Sense of Life*.

5. Review of: *Ezra Pound: Selected Poems*. Edited with an Introduction by
    T. S. Eliot. London: Faber & Gwyer, 1927.
    A Draft of XVI Cantos of Ezra Pound for the Beginning of a Poem of Some Length. Paris: Three Mountains Press, 1925.
    A Draft of Cantos XVII to XXVII of Ezra Pound. London: John Rodker, 1928.

6. *Tristram*. By Edwin Arlington Robinson. Ed. note.

7. I have learned, since drafting this essay, that he was born near Baltimore in 1906 and is a graduate of the University of Virginia.

8. John Crowe Ransom, "Painted Heads," *The New Republic*, Dec. 26, 1934.

9. *Amy Lowell: A Chronicle*, by S. Foster Damon. New York: Houghton Mifflin Co., 1935.

10. Review of *History of Art*, by Elie Faure, translated by Walter Pach. New York: Harper and Brothers, 1923.

11. Review of: *Cézanne: A Study of His Development*, by Roger Fry. New York: Macmillan, 1927.
    Cézanne, by Julius Meier-Graefe. New York: Scribners, 1927.

12. Had the Russian Revolution not happened when it did, and had Russia been able to maintain herself on the side of the Allies to the end, President Wilson's policy might have found more support at Versailles, with the result that England and France would have been defeated in their aims.

13. We would do well not to despise the quality of mind possessed by such

men. Against the triumphant materiality of their inventions, we can oppose but the feeblest intellectual weapons. Western Christianity seems to agree that they have done more for the world than the poets.

14. These terms are probably preferable to Protestant and Romantic. I use them because they convey more to my mind.

15. This phrase was, if my memory does not betray me, used by Mr. Chesterton. As this essay is being written, I understand he is providing the English translation of M. Massis' book with a preface. As I have not seen this preface, I am unable to deal with its arguments.

16. On the subject of the close parallel between the tactics of the Communist party in Russia and those of the Jesuit order, see *The Mind and Face of Bolshevism*, by Réne Fülop Miller.

Index